KING OF THE LOBBY

KING OF THE LOBBY

The Life and Times of Sam Ward
Man-About-Washington in the Gilded Age

KATHRYN ALLAMONG JACOB

The Johns Hopkins University Press
Baltimore

2 4 6 8 9 7 5 3 1

The Johns Hopkins University Press
2715 North Charles Street
Baltimore, Maryland 21218-4363
www.press.jhu.edu

Library of Congress Cataloging-in-Publication Data
Jacob, Kathryn Allamong.
King of the lobby : the life and times of Sam Ward, man-about-
Washington in the Gilded Age / Kathryn Allamong Jacob.
p. cm.
Includes bibliographical references and index.
ISBN-13: 978-0-8018-9397-1 (hardcover : alk. paper)
ISBN-10: 0-8018-9397-6 (hardcover : alk. paper)
1. Ward, Samuel, 1814–1884. 2. Lobbyists—Washington (D.C.)—
Biography. 3. Political culture—Washington (D.C.)—History—19th
century. 4. Authors, American—19th century—Biography.
5. Washington (D.C.)—Social life and customs—19th century.
6. Washington (D.C.)—Politics and government—19th century.
7. United States—Politics and government—1857–1861. 8. United
States—Politics and government—1861–1865. 9. United States—
Politics and government—1865–1883. I. Title.
PS3144.W3Z78 2009
328.73′0738092—dc22
[B]   2009009807

A catalog record for this book is available from the British Library.

*Special discounts are available for bulk purchases of this book. For more
information, please contact Special Sales at 410-516-6936 or
specialsales@press.jhu.edu.*

For Rob, Charlotte, Annie,
my mother, Doris Allamong,
and my friends

Much about the Gilded Age was only veneer-deep, but these people are the genuine, twenty-four-carat article. Even though no bribes of railroad passes or stock certificates were proffered, their loving-kindness was steadfast. As Sam's family and friends sustained him, mine have me.

CONTENTS

Illustrations follow page 90

KING OF THE LOBBY

THE RING—a five-carat deep blue sapphire surrounded by forty-two glittering diamonds—flashed each time Sam Ward gestured to emphasize a point, and he had many points to make. The ring's fire distracted the members of the House Ways and Means Committee, who were trying to concentrate on this lively witness's testimony in January 1875. The congressmen did not want to miss a word of what Sam Ward had to say. In the first few minutes, he had already made them laugh so hard that the stenographer was obliged to insert "[laughter]" into the official transcript.

This hearing was supposed to be a serious affair. The committee was investigating the latest scandal to rock the second Grant administration. The Pacific Mail Steamship Company had allegedly pried out of Congress a subsidy to carry the mail to the Orient only after greasing the skids (and several palms) with what the *New York Tribune* claimed was the extraordinary sum of one million dollars. Sam Ward's name turned up on a list of men who had profited by the deal, and he had been summoned to appear before the committee to explain himself.

The witnesses who preceded him had stumbled and sweated through their stories. Not Sam Ward. Five feet eight inches tall, stocky, with a perfectly cut suit, the eye-popping sapphire ring, a shiny bald head wreathed with a fringe of graying hair, and a flowing mustache and precisely trimmed Van Dyke beard, Sam, one reporter claimed, "fairly gleamed with good living" as he strode into the chamber with a self-assured air. His regal bearing was no accident and no surprise. Sam Ward was known to everyone in the room and far beyond Capitol Hill as "The King of the Lobby."

INTRODUCTION

ALWAYS HUNGRY for acclaim, Sam Ward savored the attention his testimony before the House Ways and Means Committee brought his way via stories in the nation's major newspapers. After his appearance on Capitol Hill, he crowed to his best friend of forty years, poet Henry Wadsworth Longfellow, that this "business which people imagined must have been unpleasant has turned out profitably . . . and has made me famous. . . . My box is full of letters of congratulations and my fingers sore with hand grips. . . . I have had offers for a book from several publishers and have felt half inclined to ramble on with my pen."[1]

Two years earlier, in 1873, Philadelphia newspaperman John Forney had observed: "What a delicious volume that famous man of the world, Sam Ward, who is every body's friend, from black John who drives his hack to the jolly Senator who eats his dinners and drinks his wine—from the lady who accepts his bouquet to the prattling child who hungers for his French candies—what a jewel of a book he could make of the good things he has heard at his thousand 'noctes ambrosianae!'"[2]

Although there were many times when he desperately needed the money a volume about his life surely would have fetched, Sam Ward never did write his autobiography. That is a pity. Such a book would indeed have been delicious, and, while any book the "King of the Lobby" wrote would no doubt have been as self-serving as his testimony, it would also have opened a window onto the lobby, as lobbyists collectively are called, in Washington after the Civil War.

Sam's reign in Washington coincided with the postwar years that have been disparaged as the Gilded Age, the Great Barbecue, the Age of Excess, and the Saturnalia of Plunder. Waves of scandals broke over the first and second Grant administrations, uncovering congressmen, cabinet members, and lobbyists in the muck on the ebb tide. Ruthless men like railroad mogul Collis Huntington arrived at the beginning of each Congress with, it was rumored, trunks full of cash with which to buy votes on Capitol Hill, while brazen representatives of shipbuilders bought the support of congressmen with stock certificates right outside the Senate and House chambers.

It is easy to lump these years together and dismiss them as an irredeemably corrupt era with little to mark it save scandal after scandal. A closer look, however, makes clear that there was much more going on in the late 1860s and 1870s than the looting of the U.S. Treasury. These were years during which the federal government and the nation were undergoing profound changes, and these transformations were the truely big story of the era. The period of transition from a prewar federal government that was relatively invisible in everyday life to a strong postwar federal government, with broad new powers reaching into its citizens' lives, was extremely rocky. While these changes were under way, conditions were ripe for the rise of all sorts of mechanisms, among them the lobby, to cope with unsettled times, and Sam Ward would succeed in Washington as he had never succeeded anywhere else before because these practices were flourishing.

This is not to suggest that these years were not corrupt. They were. There were venal politicians, rapacious robber barons, and wily lobbyists; there was contract selling, vote buying, and election rigging aplenty. There was, however, little unique or new about post–Civil War corruption except its scope and audacity. What was new was the public's awareness of corruption and a fear, fanned by an increasingly powerful press, that corruption threatened the Union for which hundreds of thousands had so recently died.

By the 1870s, as a serious depression deepened and despair over the future of the Union reached near-hysteria, everyone was looking for someone or something on which to pin the blame for this sorry situation. The lobby proved a perfect scapegoat. As is often the case, although the scapegoat bore the brunt of the blame, far more complex forces were actually at work; but in a postwar Washington that seemed to be crawling with lobbyists—one reporter did portray the lobby as "this dazzling reptile, this huge, scaly serpent"—many Americans were certain that in the lobby they had found the culprit behind the nation's woes.[3]

By 1865, the term "lobbyist" had already been used in the United States for decades, rarely favorably, to describe those exercising their First Amendment right to petition the government. In the 1820s, "lobby-agent" was the term for favor-seekers crowding the lobby of the state capitol building in Albany, and, by the early 1830s, "lobbyists" were doing the same in Washington. In his 1874 tell-all book about the capital, *Washington, Outside and Inside*, reporter George Alfred Townsend explained the origin of the term: it derived, he wrote, from the lobbies outside the House and Senate chambers, "guarded by doorkeepers who can generally be seduced by good treatment or a *douceur* to admit people to its privacy, and in this darkened corridor the lobbyists call out their members and make their solicitations."[4]

The first edition of the *Dictionary of American Politics*, published in 1892, included this definition of "the lobby": "a term applied collectively to men that make a business of corruptly influencing legislators. The individuals are called lobbyists. Their object is usually accomplished by means of money paid to the members, but any other means that is considered feasible is employed."[5]

And then there was Sam Ward, in a class by himself. Even while the popular press railed against the wickedness of the lobby in the 1870s and self-righteous politicians accused the agents of special interests of causing the imminent downfall of democratic government, the outlines of a changing lobby, a lobby still recognizable today, were beginning to take shape. It was personified by this charming and disarming son of one of New York's most distinguished families, upon whose well-cut suits no mud seemed to stick.

While the lobby has never entirely abandoned all of its old, crude, and sometimes still effective, methods, its emerging new style was more subtle, more focused on providing information than bribes, and more social. Sociability was precisely Sam Ward's forte. No one was more social than he. One reporter dubbed him not only "The King of the Lobby" but "The Prince of good livers" as well. His Washington dinners, where he brought together captains of industry, cabinet members, and congressmen for "conversation and education," were legendary: "ambrosial nights," gushed one guest. When they produced the desired results for his clients and profits for his pocket, his methods did not go unnoticed by his colleagues, who began to crib pages from Sam's book.[6]

As a host, Sam Ward was as delightful as his dinners were delicious. He carefully salted the conversation at his table with stories from his highly variegated life. *Vanity Fair* called him "the one man who knows everybody worth knowing, who has been everywhere worth going to, and has seen everything worth stepping aside to see." Henry Adams, who, while despising the lobby could appreciate this lobbyist, declared that Sam Ward "knew more of life than all the departments of the Government together, including the Senate and the Smithsonian." The son of one of New York's most respected bankers and who won then lost not one, not two, but three fortunes; a man who, while on the State Department's payroll, entered into secret agreements with the president of Paraguay; a Northern Democrat who leaned toward the South but put his life on the line to reconnoiter for the Union and his Republican friends—Sam had a deep well of experiences from which to draw.[7]

By the time he testified in 1875, the press had been hailing Sam Ward as the "King of the Lobby" for several years; "Rex Vestiari" he called himself. He earned his bread, as he tweaked his disapproving but devoted sister, Julia Ward Howe, "by the oil of my tongue."[8] The circuitous story of how this California '49er–poet–secret agent landed in Washington, how the "King" earned his crown, and how this son of wealth and privilege helped to change a questionable profession in a suspect city is one of many stories of the Gilded Age.

Sam Ward was one of the most delightful guests at the Great Barbecue, an era crowded with larger-than-life personalities. His story mirrors a hurly-burly time when anything could happen to a charming, resourceful man with a well-oiled tongue, a trove of tales, and a dazzling sapphire ring.

A note about names: Sam Ward is "Sam" throughout. The first names of his closest family members—the sisters, brothers, nieces, and nephews who were constants in his splintered life, and his wives and children, who he only wished were closer to him—are also used, to set them apart from those not related by blood or marriage. Except to his parents, Sam was almost always "Sam," not "Samuel." To Longfellow (who was sometimes "Longo" or "Longbardicus"), he was "Sambo" or "Sambolino"; to his friend James Garfield, he was sometimes "Flaccus" or "Horatius"; to friends Senator Thomas Bayard and Representative Samuel "Sunset" Cox, he was usually "Uncle Sam"; and to his friends William Henry Hurlbert and Archibald Philip Primrose, 5th Earl of Rosebery, with whom he formed an exclusive club of three, the Mendacious Club, he was most often "My Dear President." To a few he was "My Dear Ward," to the press he was usually "Sam Ward," but, most often, Sam was just plain Sam.

CHAPTER ONE

Sam Ward bobs up in Washington, 1859; the antebellum capital and the antebellum lobby; a new career revolves around dinners of "the most exquisite style"

S AM WARD, man of the world, master of cookery, mathematics, and half a dozen languages, failed financier, handsome and forty-six years old, bobbed up in Washington in mid-1859. He arrived armed with a secret agreement to lobby on behalf of the government of Paraguay, several cases of fine wines with more on the way, and a dazzling sapphire ring that he had acquired somewhere, somehow. No one else in his immediate family had ever set foot in the nation's capital, and the city did not quite know what to make of this old New York clan's first emissary. Sam seemed to know everyone of importance in town and could spout Horace for hours and sing German lieder long into the night. Before exploring how he came to be in Washington and how he came by his powerful friends, a look at the nation's capital in 1859 and at the lobby Sam was joining will set the stage for the drama of his life and career.

Sam found the Washington newspapers brimming with news about the recent trial of Congressman Daniel Sickles, who had shot and killed Philip Barton Key in cold blood within sight of the White House. Sam knew and disliked Sickles from New York political circles, and, like most of America, he knew the sordid details of the case. Sickles had married sixteen-year-old Teresa Bagioli, half his age and pregnant with his child, in 1852. They had come to Washington in 1857, when Sickles was elected to Congress, and settled into a handsome house on prestigious Lafayette Square.[1]

Within the year, Mrs. Sickles began an affair with Key, the forty-year-old United

States Attorney for the District of Columbia, son of the author of the "Star-Spangled Banner," and, according to Virginia Clay, wife of Alabama senator Clement Comer Clay, "the handsomest man in all Washington society . . . an Apollo." They grew ridiculously indiscreet, and Sickles soon got wind of the affair. On Sunday, February 27, 1859, when he spied Key loitering near his house, signaling his wife for another assignation, Sickles confronted him and shot him dead.[2]

Sickles's trial in April had titillated readers across the nation. Mrs. Sickles confessed to having intercourse on a red sofa in her drawing room; she described each piece of clothing that she took off before she "did what is usual for wicked women to do."[3] Sickles was acquitted on grounds of temporary insanity. It was the first time that plea had been used in the United States. Although there was initial approval of the verdict, consternation followed when Sickles publicly forgave his wife and took her back. Sam, arriving as the Sickleses' surprising reconciliation filled the newspapers, must have thought of his own estranged wife, Medora, off in Europe, and the rumors of her infidelity that had been filtering back to the States.[4]

Another and far happier event, this one involving friends of Sam, was also still being talked about when he arrived in the capital. Senator William McKendree Gwin, a Democrat from California, and his wife, Mary Bell Gwin, whom Sam knew from his gold rush days, were now among the leaders of official Washington society. Wealthy Southerners who had moved west, the Gwins spent an estimated $75,000 a year on entertaining, and they opened their social circle to admit Sam. A fancy dress ball they had given in the spring of 1858 was in the news once again, thanks to revelations at the Sickles trial that the affair between Key and Mrs. Sickles had moved to a new level that night.[5]

The entire evening was relived in the press. The Gwins' invitation had stressed that "no garb so well became a Congressman as the one in which he transacted the nation's business," but their wives and men with no constituents to worry about spent weeks assembling their costumes. There were Quakeresses, gypsies, Robin Hood, a matador, a quartet of Pierrots from the French legation, Highlanders, a Druid priestess, a knight. Mrs. Sickles came as a demure Red Riding Hood. Key was a dashing huntsman, with a cherry velvet jacket, white satin breeches, and high, lemon-colored boots.[6]

Fashion was much talked about by the women Sam met at the Gwins' home and elsewhere. After a string of reclusive, grieving, disinterested, or disapproving first ladies, the White House sparkled once more as a showplace for fashion under bachelor president James Buchanan's popular niece and hostess, Harriet Lane. For women, lace berthas and embroidered silk or kid gloves, reaching halfway to the elbow, were popular. Dresses were low-cut and featured small skirt hoops under yards of gauze and illusion garlanded with artificial roses, clematis, or violets. For men, black swallowtail evening dress formed the background for spectacularly colored vests of satin, velvet, and brocade and a coordinated silk cravat. For the boldest men, Sam among them, these were set off with jeweled cravat pins. On special occasions, Sam wore diamond studs in his shirt and rings on both hands. Uncle Sam, recalled Sam's nephew Marion Crawford, was the only man who could wear that much jewelry without appearing vulgar.[7]

While there were pockets of elegance, like Lafayette Square, when Sam arrived, the Washington that greeted him was not much to look at. With New York, whose teeming streets and chop houses he knew by heart, closing in on a population of one million, Washington, with only a few more than 60,000 inhabitants, including 1,774 slaves and 9,209 "free coloreds," must have seemed barely bigger than a village. Livestock still roamed the unpaved streets. Residents emptied their slops right into the gutters. One reporter described the capital as "a mud-puddle in winter, a dust-heap in summer, a cow-pen and pig-sty all year round."[8]

Sam knew London, Paris, and other European capitals well. They were long-time centers of the cultural and commercial lives of their nations. Not this capital. Washington had little past, little culture, and little commerce. It was an artificial town, created by compromise and plunked down in semi-wilderness. Its sole raison d'être was to serve as the nation's capital. Yet, although already sixty years in the making, the seat of American government looked hardly begun when Sam arrived.

Writer Mary Elizabeth Wilson Sherwood described the capital of the 1850s as "a strange jumble of magnificence and squalor."[9] Federal buildings were few and far between. The Treasury, Patent Office, and Post Office, all white, and the Smithsonian's turreted, red sandstone Castle were impressive, but marooned on widely spaced islands. The White House, with its outbuildings, fruit trees, and kitchen garden, looked like a plantation house somehow separated from its fields. The Capitol, where Sam would spend much of his time, stood sheathed in scaffolding. Its grounds were littered with marble blocks and sections of huge columns, all part of a project to add on huge extensions for the House and Senate.

The Capitol's original squat dome had been torn off, and only the base of its massive, better-proportioned, cast-iron replacement was visible. A plaster model of "Freedom," one of the last works by Sam's late brother-in-law, sculptor Thomas Crawford, destined to grace the top of the new dome, had arrived in Washington from Italy about the same time as Sam and was being cast at a nearby foundry. Another sculpture stood in the midst of construction debris on the

Capitol grounds. Horatio Greenough's seated George Washington, carved from twelve tons of white marble, had begun to crack the Capitol Rotunda's floor when it was installed in 1841, so it had been moved outside. Modeled after a statue of Zeus, Washington sat stripped to the waist, with drapery bunched around his thighs and sandals on his feet, looking cold and like the father of a very different country.

The north end of the national Mall boasted some landscaping by Andrew Jackson Downing and a clutter of lumber and coal yards. The south end trailed off into the malarial Potomac Flats. The embarrassing stump of the unfinished obelisk that was to be the Washington Monument poked up from the barren expanse. No one knew when, or if, construction, which had begun in 1847 but ceased for lack of funds and interest in 1855, would resume. In 1873, Mark Twain drenched his description of the sorry sight in satire in *The Gilded Age*: "The Monument to the Father of his Country towers out of the mud—sacred soil is the customary term. It has the aspect of a factory chimney with the top broken off. The skeleton of a decaying scaffolding lingers about its summit, and tradition says that the spirit of Washington often comes down and sits on those rafters to enjoy this tribute of respect which the nation has reared as the symbol of its unappeasable gratitude. The Monument is to be finished, some day, and at that time our Washington will have risen still higher in the nation's veneration, and will be known as the Great-Great-Grandfather of his Country."[10]

When Pierre Charles L'Enfant laid out the capital city in 1790, he included dozens of squares, triangles, and circles to showcase future monuments, but when Sam arrived, only one of them held a hero: General Andrew Jackson sat astride his implausibly rearing horse, a marvel of engineering if not great sculpture, in Lafayette Square, saluting the White House. L'Enfant had designed Pennsylvania Avenue as a wide, elegant boulevard, but in 1859 it was merely wide. The area along "the Avenue" between the Capitol and the White House did, however, look a little more like a real city. On the south side stood the sprawling Center Market, where Sam would shop regularly. The north side was lined with churches, law offices, hotels, restaurants, and shops, such as Gilman's Drug Store with Mathew Brady's National Photographic Art Gallery above it.

Hotels were a relatively new phenomenon in Washington. Only since the 1840s, when sessions of Congress lengthened and its members grew weary of long absences from their families, had demand for accommodations begun to grow as congressmen and government officials started to bring their wives to the capital. The National, Brown's Marble Hotel, and the Kirkwood were popular, but the most elegant hotel was the Willard Hotel at 14th Street and Pennsylvania

Avenue. The Willard's gilded dining rooms were famous for lavish breakfasts that included fried oysters, liver and onions, and blancmange.

Other up-scale restaurants included Wormley's, run by James Wormley, a former slave who had bought his freedom, J. G. Weaver's, Cruchet's, and Gautier's, an ultrafashionable French restaurant on the Avenue. Gautier also catered —he had catered the Gwins' ball—and excelled at sugary castles, pyramids, and pagodas. Pendleton's Palace of Fortune combined good food, a well-stocked wine cellar, and good furnishings and paintings with high-stakes gambling.[11]

Handsome private homes were scarce. Most of those that did exist belonged to the town's old Southern families. The capital's richest citizen, banker William Corcoran, who had made a fortune financing the sale of government bonds during the Mexican War, lived in one of the most elegant houses in town, opposite Lafayette Square, where his dinners and his wines were famous.

Sam had once entertained New York's social elite in his own elegant town house, and he had been entertained by the best families of Manhattan and Europe; but the high society that he found in Washington, a one-company town largely owned and operated by the federal government, was unlike any he had encountered. The city's status as the nation's capital and the absence of a large home-grown elite guaranteed that Washington's society would be unique among those of American cities. Boston might have its Brahmins and New York its Knickerbockers—families much like Sam's, recognized as leaders by virtue of antiquity and wealth—but Washington alone had an ex officio elite. Rank within it was based on elected or appointed office, regardless of the pedigree, gentility, or affluence of the occupant. Whoever held the office, no matter how low-born or venal, could lay claim to that office's assigned place at table.

The fact that Washington was the capital of a democracy, where citizens voted for their representatives, guaranteed continual turnover among this unusual elite. The revolving electoral door swept some officials out and new ones in every two years. Margaret Bayard Smith, wife of Samuel Harrison Smith, the editor of one of the town's first newspapers and a leader of its early society, poignantly noted the consequences of so transient a population in the 1830s: "I . . . live, as it were in a land of strangers. . . . The peculiar nature of Washington society makes it so." This constant roiling of the waters meant that the social elite Sam encountered in 1859 was still made up mostly of men. Unwilling and often financially unable to bring their families to a town where their tenure was uncertain, the majority of congressmen continued to winter along the Potomac alone, like a flock of all-male migratory birds.[12]

Washington's status as the nation's capital gave it another unique feature:

foreign ministers and their staff. Although many ministers regarded Washington as a hardship post, their elegant entertainments and the latest European fashions worn by the women in their delegations added sophistication to the backwater capital. Sam found a ready welcome at many of the legations. He had friends among their staff; he could commiserate in their languages; he knew how to dance their dances, sing their songs, and appreciate their food and wine.

The federal government's calendar called the tune to which Washington danced. When Congress convened in the autumn, Washington awakened. Train depots and the wharves teemed with new arrivals. With the exception of those officials' wives and daughters who came to enjoy the social season, most of the people who came to the capital each fall, such as the pickpockets and confidence men who arrived like clockwork, did not come for pleasure. They came on business—the nation's business, the people's business, or their own business. Sam Ward was among that last group.

When Sam decided to try his luck in Washington in 1859, he was following in the footsteps of a long line of men who held no office themselves but sought to influence those who did. Before the Capitol's lobbies were finished, indeed before the federal government even moved to Washington, special interest groups— shipwrights, merchants, veterans concerned with tariffs, taxes, and pensions— began lining up to exercise their First Amendment right "of the people peaceably to assemble and to petition the government for redress of grievances."

Several characteristics of the lobby in 1859 had begun to take shape as soon as the government got under way. The hired lobbyist, for instance. Petitioners seeking redress were on the scene in New York when the First Congress convened there in the spring of 1789. Almost immediately, some of them began to hire attorneys and other spokespeople to present their grievances. Boston blacksmiths hired Josiah Simpson to petition for the back pay they claimed was owed them for their wartime service; Orange County, New York, farmers paid attorney Ebenezer Hazard to draft a petition seeking compensation for wood taken from them by cold troops during the war. Some petitions pushed by hired helpers were not grievances but requests for special legislation. Miers Fisher, a prominent and expensive Philadelphia lawyer, successfully petitioned Congress to grant a patent to his client, printer Francis Bailey, for a method of printing that he claimed would produce counterfeit-proof documents.[13]

Hard on the heels of the first petitions came the first accusations of efforts to influence the members of Congress to whom the requests were addressed. In March 1790, crusty Pennsylvania senator William Maclay complained in his diary that local merchants plied his colleagues (he, apparently, was immune to their blandishments) with "treats, dinners, attentions" in an effort to delay passage of a tariff bill. Maclay also repeated a rumor about the type of man who would become a stock character in the nightmares of those who saw in the rise of the lobby the death of democracy—a congressman who would sell his vote: "In the Senate Chamber this morning Butler [Pierce Butler, senator from South Carolina] said he heard a man say he would give Vining [John Vining, representative from Delaware] 1,000 guineas for his vote. But added [']I question whether he would do so in fact[']—so do I too, for he might get it for a 10th part of the sum. I do not know that pecuniary influence has actually been used, but I am certain that every other kind of management has been practiced, and every tool at work that could be thought of."[14]

It was not long before petitioners with common cause began to band together, seeking strength in numbers. During the Second Congress, William Hull, who had been hired by a group of Continental Army veterans from Virginia seeking greater compensation for their wartime service, wrote to veterans' groups in other states, urging that they have their "agent or agents" work together with him to insure greater success for their efforts.[15]

A similar call for cooperation went out in the 1820s in the midst of one of many tariff fights. The Pennsylvania Society for the Encouragement of Manufactures and the Mechanic Arts, promoting high import tariffs, retained German immigrant Friedrich List to lobby Congress on behalf of its members. (One congressman complained that List, himself an "importation," violated the principles he represented.) Anticipating the practices of the powerful National Association of Manufacturers of the 1890s, List wrote to members suggesting that "the friends of domestic industry should meet annually to prepare the necessary legislation for Congress after discussing the measures and gathering the facts."[16]

Lobbying from inside Congress, by members on the payroll of groups with axes to grind, was also evident early on. Lobbying for and against the rechartering of the Bank of the United States in the 1830s revealed just how highly placed the bank's friends and enemies were. In 1833, no less a figure than Massachusetts senator Daniel Webster, who had been a vocal bank supporter, sent a none-too-subtle note to bank president Nicholas Biddle: "Since I arrived here, I have had an application to be concerned, professionally, against the Bank, which I have declined, of course, although I believe my retainer has not been renewed, or *refreshed*, as usual. If it be wished that my relation to the bank should be continued, it may be well to send me the usual retainer."[17]

From the earliest days of the Congress, there were individuals and groups who lobbied out of self-interest, as did the town of Providence, Rhode Island, when it sent two paid agents to petition for relief from federal impost and tonnage duties. Others were motivated by high moral purpose, like the Quakers who mounted one of the most sophisticated early lobby efforts with the goal of ending slavery. Some who came to lobby the government were charming. Like the Rev. Manasseh Cutler, who won a land deal for the Ohio Company of Associates, they offered sweet inside deals to congressmen whose friendship they cultivated. Others, like coarse, uneducated John Fitch, who invented the steamboat, offered straight talk and solid information in his bid to get congressional support for his steamboat company, and failed miserably. Destitute and demoralized after his failure, Fitch took his own life: a contemporary account claims that he accumulated twelve opium pills and took them all at once.[18]

By the 1850s, while veterans, inventors, and villages were still seeking redress of grievances, developments in the nation were increasing the volume of lobbying for other goals. As settlement spread westward, newly organized towns and counties petitioned Congress to widen rivers, deepen harbors, build lighthouses, docks, custom houses, and post offices, and a host of other improvements. The value of manufactured goods in the United States reached one billion dollars a year and, for the first time, exceeded the value of farm products. By the end of the decade, 17,000 miles of railroad tracks, the first of hundreds of thousands, snaked across the country. With fortunes to be made in this rapidly expanding industrial economy, more manufacturers and groups of producers, such as the National Association of Cotton Manufacturers and the United States Brewers Association, began sending representatives to Washington to plead their cases and protect their interests. The number of associations representing professions also began to multiply: the American Medical Association, the American Dental Association, and others were organized around goals that included putting pressure on public officials to support their interests.

New cast members, with new methods, were joining the lobbying drama in Washington just as Sam was about to appear on the stage. Captains of industry came to the capital, not only to plot strategy with their hired lobbyists, but to "work" Congress themselves. Cotton and woolen kings, rubber and reaper barons, the first of the railroad czars took rooms at the Willard Hotel, bought drinks for congressmen at the bar, and arranged for them to lose at cards at Pendleton's.[19]

Munitions magnate Samuel Colt, who kept a dozen lobbyists employed in Washington, was one of these new men in town in the 1850s. Colt's lobbying practices reflected his aggressive and imaginative nature, and it was only when he and his agents were incautious that their methods were exposed. Beginning in the late 1830s, Colt paid active-duty military officers to request his guns by name and retired soldiers to endorse them. In order to win and reward their friends in Washington, Colt and his chief lobbyist, retired general John Mason, gave out beautiful, specially made pistols in expensive, inlaid cases. Mason would identify the recipients; Colt would come to town to hand out the gifts personally. Several senators, some with experience with Colt's "peacemakers" from the Seminole and Mexican wars, helped him build his munitions empire. Texas senator Thomas Rusk worked closely with Colt from the time of his election in 1846 until his suicide, by gunshot, in 1857. Colt would draft letters endorsing his own rifles and pistols addressed to the Ordnance Department, the Secretary of War, even to the President, and give them to Rusk to sign and send. Another Texan, Senator Sam Houston, lobbied Secretary of War William Marcy on Colt's behalf. Colt's scrapbooks, which he proudly showed to potential customers, included letters of thanks and endorsement from Italian freedom fighter Giuseppe Garabaldi, Hungarian freedom fighter Louis Kossuth, Texas Rangers, U.S. Army generals, and Brigham Young, who armed his Mormon army with Colt rifles.[20]

By the early 1850s, Colt was expanding both his market and his production overseas. Beginning in 1853, he supplied guns to all sides fighting in the Crimean War. At home, he was building a huge new factory in Hartford, Connecticut. He badly needed to hold on to control of his main patent, first obtained in 1836. In 1854, the excessive zeal of Colt and his hirelings in Washington to get this crucial patent extended once more, plus rumors that he had used bribery to get a previous extension passed, brought a congressional inquiry down upon him. The investigating committee's report offers ninety-two pages describing how Colt's lobbyists were recruited, how they operated, how money changed hands, and how much.[21]

The report revealed that Colt had brought in heavy fire power for the patent campaign. Former House member George Ashmun of Massachusetts, former senator Jeremiah Clemens of Alabama, experienced railroad lobbyists Edward Dickerson and E. H. Thompson, and at least a dozen other "agents" all worked for his patent extension. They maintained a headquarters stocked with free food and drink and beautiful women, subscribing, the report concluded, to the theory that:

> To reach the heart or get the vote,
> The surest way is down the throat.[22]

Colt gave out enough boxed pistols to arm a platoon of congressmen. The investigation uncovered other inducements as well: "Money has been used . . . in paying the costs and charges incurred in getting up costly and extravagant entertainments, to which ladies and members of Congress and others were invited, with a view of furthering the success of this measure. The ladies, having been first duly impressed with the importance of Colt's pistol extension by presents of Parisian gloves, are invited to these entertainments; and the evidence shows that, while there, members of Congress are appealed to by them to favor this particular measure." Testimony also revealed "loans" to congressmen and thousands of dollars in payoffs to keep the press friendly.[23]

The result of all those gloves and guns? Failure. The patent extension was killed by the investigation's revelations. Bitterly disappointed, Colt was initially willing to spend even more money to "grease the rails" the next time his patent came up for renewal, in 1859. In a hastily scribbled note to his new chief lobbyist, Major William H. B. Hartley, Colt pulled no punches: "I have a note today from Captain Joe Comstock of which I enclose a copy—the party referred to is a distinguished leader in the Republican party & has pledged his support to our patent extensions, which if he acts in good faith united with the influence Mr. Corwin may be able to bring to bear upon the Congress we may be successful & for which I am willing to pay handsome contingent fees. I have once said that I would consent to bend myself to pay in all $50,000 to General Kerryman when the patent extension has become a law & this sum should be equally divided between the Republicans & Democrats." In the end, however, with his health deteriorating and the market for his guns booming, Colt let the drive for renewal quietly end.[24]

When preparing for what he knew would be a struggle to get his patent extended, Colt had been sufficiently worried to consider making an overture to the most powerful lobbyist in the capital, Thurlow Weed. Then at the zenith of his power in Albany and Washington, Weed was known as "The Wizard of the Lobby" and, to his enemies, as "The Lucifer of the Lobby." Weed epitomized another new and rare type of agent in Washington—the high-profile lobbyist.

Weed had been a young, ambitious newspaper editor in Rochester, New York, when, in 1823, he got his first taste of lobbying. Rochester needed a bank, and acquiring one required a state charter. Weed had championed the bank in his newspaper. He was also knowledgeable and articulate, so the townspeople sent him off to Albany with $1,000 for expenses to plead their case. Against stiff odds, Weed succeeded, and not just for Rochester but for several other clients as well.[25]

Back in New York, Weed became deeply involved in state and national politics, first as a leader of the Anti-Masonic Party, which got its start in New York in the mid-1820s and grew, in part thanks to the support of Weed's editorials. Then, in the 1830s, he became influential in the emerging Whig Party. Credited with putting Zachary Taylor in the White House and William Henry Seward in the

Senate in 1848, Weed spent more and more time in Washington, where he wrung out a steady flow of patronage for New York. When the Whig Party began to disintegrate in the early 1850s, Weed transformed himself once again, this time into a Republican, taking many fellow disaffected Whigs with him and quickly rising to power in this new political party.[26]

Charming when he chose to be, ruthless when he needed to be, Weed appreciated good food, good drink, and good cigars. (He estimated that he smoked or gave away eighty thousand cigars in his fifty-plus years of lobbying.) Weed hated slavery, and he was anti-nativist. In early editorials, he had championed immigrants and renters, advocated the extension of suffrage, and warned against government subsidization of special interests. By the 1840s, however, he had become less outspoken on such issues, and he often stood with the same vested interests against which he had once railed.[27]

Weed's portfolio, in both Albany and Washington, included steamship, ferry, and railroad lines. The People's Line shipping company paid him a handsome retainer and kept him supplied with rum, lemons, raisins, and preserves. Ship owners and merchants grateful for his help in killing a wharfage bill not only paid him well but presented him with a silver bowl and a declaration of thanks for being their "sheet anchor" in troubled legislative seas. Railroads were among Weed's most lucrative clients, and railroad stock his favorite form of payment.[28]

Like Colt's activities, Weed's lobbying efforts attracted unwanted attention and a congressional investigation, which offered another glimpse of lobbyists at work in the 1850s. A stockholders' investigation into the bankruptcy of the Lawrence, Stone and Company woolen mill in Massachusetts turned up $87,000 that had apparently been spent in Washington in 1857 to buy a tariff reduction on raw wool. Some of that money was alleged to have gone into congressmen's pockets. Although the committee could find no concrete evidence that any sitting member had sold his vote, its members noted in their report, "The committee must be permitted to say, that they have not one particle of confidence in the evidence which Mr. Wolcott [the chief lobbyist involved] saw proper to give before the committee."[29]

Testimony revealed that W. W. Stone, hoping to save his struggling company, had gone to Washington armed with carefully prepared facts and figures in hopes of persuading congressmen to lower the tariff on raw wool. Finding himself in over his head and his statistics being ignored, Stone turned to professional lobbyists for help. John W. Wolcott, Ezra Lincoln, and former House member George Ashmun, who had lobbied on Colt's behalf a few years earlier, advised him to pay high-tariff newspapers to drop their opposition to lowering the tariff and to make the acquaintance of A. R. Corbin, the clerk of the House Committee on Claims, who had a reputation for making things happen. In addition, Representative Orsamus Matteson of New York, whose own vote was frequently rumored to be for sale, recommended paying Thurlow Weed $5,000 for his influence with Republican newspapers and spending another $30,000 to buy thirty votes that he knew to be for sale in the House.[30]

Weed was called to testify. His wife was ill, and he wrote Senator Seward asking for help to avoid an appearance, but there was no way out. Under oath, he admitted receiving $5,000 from men involved in the wool tariff fight. Some of the money, he insisted, was a contribution to the Republican Party, but part, he reluctantly acknowledged, had been compensation for his services in promoting the tariff reduction bill. "In what way did you aid in promoting the passage of the tariff in 1857?" asked a committee member. Weed replied, "I have had the subject more or less under consideration for thirty years; am familiar with it, and used no other influence than argument and the presentation of what I esteemed valuable statistics in furtherance of my views. I did not use money in any way connected with that object beyond what might be considered would be strictly applicable to my expenses whilst thus engaged."[31]

That Weed, a former Whig now a Republican, who, despite his testimony, had been a long-time and well-known proponent of protection, got caught acting as a paid agent for a campaign to lower the tariff, was a godsend to his enemies. It had, hooted one, "the limping gait of a lame duck waddling out of Wall Street." Weed's friend and fellow newspaperman Horace Greeley tried to put the best face on it. Weed, he pointed out, held no office, had not sold his vote, and had not purchased any votes. Greeley protested that, while he personally would rather dig potatoes than lobby, Weed had done nothing more corrupt than change his mind on an issue.[32]

Greeley was right. Weed held no office, he had no vote to sell, nor was there any evidence that he had attempted to buy anyone else's. Nothing said that a man could not represent his own interests or get paid to represent the interests of others in Washington. Nor was there any law that said he could not give away boxes of cigars, or even guns, to congressmen. In their own ways, Weed and Colt were exercising their First Amendment right to petition.

Although neither man relished the spotlight that the investigations shone on their lobbying methods, both Weed and Colt were well-known figures in Washington in the 1850s. They represented the pinnacle of the lobbying pyramid. Beneath them, a growing army of lesser lobbyists that included bond speculators, claims agents, subsidy seekers, and promoters of schemes big and small, spread out. Unlike the earliest petitioners, often bankrolled by neighbors, who came to Washington focused on a mission, stayed for the session and buttonholed as many officials as possible, and then returned home with hands full or empty, for this new group, lobbying was a part- or full-time job. They worked for multiple clients simultaneously. There were rumors that some would lobby for both sides of an issue if they could get the work. For them, Washington was home, or at least their base of operations, year after year.

Benjamin Brown French was one of the foot soldiers of the lobby in the 1850s. He was the kind of lower-level lobbyist, derisively known as "borers," that a powerful man like Weed might enlist for a small job. Born in New Hampshire in 1800, French had read law, run a newspaper, and been elected to the state legislature as a Democrat. In 1833, he decided to try his luck in Washington, where friendly Democrats found him a position as a clerk in the House of Representatives. In 1845, French became *the* Clerk of the House, but the revolving door of the spoilsmen spun quickly, and he was turned out in 1847 by the new Whig Congress.[33]

French decided to turn his connections with men in high places and his familiarity with the House for a profit and lived the precarious life of a borer. The next five years teetered between lean and fat for the French family. In his journal entries and letters to his half-brother Henry, a judge in New Hampshire, French was confident each time Congress reconvened, certain that this would be the session during which he would find a wealthy client, make a big score, and be rewarded handsomely. Easy money always seemed within his grasp. Just how easy, he confided to his diary: "A gentleman gave me $50 yesterday just to go talk with a member of Congress 10 minutes, . . . and if a favorable report is made on the case . . . I am to have $200 more—and if it gets through Congress, probably a thousand."[34]

French was indefatigable—he wrote in his diary that he "labored like an ox"— and undiscriminating. In his quest for the big payoff, he took on all sorts of schemes, some legitimate, some questionable: Indian claims against the federal government, indemnity claims, French spoliation claims, pension claims, subsidies, patents, steamship lines, guano prospectors. Despite his hard work, the big payoff always eluded him. He spent as much time trying to chase down the fees that his clients owed him as he had in earning them. He complained to Henry, "If ever a fellow was sick of [claims] and all that sort of thing, I am that fellow." But the lobbying did not stop when French rejoined the ranks of government employees. In 1853, newly elected President Franklin Pierce, a fellow New Hampshire Democrat, rewarded French for his support by appointing him commissioner of public buildings.[35]

Two years later, after a falling out with President Pierce, French again found himself out of a job. He returned to "boring" full-time to support his family, this time specializing in private claims. By the late 1850s, French's growing unease over the slavery issue had led him into the new Republican Party. In July 1860, he was greatly relieved when his lobbying efforts on his own behalf among his new friends paid off with his appointment as clerk of the House Committee of Claims. The salary was less than he had hoped for, but he knew that he could continue to supplement it with lobbying work until something better came along. He explained the situation to his wife, Elizabeth, "My pay as Clerk will begin to run next week, and I think on $1,800 and what I shall receive *outside*, we can live till 'Old Abe' gets in and then look out!" French was still having mixed luck with his outside work. In the same letter, he complained of a failed effort: "Congress will adjourn tomorrow, and I shall rejoice to see its coattail buttons receding!" President Buchanan "has pocketed one of my clients' resolutions, and thus cheated *me* out of a hundred or two."[36]

That the number of borers in Washington had been steadily increasing did not go unnoticed. In 1852, Secretary of State James Buchanan complained to President-elect Franklin Pierce and all who would listen about the "host of contractors, speculators, stockjobbers, and lobby members which haunt the halls of Congress, all desirous . . . to get their arm into the public treasury." Their numbers were sufficient, Buchanan warned, "to alarm every friend of his country."[37]

Alarmed they were. Concern about lobbying, fanned by reports of corruption of all sorts at the local, state, and national level, was mounting. With no trace of irony, Thurlow Weed, whom many fingered as part of the problem, wrote of his unease to Hamilton Fish, recently elected Whig senator from New York, in 1852: "Was ever such corruption in high places more open and shameless, or more villainous?"[38]

For thirty-six-year-old journalist Walt Whitman, the answer was "no." The 1850s, he was certain, overflowed with unparalleled corruption perpetrated by uncountable villains, and it threatened to swamp the decent workingmen and women of the nation. In his unpublished essay "The Eighteenth President," written against the backdrop of the dispiriting presidential campaign of 1856, Whitman poured out his scorn on a long list of people he saw as destroying the nation:

Office-holders, office-seekers, robbers, pimps . . . fancy-men, post-masters, custom-house clerks, contractors, kept-editors, spaniels well-trained to carry and fetch, jobbers, infidels, disunionists, terrorists, mail-riflers, slave-catchers, pushers of slavery, creatures of the President, creatures of would-be Presidents, spies, blowers, electioneerers, body-snatchers, bawlers, bribers, compromisers, runaways, lobbyers, sponges, ruined sports, expelled gamblers, policy backers, monte-dealers, duelists, carriers of concealed weapons, blind men, deaf men, pimpled men, scarred inside with the vile disorder, gaudy outside with gold chains made from the people's money and harlot's money twisted together; crawling, serpentine men, the lousy combings and born freedom sellers of the earth.

Whitman laid the whole sorry mess at the feet of President Franklin Pierce, whom he singled out for especially repulsive invective: "The President eats dirt and excrement for his daily meals, likes it, and tries to force it on the States."[39]

Many Americans were beginning to agree with Whitman. Corruption of all sorts—venal officials, stolen elections, the spoils system, the hireling press—did seem pervasive. "Lobbyers," although just one of the culprits, had already been caught seducing the representatives of the people and attempting to subvert the democratic process, whether in Albany, Harrisburg, Washington, or elsewhere, so they were looking especially sinister and culpable.

The rank odor of corruption beginning to cling to lobbyists, even the sorry physical condition of Washington's streets paled in significance beside a much greater issue looming over the capital in 1859 that would surmount all other concerns during the next decade. Just as Sam arrived, the *Washington Evening Star*, the town's biggest booster, ran an article touting the federal metropolis's many virtues and urging visitors to come experience its charms: "Persons of wealth and taste . . . are coming more and more to appreciate the advantages and pleasures of having a home among the public men of America while the latter are assembled together. Nowhere else in this country is equal intellectual and social society within the reach of any and all respectable persons as here. . . . the lock is off and the door stands wide open for any to enter who may be so intelligent, entertaining and well-behaved as to prove agreeable acquaintances."[40]

To the men and women negotiating life in Washington that fall, the author must have seemed delusional. Even a newcomer like Sam, who was intelligent, entertaining, and well-behaved, could see that this rosy picture was bunk. Washington in 1859 was hardly an all-embracing Mecca, ready to welcome every agreeable man and woman getting off a train. The capital was a tinder box, growing more volatile each day. A deepening fissure was splitting the nation open, and the capital sat squarely on the fault line.

The Gwins' magnificent ball in 1858 had been one of the last big events in Washington at which North and South mixed socially. Despite the Gwins' best efforts, there had been an "incident" that very night. A rabid Southern partisan, Virginia Clay had, on previous occasions, refused to shake the hand of New York senator William Henry Seward, hotly telling her husband, who had begged her to greet his colleague, "Not even to save the Nation could I be induced to eat his bread, to drink his wine, to enter his domicile, to *speak* to him!" That night at the Gwins' home, she refused once again, lecturing Seward—"playfully," she claimed—about his ignorance of slavery and Southerners.[41]

From its beginning, Southerners and Southern ways had dominated the capital. Its first fine homes were built by Southerners; the first few congressmen to bring their families to Washington were Southerners; the hotels that catered to them, like the St. Charles, advertised underground locked cells for their slaves. The leaders of the small residential society in 1859—financiers and banking partners William Corcoran and George Riggs, the Tayloe and Parker families—were all Southerners. Southerners like Senators Gwin, John Slidell of Louisiana, Robert Toombs of Georgia, and Representatives Roger Pryor of Virginia and Williamson Cobb of Alabama led official society. A quarter of Washington's white residents had been born in Virginia or Maryland. Another 47 percent had been born in the District and had close Southern ties, and yet the town sheltered a national government in which Northern Republicans, with a very different point of view, were playing an increasingly prominent role. The capital's sole function was to house and service a government with which much of its population felt a diminishing kinship.[42]

As Sam and everyone else in Washington that fall of 1859 read the news of John Brown's raid on Harper's Ferry, West Virginia, followed by his trial and hanging in December, hearts hardened on both sides. Sam was dismayed but not surprised to learn that his brother-in-law, Samuel Gridley Howe, and his sister Julia were among Brown's most ardent supporters. At public events, only a thin veneer of civility remained. Harriet Lane tried to mix men and women of opposing views at her official White House entertainments, but the task became impossible.[43] Even at private dinner parties, hostesses found it difficult to honor the rules of precedence and still keep political enemies apart. Elizabeth Blair Lee, an ardent Unionist, wrote from her home across the street from the White House to her husband, naval officer Samuel Phillips Lee, about a terrible fight between Georgia senator Robert Toombs and General Winfield Scott at a dinner party in January, 1860: "Mr. Tombs . . . called the Old Hero a liar—where upon the General rushed into him—but they were promptly parted. . . . Civil war seems inevitable—even at friendly dinner parties."[44]

The arrival of two Japanese princes in May 1860 to negotiate a treaty, and a visit from "Lord Renfrew," the young Prince of Wales traveling incognito, in October, caused temporary flurries of excitement, but little could distract residents for long from the escalating crisis. The blue cockades of the secessionists sprouted on the lapels of many local men, including government clerks. If the nation did split in two peacefully, townspeople knew that Washington, on the northern border of one section, the southern of the other, would be the capital of neither, and without its status as capital, it was nothing. And if war did come, the capital, sitting on the dividing line, would be caught in the crossfire.[45]

This was the capital that Sam encountered when he arrived in 1859, the lobby he would join, and the tension he would try to keep away from his door. He brought his own political baggage along with him. Sam, like many of the wealthy men of New York with whom he had grown up, with whom he had socialized, and with whom he would found New York's Manhattan Club in 1865, was a Democrat. Although he had been away in California and South America in recent years, he had kept up with New York and national politics, thanks in part to his wealthy friend Samuel Latham Mitchill Barlow, a successful lawyer, investor, and speculator who was as powerful among Democrats as Weed was among Republicans.

Sam loathed slavery, but he was no abolitionist. He had spent more time in the South as a child, playing with his cousins in Georgia and South Carolina, than had his siblings, and he felt that he knew it better than did many Northerners. He had also come to know, through school and business and through his travels, many men who had risen to power in the South, such as Senator Judah P. Benjamin, a Democrat from Louisiana, and Vice President John C. Breckinridge, a Democrat from Kentucky. Sam believed in gradual emancipation and in compensation for slave owners. His views had cooled his friendship with Senator Charles Sumner of Massachusetts and caused a chill in his relationship with his favorite sister, Julia, who shared her husband's passionate abolitionist stance. Sam and Samuel Gridley Howe, his least-favorite brother-in-law, were barely speaking, but Sam had regarded him as a bully and a fanatic for some time anyhow. Sam and his best friend, Henry Wadsworth Longfellow, who, while less outspoken, sided with the Howes and Sumner, pointedly skirted the issue of slavery altogether in their letters.

Bankrolled by Baring Brothers, a British banking house, by the president of Paraguay, and by his friend Barlow, Sam rented a small house, 258 F Street, from the latter, stowed his political and philosophical bundles as best he could, and began to give the intimate dinners that would make him a legend. His "evenings" of fine food, wine, and conversation were means to ends, the ends being whatever his clients wanted and could pay for—a positive resolution to claims, favorable exchange rates, tax and tariff relief, political gossip.

Sam's gatherings were successful as much for their excellent fare as for their eclectic guest list. He had a real talent for friendship, a genuine curiosity about the world, and an openness to all points of view. During his forty-six checkered years, he had made and kept many friends from all parties, all parts of the country, and all walks of life, seeing the good in all sorts of "characters." Many of them, as disparate as William Gwin, a slave-owning Democratic senator from Mississippi, and William Henry Seward, an abolitionist Republican senator from New York, were now in Washington in positions of power. While many hostesses had tried and failed at the feat, Sam managed to keep his house neutral territory, where old friends and new ones on all sides of the issues of the day could gather. Gwin, Seward, Senators Stephen A. Douglas of Illinois, Milton S. Latham of California, Robert M. T. Hunter of Virginia, and Jefferson Davis of Mississippi, a combination of moderates and hotheads, could dine together without coming to blows.[46]

Senator Latham and Sam knew each other from their days as '49ers in San Francisco. When Latham arrived in Washington in early 1860 to take his Senate seat, he called on Sam, "a most remarkable man," and was quickly added to his guest list. On Sunday, March 25, 1860, Latham recorded in his diary that he had dined at Sam's with Baron Salomon de Rothschild of the French banking dynasty, Gwin, Representative Samuel "Sunset" Cox of Ohio, and the editor of the pro-Buchanan newspaper *The Constitution*, William Browne. Latham was not naïve. He knew that Sam had a purpose for the evening, but at night's end he still did not know what it was, only that he had had a delightful time.[47]

Within months of his arrival, Sam was moving among the upper echelons of Washington society. He was a guest at dinners with Secretary of the Treasury Howell Cobb and Secretary of the Interior Jacob Thompson. Senator Latham and Senator and Mrs. Gwin were aboard when Sam organized a cruise down the Potomac in April to picnic at Mt. Vernon. Sam's guest of honor was Harriet Lane. Sam also included Latham at a dinner in early May at which his guest of honor was General Winfield Scott, an old family friend. It was a great honor for Sam that General Scott, who was seventy-four and enormously fat and who rarely dined out, accepted his invitation; but Scott styled himself a connoisseur of fine food and wine, and he knew that both awaited him at Sam's house.[48]

Gwin, Browne, Kentucky Senator John J. Crittenden, and John Van Buren, son of the former president, were the other guests that night at what Latham called "one of the most interesting dinner parties ever assembled." The dinner was "got up in the most exquisite style, and the wines were pronounced by General Scott and Crittenden as very rare and exquisite in taste." It ended with a most dramatic dessert, "a pyramid of candies representing the different battles in which General Scott had been engaged, surmounted by the Goddess of Liberty with the American flag in her right hand and in her left the scales of justice." This tribute of Sam's must have warmed "Old Fuss and Feathers'" heart, because the general stayed late, reminiscing about Andrew Jackson and sharing stories about his great victory at Chapultepec in 1847.[49]

A few days after this dinner, Sam described it in detail to Julia and boasted, "Bohemia is rising in the world."[50] Julia could not have missed the dig. She had been desperate for Sam to give up his boom and bust life, running from creditors and disappearing on secret missions. "Keep to the things that are left you," she had pleaded, "they include all the best things—health, uncommon talents, acquirements and accomplishments, and friendship. Save these things from the wreck. . . . Begin a right and simple life with the capital you have—yourself." She thought he might lecture on his experiences in the West, write about the Potoyensee Indians with whom he had lived, become a professor—all were more respectable than the life he had been leading. "Come back," she had begged, "to the old Puritan morals, the only ones for the Anglo-Saxon race. Shake yourself loose from this nightmare. Wake up, and find yourself all that you ever were—the honest son of an honest man. . . For God's sake, my dear brother, listen to these true words from a heart true to you."[51]

Julia had been relieved when Sam had finally come back East in the spring of 1859 and had hoped for a moderation of his behavior. But he had no intention of hewing to the old Puritan morals; he had had enough of those when they were forced on him by his father. He also had no intention of becoming a poorly paid professor; he had heard enough about that life from Longfellow, who taught at Harvard. Sam decided to apply the attributes that Julia had enumerated to a profession that scandalized his sister. As soon as he was settled in Washington, he wrote teasingly to "My Dear Old Bird," crowing of his successes, making sure she knew that he was in demand, and dropping names and hints of his importance: "The other day at the State Department they asked me to put a Protocol into Spanish. I did it offhand, without Grammar or Dictionary, and my work remained without a single correction. . . . I have my own crockery and a set of silver marked S.W., which I earned by the sweat of my brow and the oil of my tongue." He signed his letter, "Your own, Sambo."[52]

Sam was indeed busy earning his crockery. He was secretly working for Paraguay's President López to protect that country's interests and shepherd a new treaty through to ratification. For his efforts, he was receiving payment of £100 a month, funneled through López's London bank accounts. Sam and President López conducted their clandestine correspondence using pseudonyms: Sam signed himself Pedro Fernández, while López became Nicolás Pérez. At the same time, Sam was drawing a paycheck from the U.S. State Department as secretary and translator for the arbitration commission meeting in Washington to consider claims and counterclaims between a group of Rhode Island businessmen and the government of Paraguay. By the time the treaty was ratified in March 1860, and the dispute settled resoundingly in favor of Paraguay in August, Sam had earned almost $18,000 from a delighted López, even though there was little evidence to suggest that Sam actually swayed the final decision beyond using his friendship with journalist William Henry Hurlbert to stop the vilification of Paraguay in several influential newspapers.[53]

In addition to his work for President López, Sam had several other irons in the fire that spring. In April, he closely followed the news from the Democratic national convention in Charleston, relaying every tidbit he could glean from his sources there to Barlow in New York and other Democrats in Washington.[54] In May, at the close of a letter to Julia, Sam promised, "I shall get Crawford's doors taken." Sculptor Thomas Crawford had designed the massive pediments for the new Senate wing of the Capitol and the statue that would crown its new dome, but, at his death from eye cancer in 1857, the commission for the massive bronze doors for the Senate wing was in limbo. Just how he got Crawford's doors "taken" was never clear, but Sam claimed credit for getting the sketches accepted and paid for, and his widowed sister Louisa was grateful.[55]

Throughout the spring, summer, and fall of 1860, Sam was busy watching out for Barlow's business interests. Barlow had backed Buchanan for the presidency in 1856 and thus had enjoyed great influence in Washington for the past four years. He realized, though, that his inside track might run out in the upcoming fall elections, and he was eager to extract all of the favors he could in the months remaining.

Barlow was already heavily invested in railroads, shipping, international finance, and real estate. In 1860, he thought he saw an opportunity to increase his fortune through mining in Latin America, where Sam could prove especially helpful. Sam was happy to oblige for an unspecified fee, suggesting men in Washington and Mexico to whom Barlow should write and relaying information that he picked up at the State Department.[56]

A flurry of letters between Sam and Barlow discussed a number of domestic projects with which Barlow needed Sam's help. One big real estate deal in which

Barlow and a consortium were trying to sell buildings and furniture to the government would net Sam and Barlow $15,000 each. "My dear Barlow," Sam wrote, reporting on his progress, "it has taken me a week to corral my Congressional elephants and I am at length able to write you favorably touching both your projects. I can get the furniture bill passed any day." Sam signed several of these confidential letters, "In haste, yours fraternally, S.W." Sam and Barlow both belonged to New York's Holland Lodge of Freemasons. On his most sensitive letters to Barlow, Sam wrote across the top, "On the □," a Masonic sign imposing the strictest secrecy.[57]

By the fall of 1860, the upcoming presidential election loomed large, consuming Sam and Barlow and most of Washington and the nation. Even though residents of the District of Columbia could not vote, partisans of all four candidates—Stephen A. Douglas, supported by Sam, Barlow, and other Northern Democrats; John C. Breckinridge, championed by Southern Democrats; Constitutional Unionist John Bell; and Republican Abraham Lincoln—held torch-lit parades through town. Sam sent all of the gossip he could pick up to Barlow, conferred with Gwin, and commiserated with Seward, who had thought that the Republican nomination had been his.

Tension mounted everywhere as election day approached. Still, Julia must have been taken aback by the uncharacteristically harsh language Sam used in an emotional letter to her on October 20, in which he seemed to brand her and her husband, who was at that very moment off in Canada evading charges of complicity in arming John Brown and his men, as demagogues: "I don't like the looks of things in Washington, and know that we shall have trouble with the South if Lincoln carries New York. . . . The North is playing with fire and a powder magazine, and I expect to see the day when an abolitionist will be as obnoxious as were the members of the Hartford Convention half a century ago. . . . Since the first winter of the Pilgrim Colony, New England will not have suffered so much as from the financial miseries entailed upon her by fanaticism."[58]

On election night, November 6, when news of Lincoln's victory reached the capital, a mob attacked the Republican headquarters. Local secessionists draped their houses in black. A shadow fell across everything in Washington, including Christmas preparations. Shopkeepers decorated their windows, and Gautier encouraged early orders for holiday cakes "both pound and fruit" in vain. The dry goods store Lammond's ran an advertisement claiming, "Readers, the Union is in danger, but by buying your holiday presents at Lammond's, you *may* save it." Nevertheless, sales flagged. Few were in a festive mood.[59]

On December 20, outgoing President Buchanan, vilified by Southerners and

Northerners alike who were disappointed by his inaction, attended a Washington wedding. As he sat in the parlor amid the hot-house flowers, he heard a commotion in the hallway and asked a woman nearby whether the house was on fire. It was, in fact, the Union that was in flames. The shouts came from outside, from those rejoicing over the news of the secession of South Carolina.[60]

Sam Ward's life was about to take another turn.

CHAPTER TWO

A prestigious pedigree and a promising start; loves and losses; a fortune squandered; roughing it with the '49ers; secret missions, secret agreements, and a new beginning

WHEN THE *Evening Star* noted of Washington's fluid society in 1859 that, "the lock is off and the door stands wide open for any to enter who may be so intelligent, entertaining and well-behaved," it read like a personal invitation to Sam Ward. He was all of those things, as well as a new-made man on the make. Washington might be jittery with sectional tension and there were already lobbyists aplenty, but none would prove to be quite like Sam Ward, who was ready to follow the trail that Thurlow Weed, another suave New Yorker, had marked with the smoke of excellent cigars and to blaze his own.

So, where had Sam been all those years before 1859? And how had he acquired his seemingly endless trove of anecdotes about the Wild West and the Bonapartes and his knowledge of Euclidean geometry and German wines? The road that led him to Washington was full of detours that included love, loss, fortunes won and lost, exile, and aliases.

Samuel Ward, the fourth in a distinguished line to bear that name, was born on January 27, 1814, in New York City. He arrived as the city was tense with fear that the British, with whom the young nation was again at war, would blockade its harbor and torch its buildings as they had barely thirty years before. This time, however, the British ships sailed past New York, headed for the Chesapeake Bay and the new federal capital, which they burned instead. Among his ancestors, the new little Ward claimed a captain in Oliver Cromwell's cavalry, two colonial governors, a member of the Continental Congress, two officers in George Washington's army, and Francis Marion, the "Swamp Fox." Between his mother's and his father's families, he was related to Wards, Greenes, Cutlers, and McAllisters, all prominent families of the North or the South.[1]

Sam's father was a young New York banker when he was smitten by sixteen-year-old Julia Cutler. They married in 1812, and Julia had her first flare-up of what was almost certainly tuberculosis in the spring of 1813. Sam's birth in 1814 began a cycle of pregnancy and illness: another son, Henry, was born in 1818; Julia in 1819; Marion in 1820; Louisa in 1821; and Annie in 1824.

Mrs. Ward worried that her first born seemed small and pale, so he was sent off to his grandfather Ward's farm on Long Island for much of the year. Sam adored the old colonel, who loved him back. From his grandfather, Sam claimed, he gained his love of learning and his lifelong curiosity about all things edible, which began with the stewed skunk the Indians who worked his grandfather's fields let him sample. Sam apparently never recognized another lifelong trait, credulousness, demonstrated in another story from his childhood. Sam and a mulatto boy named Bilbo, who worked on the farm, plotted to run away and join a band of pirates. All they lacked was money, but Bilbo had the solution. As Sam told it, "he induced me to put a penny a week in a certain hole in the ground where, he declared, at the end of the year I should find the fifty pence turned into gold by incantations known only to him." Sam was stunned later to find not gold, not even the pennies, but a pile of white pebbles. Similar tricks, for much higher stakes, would be played on him many times.[2]

When Sam was ten, his parents sent him off to Massachusetts to the Round Hill School, a progressive new school run by former Harvard professor Joseph Cogswell and George Bancroft, the future historian and U.S. minister to Great Britain, and based on a German philosophy that espoused developing the whole person. Within months after he arrived, Sam's mother, just twenty-eight years old, died of puerperal fever, three days after giving birth to his sister Annie. There was no time to fetch Sam from school to say goodbye.

Sam's father was devastated. Unable to bear the memories it contained, he sold their house with all its furnishings and moved his young family to Bond Street. He turned to religion and threw himself into good works. He gave up cigars and took up temperance and, to the horror of his brothers and friends, destroyed all of the wine in his well-stocked cellar. His neighbor, diarist Philip Hone, recalled, "He became all of a sudden a total abstinence man, at a time of life when the experiment was dangerous, and drank nothing but water." Banker Ward also became morbidly obsessed with his children's physical and spiritual health. Her father, Julia recalled, "carefully and jealously guarded [us] from all that might be represented in the orthodox trinity of evil, the world, the flesh, and the devil. . . . He dreaded for his children the dissipation of fashionable society, and even the risks of general intercourse with the unsanctified many."[3]

Off in Massachusetts at Round Hill, Sam mourned his mother alone. He begged to come home. So homesick was he that he drew little hearts on the bottom of a letter and wrote, "For father, the largest part of my heart." "O, dear father," he wrote as his twelfth birthday neared, "I want to see you so much that I would give anything that it is in power to give, in order that we might mutually soothe one another's afflictions." In reply, he got a lecture: "My darling son—Your twelfth birthday fills Father's heart with the thought of your angel mother, blest in Heaven. For her, for your poor Father, for yourself and for your friends, strive to be all that is virtuous, good and wise. . . . relax not, dearest boy." In letter after letter to his father, Sam beseeched him for sympathy, for solace, for approval. All his life he would seek affection and praise from his family and friends.[4]

Headmaster Bancroft, who did not like Sam one bit (Sam detested "Old Bancroft," who was all of twenty-seven), identified other traits in his student. Sam excelled at subjects neither his father nor Bancroft valued: he picked up modern languages easily; he drew beautifully. In mathematics, a subject Mr. Ward did appreciate, Bancroft was sorry to say that Sam did not "excel, nor would he," a prediction Sam would soon prove wrong. In his final report to Sam's father, Bancroft conceded that Sam "has no malice and no obstinacy," he is "manly, correct, open, confiding, pleasant." Sam would have been thrilled to hear these positive words from his stern teacher, but he was not told. Bancroft had warned Mr. Ward against offering Sam encouragement: "Praise injures him. . . . it makes him first confident, and then of course careless."[5]

At Round Hill, Sam also revealed a talent for friendship. His willingness to instigate a prank and suffer the consequences if discovered, his loyalty, and his sensitivity to the needs of others made him popular with his classmates, whose friendship would stand Sam in good stead in later years. They were an impressive group of boys representing the leading families of the nation: Amorys, Appletons, Grays, Perkinses, and Peabodys from the North; Habershams, Bullocks, Tilghmans, Gilmors, Pickneys, Izards, and Rutledges from the South. Sam noted especially Theodore Sedgwick and John Lothrop Motley, a future historian and lawyer and an ambassador-to-be, and Henry Bellows, who would organize the U.S. Sanitary Commission during the Civil War.[6]

Sam graduated from Round Hill in 1828 and went home to New York. The family to which he returned was growing increasingly prosperous. Samuel Ward was a chief partner of the rock-solid Wall Street banking house of Prime, Ward, and King. Sam's father, his four uncles, and his grandfather were spread out along Bond Street in a row of handsome townhouses. Although his father's socializing tended to be sober, conservative, and infrequent, all of the Wards were part of New York's social elite. Sam met a host of prominent and rising men around the various Ward dinner tables—Washington Irving, James Fenimore Cooper, Hamilton Fish, Thurlow Weed, William Henry Seward, John Jacob Astor—whose paths would cross with his in the coming decades.[7]

Although only fifteen, Sam easily passed the entrance examination to Columbia College (now University). There, for the first time in his life, he had leisure (classes took up little of his time) and, thanks to a modest allowance from his father, money. Putting both to good use, he and his new friends got to know every oyster cellar in Manhattan. Sam's favorite spot was a new little café on William Street run by Swiss brothers John and Peter Delmonico and patronized by homesick Europeans: "I reveled in the coffee, the chocolate, the *bavaroises*, the *orgeats* and the *petits gateaux* and the *bonbons*."[8]

Like his Round Hill friends, Sam's college friends would crop up again and again in his life. Some were fellow members of Columbia's Philolexian Society. Theodore Sedgwick, Sam's friend from Round Hill, was a member of this literary and debate group, as were many of the sons of New York's first families, names like Fish, Hone, Chauncey, and King. After two and a half years of this education in good living and camaraderie, Sam graduated from Columbia College in the summer of 1831 at seventeen.[9]

Sam, who had been more devoted to "*bonbons*" than books at Columbia, proved to be a better scholar after graduation. Perhaps to avoid joining Prime, Ward, and King, as his father expected of his oldest son, he threw himself into the study of mathematics and begged to go to Boston to study with the great navigator Nathaniel Bowditch and his mathematics professor from Round Hill, Benjamin Peirce, then at Harvard. Already demonstrating skill in the subject, he began publishing a little magazine of problems and puzzles called *The Mathematical Diary*; edited a new edition of J. R. Young's *Algebra*; wrote two scholarly articles, one on the doctrine of probabilities and the other a review of a biography of John Locke, for the prestigious *American Quarterly Review*; and landed a spot on the board of examiners that grilled cadets at West Point on their mathematical proficiency. A week after he returned home from West Point, two gentlemen from the military academy called on Samuel Ward to offer his son the post of assistant professor of mathematics, with a salary of $1,500 per year *and* a furnished house. Sam was eighteen years old.[10]

His father was astonished, but Sam was thrilled and ready with a counter-proposal: while he was at present inadequate to the task, with a year of studying military engineering in Europe, he would be equipped to do his father proud. Sam's powers of persuasion must have already been irresistible. For a young American, a teenager, to go abroad alone to study was still rare, but soon Samuel Ward was taking his son to visit Albert Gallatin and other prominent New Yorkers to collect letters of introduction to the eminent men of Europe. From his father, Sam received the most important letter of all, an unlimited letter of credit for Hottinguer et Cie., the Paris correspondents of Prime, Ward, and King.

Sam sailed from New York harbor in mid-October 1832. By late November, he was happily settled in Paris, what he called "the city of sin and science" in his first letter home. Instead of studying mathematics at the Sorbonne, he threw himself into learning all about Parisian society. By spring, he was spending sums that left his father staggering. In one of his ingratiating letters home, signed "Your affectionate and steady son," he explained that music, of which he had become passionately fond, was basically mathematics, and it was only to grasp this complex interrelationship better that he had hired not one but two music teachers *and* purchased a piano.[11]

Sam's letters and pocket diaries offer a glimpse into his personality during this time in Europe, which he considered the most important of his life. He was alternately overindulged and then chided for his lack of restraint by his father, whom he loved, feared, and often deceived. Sam craved praise and affection, and he also gave both effusively and sincerely. He always believed the best of the people he met. He was a spendthrift, whose promises to reform always came to grief. He cherished lofty aspirations, but he had an aversion to hard work. Sam was also a romantic, deeply moved by art, music, poetry, prose, drama, beautiful women, and lovely vistas. He was charming, handsome, well-dressed, well-read, well-mannered, and well-spoken. He graced every drawing room he entered and beguiled everyone within earshot.[12]

Somehow, Sam convinced his father to let him extend his stay again and again until the original one year in Paris turned into three more in Heidelberg. The pretext was to study with the great German men of science, but, in fact, he worked even less there than he had in Paris. In Sam's eyes, these were years well spent. He acquired new skills: he learned German and polished his French, learned to dance the mazurka and mastered the guitar, and memorized endless verses of German lieder. In Paris, he dined at something new to an American, a real restaurant with tablecloths and individual menus. He ate at the very best such establishments and developed a taste for subtle sauces and exotic vegetables like endive and eggplant. He also met interesting new people like Franz Liszt,

Niccolò Paganini, and drama critic Jules Janin, who introduced him to the prettiest actresses and greatest actors in France. Although Janin would not confirm it, many believed Sam to be the American in Janin's *The American in Paris*, published in America in 1844.[13]

In Paris, Sam called on the great mathematician Legendre. In Göttingen, he met Karl Friedrich Gauss, the astronomer. In Dresden, he had his portrait painted by the court painter, Carl Christian Vogel von Vogelstein. In Berlin, Sam convinced the American minister, Henry Wheaton, to name him secretary of legation so he could gain entrée to the best parties. He caught a glimpse of Jerome Bonaparte and talked at length with his brother, Joseph. And there were girls—the name Florentine appears most often in Sam's little red pocket diaries, but it shares the pages with Josephine, Paquita, and Jeanette and notes on copious amounts of champagne washing down breakfast, dinner, and supper.[14]

Sam literally dined out for decades on stories of the men and women he met during these years, but one encounter especially enriched his life. During his last spring in Heidelberg, at a small reception, Sam met Henry Wadsworth Longfellow, a young widower from Maine preparing to take up a post at Harvard. That night, Sam wrote, he made "a friend in whom I never failed to find the most tender and loving sympathy." The friendship sustained both men for nearly fifty years.[15]

Interspersed with the new people, places, foods, and wines Sam encountered, there were some new ideas about science and mathematics. He earned a doctoral degree in mathematics from the University of Tübingen, an uncommon accomplishment for an American of twenty, and his dissertation was written in Latin. In letters home, he outlined his grand plans to write on mathematics, astronomy, geology, and philosophy, as well as fiction, poetry, and biography. Sam was certain that renown lay in store for him. To his fellow student and new friend Charles Mersch, he wrote, "I must be *aut Caesar aut nullus*" (I must be Caesar or nothing).[16]

In Sam's father's eyes, these years away from home were not only wasted but dangerous and enormously expensive. Nearly every letter he wrote to Sam coupled a rebuke for excessive spending with warnings against pursuing a purposeless life of indolence and a plea to come home. Nearly every letter Sam wrote to him included a contrite apology but no sign of actual reform. In response to one scolding letter, Sam promised, "Careful economy and rigid self-denial shall somewhat atone for my carelessness." But self-denial was alien to Sam's make-up. Soon thereafter, he bought a coach.[17]

Tired of excuses and genuinely pining to see his oldest son, Samuel Ward finally ordered Sam home in early 1835. Sam, desperate to avoid what he referred to as the "involuntary servitude" that awaited him in New York, promised to come in May, then July, then September. Finally, in the spring of 1836, Sam could stall no longer. The long-suffering bankers at Hottinguer's presented him the bill for his four years of "study": 81,000 francs, roughly $16,000—akin to $400,000 in 2000—an enormous sum for a young student to have spent. This was serious, and Sam knew it. He outdid himself in effusive prose in a long preemptive letter to his father: "Must my gray-haired sire still labor, in the meridian of his life, while I, who am young and inhale inspiration, genius, with God's air, inhale them but to impoverish him? . . . Here I lie on this sad earth when vainly I would soar! Adieu, dearest father! Thank thy loved sire, my dear grandfather, that until past the age of folly thou atest Spartan bread!" Sam was actually lying on a comfortable bed at the Hôtel des Princes! To Mersch, he boasted: "Yesterday a letter of eighteen pages to my father, a sublime epistle . . . I am possessed of the desperation of genius." Sam landed back in New York on September 25, 1836. Was it merely coincidence, he wondered in a letter to Mersch, that the Bible verses read from the pulpit on his first Sunday home should be the story of the Prodigal Son?[18]

Sam returned to a home he had never seen. While he was away, his father had built an austere but elegant mansion, what his neighbor, Philip Hone, called a "noble house," on the corner of Bond and Broadway, the expanding city's most prestigious address. Known within the family as "The Corner," the new house included the first private picture gallery in New York City. Sam was deeply touched to find that his father had also included a library specifically to hold all of the books that he had bought and shipped home over the past four years.[19] George Templeton Strong, then a seventeen-year-old student at Columbia whose family and the Wards were friends, offered his snide opinion of the Ward library and Sam in his diary on April 7, 1837: "Walked up with the two Wards to see the library Samuel Ward has brought out from Germany with him. . . . In point of show it is certainly the finest I ever saw, a great majority of the books being in the finest possible condition as to binding and typography. . . . It is a splendid collection though I fancy more for show than use."[20]

Samuel Ward hoped that this new home would be a self-contained oasis for his family. The formidable cast-iron fence that surrounded it made tangible his desire to keep the temptations of the wider world at bay. Henry, eighteen, was about to graduate from Columbia, where Marion was also a student, but Mr. Ward had been successful thus far in keeping his daughters, the "three graces of Bond Street," fairly sequestered. Annie was just ten and Louisa thirteen, but Julia, seventeen, was already chafing for wider horizons. "My dear father, with all his noble generosity and overweening affection," Julia recalled, "sometimes appeared to me as my jailer." She was thrilled to have her worldly brother back home as an ally; his return "opened the door a little for me."[21] Just as Samuel Ward had feared, Sam came back bursting with new music, dances, books, recipes, friends, and all of the European frippery of which the elder Ward had a horror. It was Sam's new ideas, however, especially those about what he regarded as a rich man's obligation to foster convivial culture, that clashed most sharply with his father's views. Julia described one debate between father and son shortly after Sam came home:

> My dear eldest brother held many arguments with him on this theme. . . . On one occasion the dispute between them became quite animated.
> "Sir," said my brother, "you do not keep in view the importance of the social tie."
> "The social what?" asked my father.
> "The social tie, sir."
> "I make small account of that," said the elder gentleman.
> "I will die in defense of it!" impetuously rejoined the younger.
> My father was so much amused at this sally that he spoke of it to an intimate friend: "He will die in defense of the social tie, indeed!"[22]

In New York, Sam tried to settle in to a life in which he hoped to pursue two demanding careers at once: scholarship, which he loved, and banking, which he loathed. How hard could the work of finance be, he wondered. Prime, Ward and King was booming. He bragged to Mersch that the firm had made $216,000 the previous year.[23]

Sam initially thought he was doing splendidly. After three months on the job, he crowed to Mersch, "I am making amazing progress in business and am told that a year from now I shall be made a member of the firm."[24] Julia recalled his start a bit differently. She wrote of Sam's shove into the banking world: "He decided, with some reluctance, to pursue this course. . . . His first days' performance at the office was so faulty that my father, on reviewing it, exclaimed, 'You will play the very devil with the check-book, sir, if you use it in this way.'" Always Sam's champion, she continued that he had "applied himself diligently" but "without developing a taste for business pursuits," which was a considerable understatement.[25]

In long letters to Mersch, who was waiting in Luxembourg for word to come to New York to begin their joint scholarly projects, although Sam sometimes exalted, he more often despaired: "Sometimes it seems as if my day had come—and gone. . . . In the office of an American banker, one can but feel that every day is a day lost."[26]

Longfellow was a bright spot in the bleak picture Sam painted. Many weekends, Sam would take a steamer up to Cambridge or Longfellow would come down to New York to enjoy the luxury at The Corner. When not visiting each other, Sam and Longfellow exchanged frequent letters. At the beginning of their nearly fifty-year-long correspondence of hundreds of letters back and forth, Longfellow wrote, "You will write me soon, I trust; and when the shuttle of thought gets once fairly in motion, we will weave such a motley and gorgeous epistolary tapestry, as has never yet been woven on the 'loom of time.' What do you think of that?" Sam thought that was a fine idea. Their letters, in which they poured out their joys and fears, are filled with the language of the intimate male friendships, sanctioned by the culture that celebrated them, that enriched the lives of many nineteenth-century men. Sam and Longfellow's friendship was unusual only in that it endured with unabated warmth for so many decades.[27]

Sam saw Longfellow as his link to the world of academe, a world he still felt certain was right for him. Longfellow knew better. Fondly but accurately sizing up Sam's personality, Longfellow wrote of him to a friend, Sam's cousin George Greene, that "he is wholly unfitted for going through the drudgery of a professor's life." At the same time, Longfellow appreciated that Sam could never throttle down his "sixty-horse-power temperament" to the pace of the counting house. What neither Longfellow nor Sam's father nor Sam had was a solution to this dilemma.[28]

Sam's father loved him deeply and worried about him incessantly. He could see that Sam was not happy, and he probably knew in his heart that Sam was not cut out to be a banker, but his response was to redouble his efforts to make him one and to lecture Sam constantly about the virtues of hard work and prudence. His warnings fell on deaf ears, and Sam's balancing act, teetering between scholarship and the counting house, continued unresolved. In later years, Sam looked back at the choice he had failed to face straight on: "At the inception of my career I committed its first grave error: instead of following the Divine precept, 'No man can serve two masters,' I took for my motto the false doctrine of Molière's Tartuffe: 'Il est avec le ciel des accommodements,' and imagined that the duties of my new calling need not interfere with the prosecution of my old one. My love for the latter was sincere, but I ought to have felt that if the former were as degrading as my mistaken vanity fancied it, I should have had the manhood to reject it; or, having adopted it, the loyalty to make it my chief pride and duty."[29]

While Sam saw his mistake in hindsight, in the moment he was burning his candle at both ends. He swore to Mersch that he studied "during all my spare time from 5 to 8 in the morning, from 9 to 10:30 in the evening."[30] His diligence paid off. To his delight and his father's surprise, New York's new Stuyvesant Institute, an association for the diffusion of knowledge, invited him to give its opening lecture. Sam chose as his theme the importance of the sciences to the nation's future.[31]

The success of his talk spurred Sam on. "Women no longer appeal to me—the thirst for knowledge alone devours me," he enthused to Mersch. "Gaiety, pleasures, charming young creatures, daughters of flaming youth . . . I see them no more. . . . I shall not marry before I am at least thirty, except to ambition." Mersch must have been surprised indeed when one of Sam's next letters, written just shy of his twenty-fourth birthday, brought word of his engagement to seventeen-year-old Emily Astor: "I am the happiest of mortals, I do not know what good fairy presided at my birth, but if there ever was a Fortunatus it is your friend Sam."[32]

Despite his claims, Sam had not spent *all* of his time in his library or at the bank. He renewed his acquaintance with the Delmonico brothers and patronized their restaurant, the first in the city, which they had opened in his absence. Young, handsome, cosmopolitan, the oldest son of a rich man, he was invited to every fashionable soirée, dance, and party by hostesses eager to have him grace their drawing rooms. At one of these parties, Sam met pretty, blonde, fun-loving Emily Astor, granddaughter of gouty John Jacob Astor, the richest man in America.

Emily's father, William Astor, who had also studied in Heidelberg and had also begged his father to let him stay longer, but who had obediently come home when ordered to take his place in the family business, was not entirely happy with his daughter's flashy young suitor. Sam's family was wealthy but not in the same league as the Astors. Sam, however, ascertained that it was really John Jacob Astor whom he had to win over. Emily was her grandfather's favorite grandchild; he loved to hear her sing the old German songs of his boyhood, the same songs that, to the old man's delight, Sam could sing by heart. One of the young New York Livingston girls shared the news of Sam's success with a cousin: "I presume you had heard of Emily Astor's engagement to young Ward. . . . He is said to be very clever and well informed—he is certainly very amusing. . . . I should not omit as a recommendation of the match . . . that Ward's father is considered one of the wealthiest men in New York, and old Astor's motto is you know *a little more.*"[33]

Sam and Emily were married at her parents' house on January 25, 1838. Julia claimed that the wedding was "the most cheerful that I ever saw."[34] Two days later, Sam wrote to Longfellow of his happiness: "The visions of hope and youth and loveliness have become one glorious, thrilling reality; out of the perfumed incense I have so long burned to my unknown divinity, the goddess herself hath appeared."[35]

The months that followed were some of Sam's happiest. He was doing tolerably well at Prime, Ward, and King; his father eased up on his hectoring; he was giving lectures, writing reviews and essays, helping to underwrite a new magazine, *The New York Review*, and gaining a reputation as a young man of letters. A mark of the increasing esteem in which Sam was held was his inclusion in a ten-lecture series presented by the Mercantile Library Association in late 1840. Lecturers included Horace Mann, Longfellow, Ralph Waldo Emerson, and "S. Ward, Jr., a young merchant, rising rapidly to fame."[36]

Sam had a wife he adored and who adored him. Young, rich, and popular, they were one of the golden couples of the city's elite. To Julia's delight, Sam and Emily lived and entertained at The Corner after their wedding and included her in their parties. Sam's household account books from these months document their expenses as they set out to furnish their own home nearby at 32 Bond Street, a wedding gift from Sam's father. There were purveyors' bills for marble mantlepieces, carpets and draperies, teapots, rose bushes, candlesticks, books, and champagne (one dozen bottles—$12). Then an entry appeared for a pink baby's hat and infant dresses, then another for washing three dozen diapers every day ($3.50 for a month). Emily and Sam's first child, a little girl, was born on November 9, 1838. They named her Margaret after her grandmother Astor, but everyone called her Maddie.[37]

The first dark cloud to cast a shadow on Sam's happiness was his father's unexpected death in November 1839. The obituary in the *New York Sun* echoed those in several newspapers, calling Samuel Ward a "merchant of active energy, extended views, unbounded enterprise, and inflexible integrity . . . plain in his habits and prudent in his conduct, he was a model of mercantile munificence." His neighbor Philip Hone said of him, "He was a rich man, and made a good use of his money." To Sam, his father had been a conscience and a restraining hand. Although the two had often disagreed and Sam had long chafed at his father's conservative values, he missed him terribly. He poured out his sorrow in letters to Longfellow: "I am as one shipwrecked." "I am as a child of some old soldier of feudal days to whom devolves the two-handed sword of his sire who perished in the battlefield." "We continue the firm and his place will be mine as soon as I can fill it which will not be until we see miracles again. . . . God help me."[38]

There would be no waiting for miracles. Sam took his father's place at Prime, Ward and King almost immediately. His brother Henry, twenty-two, who understood and loved the business, joined him, and Sam relied heavily on him. Less than a year later, however, Henry caught typhoid fever and died within days in Julia's arms. Sam was still reeling from his death when the next month brought news of the hideous death of Nathaniel Prime, the retired founder of the bank and a close family friend. Sam wrote to Longfellow: "Old Mr. Prime committed suicide yesterday, by cutting his throat with a razor." (Prime had become delusional and imagined that he had lost all of his money.)[39]

There was one bright spot that fall. In October, Sam wrote Longfellow that "Toward Christmas I am promised, God willing, another Bairn." On February 16, 1841, he dashed off a joyous note announcing the arrival of his first son and noting that mother and baby were doing "extremely well." Two days later, another note, this time barely legible, brought the heartbreaking news that an infection had set in and Emily had died "after but an hour's warning." On February 21, Sam wrote again, ending with an ominous postscript: "I fear we shall not be permitted to raise the little boy." The next day's letter confirmed that prophecy: "A little after three o'clock this morning our little sufferer left us to join his mother. . . . God knows what will become of me."[40]

Sam found himself executor of his father's several-million-dollar estate, partner in one of New York's most prestigious banking firms, guardian of his three high-spirited sisters, all of whom moved in with him, a widower, the father of a two-year-old girl, and still only twenty-seven years old. He shared his misery with Longfellow in almost daily letters, but in one he put his finger on the tonic that would see him through this dark time: "I am a little changed, but there is something left of me."[41] Although badly shaken, Sam's basic nature—his appealing as well as aggravating qualities—had not changed. His optimism would slowly return; his generosity of spirit and romantic nature would resurface, as would his need for approval and to be loved, his desire for wealth and his unwillingness to work hard to get it, and the dangerous combination of financial ineptitude and eagerness to take risks.

At first, Sam mourned by throwing himself into his studies, but before long he was taking singing lessons again. He began reporting on everything from Maddie's developing language skills to his sisters' first love affairs in newsy letters to a host of friends and to his brother Marion, a successful young businessman in New Orleans. Almost daily letters were received from and mailed off to Longfellow in Cambridge, and many of Sam's ended with "Give my love to the boys."[42]

"The boys" were three of Longfellow's closest friends: Cornelius Felton, once Sam's teacher at Round Hill, now Longfellow's colleague at Harvard, where he was professor of Greek; Dr. Samuel Gridley Howe, the oldest of the "boys" at forty-one, who fought in the Greek revolution and was the founder and director of the Perkins Institution for the Blind; and Charles Sumner, a rising young Boston lawyer, who had traveled in Europe and could speak almost as many languages as

Sam. After Emily's death, they welcomed Sam into their circle. Many weekends, he caught a steamer up to Boston, where the group would smoke cigars, drink German wine, and talk for hours in Longfellow's rooms at Craigie House. Other times, they all trooped to New York to stay with Sam. They were not rich men, and they were all a bit agog at Sam's gracious life style. After one group visit, Sumner wrote Sam with thanks: "We all returned plethoric with happiness." Felton, writing to Longfellow in Europe about his and Howe's recent visit with Sam, noted: "We enjoyed this visit beyond anything this mortal life often turns up. . . . Howe says he has never experienced anything like it except two or three expeditions against the Turks." "Such meetings are the wine of life," Longfellow wrote to Sam.[43]

In the letters that circulated among the five friends, they discussed books, poetry, ideas, and philosophy. There was no mention of politics or banking, but there was a good deal of talk about love. Howe hated to be laughed at and so was left alone, but the others teased one another about crushes on actresses, pried for information, and gossiped about acquaintances and about each other. At different points in time, Howe, Longfellow, and Sumner (but not Felton, who was married) was each suspected of being in love with one or another of "the Three Graces," Sam's sisters. Felton suggested that each of them marry one of the young women.

Howe took Felton up on his suggestion. After a stormy courtship, he proposed to Julia, who was nearly twenty years his junior, as blond as he was dark, as different from him in temperament as could be imagined, and equally strong-willed. Completely smitten, she accepted. Although Sam professed to be pleased for both of them, he was worried. He saw flashes in Howe of his father's cold authoritarianism. When Howe suggested that Julia was not docile enough and objected to her desire to continue to write after their marriage, Sam wrote him in hot defense of his sister. If Julia drew well, Sam admonished Howe, surely he would exhibit her work; "Why should not a fondness for history and philosophy be also an attribute of the mother of his children—or poetry be welcome when it gushes from the 'wellspring' of a nature imaginative yet reasonable, aspiring though gentle?"[44] A fissure in Sam's friendship with Howe opened then, and it grew wider over the years.

Despite Sam's misgivings, all of "the boys" were on hand on April 26, 1843, for the wedding in New York. To Howe's intense annoyance, both Sam and Marion, who thoroughly disliked Howe and called him a "confounded bit of Boston granite," recommended to Julia that she become, after her marriage, Mrs. Julia Ward Howe, rather than Mrs. Samuel Gridley Howe.[45]

None of the boys teased Longfellow about Fanny Appleton. He had been desperately in love with her for seven long years, during which she had remained frostily aloof. After Julia and Howe's engagement, there were the first glimmers of hope, and Sam even ventured an allusion: "There has been a recent eruption of Mt. Etna after a stillness of many years in its crater." Fanny had, in fact, thawed at last. Howe was on his honeymoon, but the rest of the boys were together in June for a second wedding, this one in Cambridge, with Sam as toastmaster.[46]

That left Sumner and Sam. Although Sumner had opined to Sam the year before, "I wish I could find somebody to love," by the time of Longfellow's wedding, when Sumner was thirty-two, he was telling them all that he was going to wait to wed until he was forty. In fact, he waited until he was fifty-five, and the union was unhappy and brief.[47] Sam, however, made no such vow. Handsome, a rich widower for two years, and not yet thirty, he was one of the best catches in New York. There had been rumors for months among the boys that he had already been caught.

Sam had fallen for a beautiful young woman from New Orleans named Medora Grymes, who had appeared in New York for the 1842–43 winter social season. Her mother, Suzette Bosque Grymes, a fortune-hunting shrew, had brought her two spoiled daughters to New York to find rich husbands who could support them in the style to which their indulgent lawyer-gambler father, John Randolph Grymes, had accustomed them. Medora, described by one artist as the "incarnation of Aphrodite," had quickly found a dozen suitors. By the time she met Sam, she was already engaged to a much older, well-off Frenchman. That, however, did not deter her mother, who was eager for a younger and even richer son-in-law. She enlisted the aid of her husband, who proclaimed that he could not condone the first match because of the age disparity, and the engagement was broken.[48]

No one but Sam and Suzette Grymes believed that Medora was the woman for him. Marion, who knew a great deal—little of it good—about John Grymes and his family, wrote to Louisa from New Orleans of the family's checkered background and Medora's shallow intellect. He thought Medora was a schemer, and he was certain that Sam was making a big mistake: "Sam is entirely beyond our control, and indeed beyond self-control. Something must sober him a little, for he is perfectly among the clouds." Marion encouraged Louisa to show Sam his letter but underlined a warning: "Do not, however, trust this letter out of your sight, for should M——— know that I have endeavored to thwart her wishes, it would sow the seeds of a deadly discord between us which could not but make Sam unhappy."[49]

Sumner, Howe, and Longfellow, who all met Medora in Boston, were impressed by her beauty but by little else and told Sam so, although Longfellow, happy at last, couched his concern in the gentlest of terms.[50] Julia, horrified that Sam had pursued Medora while she was engaged to another man, was more blunt. In Europe on her honeymoon, she heard the rumors and derided Sam in a letter to Louisa: "I am given to understand that he is making a donkey of himself by sending Medora Grymes bouquets which she gives away, boxes, and a riding whip which he himself deserves to feel."[51]

Deaf to all cautions, Sam proposed and Medora accepted. The Astors were livid, viewing the match as a slight to Emily's memory. When news reached their summer estate where Louisa and little Maddie, nearly five years old, were visiting, the Astors had Louisa shown to the door with her suitcase behind her. They demanded custody of Maddie, threatening her vast inheritance if Sam refused. He acquiesced. If he ever wrote a word about his decision to relinquish his daughter, it does not survive.[52] Maddie was in the Astor camp for good, and the Astors never had a good word for Sam. The gulf that opened between father and daughter would never be forded.

Sam Ward and Medora were married before a small group of family and friends, including Longfellow and Sumner, on September 20, 1843, on Staten Island at the mansion Suzette Grymes had pretentiously named *Capo di Monte* but everyone else called Grymes Hill. Shortly afterward, New Yorker Henry Brevoort wrote a long letter to Washington Irving, who was serving as the American minister to Spain, sharing the latest gossip, much of it about their mutual friend Sam, the Astors, and the jilted Frenchman: "Old Mr. Astor still holds out [he was eighty], and is better, body and mind, than he was before you left us. An untoward event has just happened in his family, which has stirred his ire, a thing which always does him good. Master Sam W—has married Miss Medora Grymes." He concluded: "Sam, albeit not one of the wisest of men, has probably made a silly match." Fanny Longfellow, a happy bride herself, had initially taken Sam's part, but, after the wedding, she wrote of her misgivings to a friend: "I do not think Sam is very wise, but prefer to hope now that he is married, that he may make her too happy to go astray." Sam had no doubts at all. To the honeymooning Howes, he wrote: "I am as happy and serene as it is possible for a man to be."[53]

Sam and Medora graced every major society party that winter except those at the Astor mansions, and they entertained often themselves. When Medora bore two sons in quick succession—Samuel, called Wardie, in 1844, and John Randolph in 1845—Sam was ecstatic; his home life was happy again. His business life was anything but. Urged on by Medora, Sam wanted more than ever to make a lot of money and retire from business. Supremely confident of his abilities, he saw speculation as his ticket to freedom. Marion wrote increasingly stern letters from

New Orleans, warning Sam to go slow. Alarmed by Sam's recklessness, James King pulled out of the firm at the end of 1846. In September 1847, Wall Street was stunned by news that Prime, Ward and Company had collapsed. Rumors about the cause of the smash up filled the financial papers for days, but in the end the blame was heaped upon Sam, whose speculation in commodities had caused the debacle. Marion could not help Sam fend off critics; just as the disaster unfolded, he died suddenly of yellow fever in New Orleans.[54]

Several million dollars were gone and thousands more were owed to creditors. Sam had sullied his father's name and he had squandered his *and* his sisters' inheritance. Julia initially defended him, weakly arguing that the more sober partners "should have looked after him sharply and restrained him." Sam took the same tack, but his whiny attempt to deflect censure elicited little sympathy from his uncles and none from his brother-in-law.[55]

Broke, Sam was forced to rent out 32 Bond Street. He, an extremely resentful Medora, and their sons moved into Grymes Hill, where Sam had to endure his mother-in-law's unrelenting criticism. In the fall of 1848, Suzette Grymes packed up Medora and the boys and sent them off to New Orleans and threw Sam out. At thirty-five, he was bankrupt, homeless, estranged from his uncles and ridiculed by his wife's family, and casting about for some way to earn a living. He wrote to Longfellow, who had been the soul of tact in his letters after the crash, asking, "What does the *North American* pay? Would they like an article upon Gastronomy? . . . I want to turn a penny."[56]

There was not much money in writing, and conventional solutions to Sam's money woes, such as hard work at a regular job, held no appeal. An adventure, however, that would both get him out of New York and restore his fortunes could be just the ticket. In the California gold fever that was sweeping the nation Sam saw his opportunity. He would join the '49ers rushing to the Pacific coast. Even after his recent debacle, Sam found it easy to raise a stake among rich New Yorkers. After a quick trip to Boston to say goodbye to Julia and a line to Longfellow—"Adieu, dear Longo. Write to me when you have time and inclination."— Sam and his Southern cousin Hall McAllister cast off aboard one of the Pacific Mail Steamship Company's newest steamers, the *Panama*. Sam was free at last from the confines of the counting house, and he would never go back.[57]

Sam claimed that everyone aboard the *Panama* was horribly seasick except him and Captain David Dixon Porter. Their shipmates included William McKendree Gwin, the Mississippi planter with designs on becoming one of California's first senators; Major Joseph Hooker, off to a new military assignment; and Jessie Benton Frémont, who would always remember Sam's chivalry, and her little daughter, on their way to join John C. Frémont. Sam's path and theirs would cross again and again. Sam made friends on every deck and in every port. Rio de Janeiro fascinated him. When their ship docked in San Diego, Sam and Hall disembarked long enough to find the Bryant and Sturgis hide-house that Richard Henry Dana had described in *Two Years Before the Mast*.[58]

Sam's band of adventurers grew. Hall McAllister, who would become one of San Francisco's most prominent lawyers, sent bags of gold dust back to Savannah to entice his younger brother Ward, just twenty-three, and his lawyer father to join him and Sam, which they did. While Hall, who would spend the rest of his career in California, and Sam thrived in the rough and tumble West, Ward did not. He stayed for two years before returning east, where he would become the self-appointed arbiter of New York's high society, the "snob of snobs" to his detractors, and make Mrs. William Backhouse Astor, Jr., Sam's former sister-in-law, its queen. For his part, Sam convinced his brother-in-law Adolphe Mailliard (Annie had married the Frenchman in 1846) and his friend Charles Mersch to join in their California adventure.[59]

Neither Sam nor his friends and family had any intention of standing in icy streams sluicing for gold. Hall hung out his shingle as a lawyer, and Sam invested the capital they had collectively managed to raise in pipes and saws, everything that miners would need, and set up shop in a tent on the rowdy San Francisco waterfront. Sam's curiosity about other cultures and his fluency in several languages made him a popular storekeeper with the Belgians, Chileans, Mexicans, and French living the bachelor life beside men from the American Midwest and East in the gold fields. He plowed his share of the profits into the town's booming real estate market and soon boasted that he had made a quarter of a million dollars in just three months. Although a busy businessman in a boom town that was 97 percent male, Sam did not forget the importance of the "social tie" that he had once sworn to defend. When he and other San Francisco merchants decided to hold a banquet, the only building available was a low and dark warehouse. Astonished guests arrived that night to find two rows of toga-clad marble statues, each holding a flaming torch—stevedores that Sam had hired, stripped to the waist, and whitewashed.[60]

On May 4, 1851, Sam's new fortune went up in smoke when a swift-moving fire destroyed all of his wharves and warehouses and everything stored inside. He was broke again, with creditors hounding him once more. This time, he headed for the hills. He took a job as a ferry operator at a tiny outpost 200 miles east of San Francisco, and lived on horsemeat, parched corn, beans, and coffee. His nearest neighbors were the Potoyensee Indians, whom he befriended and defended, studying their cuisine and language and sending samples of Potoyensee verb conjugations back to Felton at Harvard. In a long, pensive letter to "Dudie" (Julia), Sam soberly took stock of his worldly possessions: a mule, a saddle, a bridle, a revolver and a double-barreled gun, two trunks containing worn-out clothes, his father's watch, two rings, a locket with his siblings' hair, three or four ounces of gold, and a few books, one a copy of Horace.[61]

Still broke but bored with frontier hardships, Sam headed back to San Francisco, where he got caught up in the schemes of American and French adventurers making sporadic raids into Mexico. He claimed that he smoked cigars with Santa Ana, saved some Frenchmen from death before a firing squad, colluded with American filibusterer William Walker, and taught the redowa, a dance at which he excelled, to delighted ladies in the Mexican capital.[62] The next word Julia had from Sam was a brief note announcing that he was sailing for France to act as a negotiator between European investors and American and Mexican interests.

Just what this mysterious mission was all about, or what he was doing a few months later in Nicaragua and Costa Rica, and then back in Europe, where he visited with Henry James, who was traveling with his two sons, William and Henry, Sam never revealed. But when he resurfaced in New York in the summer of 1855, he was in the chips again. Medora, back on Staten Island with her mother, asked no questions—as long as Sam was rich, she was happy. Sam, however, may have had questions for her. He must have heard the rumors about Medora, who until recently had been living in Europe with the boys and her mother. George Templeton Strong wrote in his diary what was being said *sub rosa* in New York social circles: "Mrs. Sam Ward, who's living in Paris while her husband's in California, said to be the mistress of a Russian Prince."[63]

Still looking to make a fast buck, Sam plunged back into speculating on Wall Street, again with no success. His funds soon dwindled and with them what was left of Medora's affection. Early in 1856, Sam admitted to Julia that the breech between them had become unbridgeable—"I fancy my goose is cooked."—and that his financial situation was a shambles.[64] Longfellow, who had so often been on the receiving end of Sam's largesse, was startled to receive from him a plea for a quick loan. Sam was about to slink out of New York, leaving his creditors behind once more.[65]

This time, with the help of his new friend William Gwin, who had indeed become one of California's first senators, and his old New York friend, lawyer, investor, and wealthy Democrat Samuel Latham Mitchill Barlow, who had influence in Washington, Sam, now forty-four, finagled a berth on an official diplomatic mission to Paraguay, complete with salary ($1,500 a year), as its secretary.

Though political connections had snagged him the post, he was well qualified: Sam was the only member of the entire expedition who spoke fluent Spanish.[66]

The diplomatic and naval mission Sam joined was an effort by the United States government to settle a complicated, long-running dispute and to rescue the investments of American stockholders in a Paraguayan navigation scheme. The mission merited such a formidable force—a flotilla of nineteen ships carrying two hundred guns, twenty-five hundred sailors and marines, plus Sam and the negotiators—because a Paraguayan naval ship had fired on a U.S. naval ship, the U.S.S. *Water Witch*, in 1855, for which an apology was now demanded. However grave the mission, Sam was just happy to be aboard. He had a wonderful time, especially at the ports of Buenos Aires and Montevideo, where he sampled the local wine and food.[67]

To everyone's surprise, negotiations in Asunción were quickly and smoothly completed. The government of Paraguay apologized for the *Water Witch* incident; it agreed to submit the claims of the navigation company to arbitration; and a new commercial treaty with the United States was even drafted. Sam somehow convinced both the American delegation and Paraguayan president Carlos Antonio López that he was largely responsible for the happy turn of events, and he may well have been. He sailed home carrying silver utensils for making maté in his trunk, wearing a ring set with a large sapphire and diamonds on his finger, and with something else even more valuable. Behind the back of the American commissioner, Sam and President López had negotiated their own personal compact. In his pocket, Sam had a secret agreement, sealed with a £1,000 payment, to lobby on Paraguay's behalf in Washington. He landed in New York on May 9, 1859, and stepped ashore to begin a new career.[68]

CHAPTER THREE

Sam, alias "Carlos Lopez," reconnoiters deep inside the Confederacy; dispatches to help the Union from New York City; back to Washington "to get some money"

ARD ON THE heels of the news that South Carolina had seceded came rumors that the South would attempt to take over the federal government before Abraham Lincoln could be inaugurated. Word got back to Sam and everyone else in Washington that, on Christmas Day, the *Richmond Examiner* had brazenly asked, "Can there not be found men bold and brave enough in Maryland to unite with Virginians in seizing the Capital in Washington?" The Capitol building was checked for explosives every night.[1]

Any hope that the unraveling strands of the Union might yet be rewoven dimmed in the new year when, on January 21, 1861, senators from Alabama, Florida, and Mississippi delivered their valedictories and stalked out of the Senate chamber. Among the weeping Southern women who packed the Senate gallery sat a tearful Virginia Clay, watching her husband take his leave. Of their last days in the capital, Mrs. Clay later recalled: "From the hour of this exodus of Senators from the official body, all Washington seemed to change. Imagination can scarcely conjure up an atmosphere at once so ominous and so sad. . . . Farewells were to be spoken, and many, we knew would be final. Vehicles lumbered on their way to wharf or station filled with the baggage of departing Senators and Members."[2]

Rumors of plots to assassinate President-elect Lincoln before he could take the oath of office also surfaced. General Winfield Scott, a Virginian but not a secessionist, ordered 650 regular soldiers to the capital. For his loyalty to the Union, he was burned in effigy at the University of Virginia and received death threats himself. March 4, 1861, inauguration day, dawned sunny but raw. Rooftops along the Pennsylvania Avenue parade route bristled with soldiers and their rifles. The cavalry unit flanking the carriage carrying Lincoln and President Buchanan to the Capitol for the swearing-in ceremony kept their horses dancing to deprive any sharpshooter of a clear line of sight.[3]

Sam was among the crowd on the east side of the Capitol that morning. With a soldier posted in every window and more said to be concealed beneath the platform on which he stood, President Lincoln took the oath of office without incident. His inaugural address contained reassuring, not inflammatory, words: "We are not enemies, but friends." Hope for averting civil war was still alive, and it was shared by Sam and his friend New York senator and secretary-of-state-designate William Henry Seward.[4]

Despite his Southern leanings and his many friends and family in the South, there was no question that Sam would remain loyal to the Union. Having only recently arrived on the scene in Washington, he planned to stay and help in any way he could. On February 15, 1861, Sam wrote to Samuel Barlow, asking to continue the lease on 258 F Street.[5] On February 16, he wrote to Seward, "Dr. Gwin dines alone with me today at five and thought that, if not elsewhere engaged, you might find it a relief from cares and questions to join us, which I should esteem a great pleasure as well as a high honor. There will be no other guests." Despite the note's casual tone, the meeting that evening was anything but.[6]

Sam had shared tips about railroad stocks and other investing opportunities with Seward, a fellow New Yorker whom he had known for years and liked, despite their political differences. Now he was about to become useful to him in a much more important way.[7] Seward was in a tight spot. As secretary of state, he would need both to steer the new president, whom he regarded as naïve, on a conciliatory course and also to convince the leaders of the Confederacy that, as he sincerely believed would be the case, it was he who would actually be guiding the president's policy and that that policy would be one of peace.

Seward could hardly, however, communicate directly with Jefferson Davis and Confederate leaders in Montgomery. He needed a go-between, someone these Southerners would trust, and he had hit upon his Senate colleague from California, William Gwin, who still owned land and slaves in Mississippi. Though reluctant, Gwin had agreed, but both men knew that they could not be seen conferring. Gwin suggested their mutual friend, Sam Ward, as their cover. Writing of this period twenty years later, Gwin explained, "By this time it was difficult for Mr. Seward and myself to have interviews without exciting remark, and a 'mutual friend' was therefore selected as our go-between." He and Seward would be just two among the many men who dropped in at Sam's home for a good dinner.[8]

Brief notes suggesting or requesting meetings were soon passing among the homes of the three. Sometimes Sam's notes came with a gift. One message vouched for the soothing effect that the wine he was sending Seward had already had "upon our friend Dr. Gwin in some of his most irascible moods." Claiming that the vintage also promoted virtue, Sam added, "I wish I had a shipload of it to send to Montgomery."[9] On the theory that "to the navigator, the faintest scud may sometimes prove the direction of the upper currents," Sam also sent along to Seward all sorts of news that he picked up from his other dinner guests, correspondents, and friends in the capital. With his note about the clouds, he enclosed a letter from a Southern friend with the request, "Please tear up after perusal."[10]

On inauguration day, in a long letter marked "PRIVATE," Sam sent Seward extracts from a letter he had just received from Barlow in New York. Barlow, in turn, was relaying in his letter to Sam news he had just received from a source high up in the Montgomery hierarchy—Confederate attorney general Judah Benjamin. Benjamin, who may have intended his message to be passed on, had told Barlow "in the most emphatic manner as to the dissatisfaction of the government in Montgomery with things at Washington and their intention *not* to await events." In addition to forwarding the unsettling news, Sam sent four more pages of information about the inner workings of the Confederacy that he had gleaned from his own sources—the names of recent appointments in Montgomery, details about the Confederate Constitution, sentiment in England and France. The long communication ended with "Dr. G. desires to see you and begs you will be kind enough to send me word as early as you please at what hour it will be convenient for you to meet him at 258."[11]

The arrival in Washington of three Confederate commissioners, all friends of Gwin and acquaintances of Sam, right after the inauguration to negotiate for the peaceful surrender of federal forts in Southern territory prompted a flurry of notes back and forth. Seward was trying every which way to avoid meeting them and, through Sam, was asking Gwin both to help put them off and to send him news from inside their camp. At first, Gwin complied, but then he balked. He began to question whether Seward really had the president's ear. Unwilling to stall the commissioners any longer, or, worse, possibly to mislead his Southern friends about the administration's real intentions, Gwin left town. Over the next few years, Sam would try to help Gwin and his wife as their fortunes plummeted, but now he was about to prove more immediately useful to Seward.[12]

While the plot thickened in Washington during January of the secession winter, the first installment of a highly entertaining series entitled "Incidents on the
River of Grace" appeared in a sporting publication called *Porter's Spirit of the
Times*. Wry, sometimes hilarious, prose told the picaresque tale of a '49er chasing
reports of gold among the quartz deposits in a remote area of California in the
summer of 1851. The first paragraphs introduced readers to four dispirited fortune seekers and the four stout nags that, after "a consultation among themselves," saved the day by getting their hopelessly lost riders, whose thirst had
become "Homeric" in magnitude, to a river bank.[13]

The next installments brought exciting tales of raging floods, stage coach
robberies, and angry Indian chiefs. There were frequent references to food (the
butchering of a cow, followed by "such gourmandizing as you read of in Ulysses'
description of the supper of the Cyclops") and vivid character sketches ("a small,
spare weasel of an Eastern man.") Potoyensee Indian practices, such as the "in-
cineration" of their dead, were described in vivid, sensitive detail.[14]

The author of these gripping tales? He signed himself "Midas, Jr.," but it was
Sam, slyly referencing his former father-in-law, William Backhouse Astor, known
as "Midas" in the New York press. Sam had followed Julia's nudging to write
about his western adventures after all, although *Porter's* was probably not the type
of venue she had in mind. How much money Sam may have earned by his pen is
unknown. Where he found the time to write these tales, each consisting of several
thousand words, is hard to imagine: he had been working for the Paraguayan
claims commission that spring and summer; he was watching out for Barlow's,
Paraguay's, and Baring Brothers' interests; and he was acting as go-between for
Seward and Gwin.

What is clear, however, is that suddenly something intervened. The series
abruptly ended with the fourteenth installment on April 23, 1861. The editor of
Porter's apologized to his readers: "The illness of the author is our excuse." But
Sam was not ill. Far from it. He was about to embark on another adventure, this
one even more exciting and potentially more dangerous than his months along
the River of Grace.[15]

On April 9, in another letter marked "PRIVATE," Sam wrote to Seward: "I have
resolved—perhaps under the inspiration of vanity—to set forth for Montgomery
on a peace errand in the morning— . . . and should esteem it a great favor if you
could afford me the honor of a five minute interview this PM at any moment
convenient to you."[16] When they met that evening, Sam must have gone over his
plans with Seward and gotten his approval or, at least, acquiescence. They also

must have agreed on the details and ruse for their future communications and talked about Sam's companion for this trip to the heart of the Confederacy, *London Times* correspondent William Howard Russell.

After his dramatic, up-close coverage of the Crimean War in 1854 and 1855, Russell was regarded as the father of all war correspondents. In the spring of 1861, when the *Times*'s editor found it hard to credit dispatches from his reporter in New York that the American Southern states really meant to secede permanently, he sent Russell to get the real story. Russell already had at least one friend in the States; he had met Sam in London the year before. Russell recalled their meeting:

> One night in the summer of 1860, I think, I was sitting alone in my study, when I heard a ring at the front door, and as it was past 10 o'clock, and as I was not expecting visitors, I said to the servant, "Not at home." But the door was already open, and a voice I loved dearly cried: "Only five minutes, William; I have brought an American friend who desires above all things to see and know you!" It was Thackeray who spoke, and he was always welcome. Taking my hand and putting it in the palm of his companion's, he said: "This is Mr. Sam Ward, of New York, nominally a citizen of the world—the rest you will find out for yourself." It was near 2 o'clock in the morning ere the visitors left.[17]

As soon as Russell landed in New York in mid-March, the two were reunited. Sam introduced him to many of his friends, mostly Democrats, and arranged for Barlow to give a dinner in his honor. When Russell continued on to Washington, he made 258 F Street his headquarters. Sam took him to meet Charles Sumner and introduced him to Seward, who introduced him to President Lincoln, the Cabinet, and plenty of Republicans.[18]

After two weeks of dinners, parties, and interviews in the capital, Russell was eager to see for himself the mounting crisis from the Southern perspective, and he needed a guide. Sam knew that Seward wanted news about sentiments and activities in the South, and Sam had a wide network of family and friends there. Hence, his private letter to Seward on April 9 and the next day one to Barlow that read: "I am off for Richmond in the morn. . . . I am *convinced* Mr. Seward is sincere in his assertion that 'no hostilities will be provoked by any of the war movements which have been in progress for the last few days.' How I know this, no matter [his source was Russell]—I do know it and recommend you to keep cool and buy stocks, and if they drop to go on buying."[19] How sure was Sam of this, Barlow asked in reply by wire. Barlow had heard that Thurlow Weed, who was very close to Seward, was selling. Sam put the question to Russell, who had dined with Seward the night before, and wrote back to Barlow, marking his letter both "PRIVATE" and "On the □": "My belief in the pacific policy of the administration was derived from Seward's intimations to Gwin in the first place, and in the second by the whole tenor of his discourse to Russell, with whom he has had four long interviews. . . . If I am wrong, I have been *fooled*, and Mr. Seward is keeping the truth for the benefit of his friends. . . . But I can hardly believe that the Secretary would send for a man like Gwin and pour volunteer lies into his ear, or that he would solicit the presence of Russell to deceive him with purely fictitious revelations!"[20]

Although he was most certainly "fooled," and Barlow, because he had listened to Sam, was out an unspecified amount of money, Sam chalked it up to Russell's misreading of Seward and the secretary's misreading of Lincoln. He could not bring himself to believe that Seward would withhold information from, or intentionally deceive, his friends. Actually, a news blackout kept from Sam, Russell, Barlow, and almost everyone else the fact—known to Seward—that, even as Sam wrote, expeditions were on their way to reinforce Forts Sumter and Pickens. On April 11, Sam boarded a train heading South. Before dawn on the morning of April 12, Confederate General Pierre G. T. Beauregard ordered his batteries to open fire on Fort Sumter.

Fort Sumter was in flames when Sam's train pulled into Charleston. He got there in time, he claimed, to see the flag of the United States shot down, which made the blood of his Revolutionary War–veteran ancestors boil in his veins. Nevertheless, as soon as Russell joined him, Sam set about introducing him to the elite of Charleston. Some were kin and some were friends from as far back as Round Hill days; among them were Beauregard, who had danced with Sam's sisters in Newport while a cadet at West Point, South Carolina governor Francis Pickens, and elderly lawyer James Louis Petigru. Sam and Russell were wined and dined all over town, and each listened carefully to all that was said. Both were taken aback by the virulence of their tablemates' professed hatred of Yankees. Russell's gleanings found their way into his dispatches. By prearrangement, Sam's found their way into long, secret letters to Seward.[21]

For Sam to send reports from deep inside the Confederacy back to the secretary of state in Washington was a tricky business all around, and both men knew it. Seward would be embarrassed if it was revealed that he was corresponding with a Democrat previously soft on the South. Sam, if discovered, would fare much worse—he might be hung as a Northern spy. Probably at their meeting on April 9, Seward and Sam agreed that his letters, smuggled out under cover of Russell's dispatches to the *Times*, would be addressed to Seward's loyal friend and subordinate at the State Department, George Ellis Baker. Sam would use a pseudonym that he no doubt suggested and enjoyed, "Charles Lopez."[22]

Sam's, or Charles Lopez's, first of more than fifty letters to "My Dear George," on April 19, 1861, contained a richly detailed account of the fall of Fort Sumter and information on fortifications, including the number and names of the ships, all potential privateers, in Charleston's harbor. Action was needed, and immediately, Lopez warned Baker: "While you are planning, these people are acting. . . . I feel convinced that the people *here* will *never* come back. They are as ready for the stake as the Smithfield martyrs."[23]

In his next letter, on April 25, Lopez tried to squash what he knew to be a widely held belief in the North, that if war came the South would be quickly crushed. Southern troops were already on the move, he wrote; "I hear that two Louisiana regiments have gone up to Memphis." The resignations from the U.S. military of men like Robert E. Lee and Albert Johnston especially alarmed him: "These men know all your secrets—all your power and all your weakness—and they have every deviltry of war at their command."[24]

On May 2, from Savannah, where he had many well-connected relatives, Sam sent an eleven-page letter stuffed with information about the quantity, caliber, and placement of Fort Pulaski's armaments, along with some gossip—Sam knew that Seward would enjoy the rumor that he and President Lincoln had taken to drink.[25] Moving on to Macon and then Montgomery, Sam and Russell met with President Jefferson Davis and other high-ranking Confederates. Sam wrote on May 9 of the shortage of a crucial item in the recipe for war—gun powder: "They have all the ingredients save sulfur, which they hope to get from Mexico."[26]

Sam and Russell moved on to Selma and then Mobile, where they were harassed for the first time by a vigilance committee. Sam's friends there vouched for and entertained them, but both were shaken. Pressing on, they found New Orleans feverish with military activity. Russell claimed that he could not find a seamstress to mend his shirts, so busy were they sewing Confederate flags. Sam introduced Russell to soft shell crabs and pompano before they set off up the Mississippi River, stopping frequently to be entertained at vast plantations where they saw up close gangs of slaves working cane and cotton fields and slaves being sold.[27]

After Baton Rouge and Natchez, they landed at Vicksberg and took trains to Jackson and then Memphis, where Sam dispatched a long letter almost wholly about military preparations: which forts had slight defenses and which were strong, how many regiments and with what they were armed. He emphasized again and again that beating the Confederates would not be easy. The soldiers and defenses he had seen were formidable: "These fellows are spoiling for a fight, and talk with a ferocity which, although heightened by whiskey, I am sure they feel."[28]

Russell was growing increasingly worried about being trapped behind Confederate lines and cut off from his newspaper. If he knew the contents and the real recipient of Sam's letters to Baker, that must have added to his uneasiness. Sam and Russell decided to head north, and Sam's next letter came from Cairo, Illinois, on June 21. Once safely back in Union territory, Sam dropped the Lopez-to-Baker subterfuge. He signed his letters "Sam Ward," but he continued to stress what Seward did not want to hear—a difficult road lay ahead:

> I cannot better explain my view of the difference between the aggressive tiger men of the South and your soldiers fighting for an abstract question than by reminding you that I have seen Billy Mulligan on two occasions clear out a bar room. These men, with their yells and Bowie knives and bloodthirsty manners, will take by surprise the bravest men who are unused to such riot. . . . should a meeting take place tomorrow, it would be the odds of horned cattle against beasts of prey. Nothing but the mob of Paris in the Reign of Terror can equal the savage ferocity and sanguinary bitterness of the Southern troops. Your men will get their blood up by and by and prove the more unrelenting of the two, but it will take lots of blood to bring them to such a diapason.[29]

Sam used the same letter to rail against the political generals receiving commissions right and left. He found the whole idea alarming, but, in one case, absolutely disgusting. He hooted at news that Daniel Sickles had been commissioned a brigadier general: "Dan Sickles at the head of a brigade of 5000 men! Good God! Fancy him caught in a tight place by Davis, Beauregard, Lee, or Whiting! Do you believe in miracles and that the Lord of Hosts will select Sickles' head and heart as His tabernacle for the nonce?"[30]

By way of Chicago and Niagara Falls, Sam and Russell arrived in New York on July 2, 1861, and completed their circuit a few days later in Washington. Both were astonished at the changes three months had wrought in the town. After several panics in the spring over reports that the capital was about to be overrun by marauding Southerners, the first of the troops summoned by General Scott to protect the capital had finally arrived. Sam almost certainly knew soldiers in the Seventh New York, made up of men from the best families in Manhattan, who were said to have marched off for duty with sandwiches from Delmonico's.

In the first weeks after the fall of Fort Sumter, many of Washington's secessionist families packed their trunks, shuttered their homes, and departed. Southern-sympathizing civil servants and army and navy officers resigned and left town. Trains leaving Washington were full; those arriving, nearly empty. Then the ebbing tide turned, and trains full of soldiers, some of the seventy-five thousand troops that President Lincoln had called up for three months' service, pulled in. The first to arrive were quartered in the Capitol, in the Patent Office among the cases of models, and at the Treasury. Supplies also began to arrive. Tons of coal piled up and herds of cattle crowded into the Navy Yard, where there was not enough dock space for all of the ships bringing still more.

By the time Sam and Russell returned in July, there were encampments everywhere. Buglers woke up the whole town with reveille. Russell saw much military activity but little order. He began to have his doubts about the Federal army, and a tour of the camps on the Virginia shore confirmed his misgivings. Russell knew armies, and this one was as yet no match for the troops he had just seen in the South. He said as much in his dispatches to London, which, when word trickled back, caused consternation throughout the North.

In July 1861, the editor of *Porter's*, apparently forgetting his earlier excuse that Midas, Jr., was ill, announced to his readers that, "Our correspondent 'Midas, Jr.' has returned from his wanderings, and we anticipate a speedy renewal of the interesting series in our volumes." However, no more installments ever appeared. Midas, Jr., had indeed returned from his wanderings, but he was too busy with the present to look back.[31]

Once again, Sam conferred with Seward, who either suggested Sam's next move himself, or, more likely, approved of the plan when Sam proposed it. Sam headed for New York and took rooms at the New York Hotel, a favorite with Southerners and Copperheads, Northern Democrats opposed to the war. On July 7, a new stream of letters began flowing to Washington, some from Lopez (now Carlos instead of Charles) but some in his own name, sometimes addressed to Baker, sometimes to Frederick W. Seward, the secretary's son, and sometimes to the secretary himself.

Sam's letters from New York were filled with his own opinions and suggestions and with rumors and tips he picked up all over town but especially in the hotel lobby and bar. The hotel was, Sam wrote, a "good gleaning ground"; but he knew that some of what he heard about the situation in Mexico, the British and French attitudes toward the American crisis, and the situation in the South might not be true. He sent everything along to Seward anyway unfiltered, with a caveat: "I have no time to sift the truth of such matters as command my attention, when it is so easy for you to verify them."[32]

It was July 15, 1861, when Sam wrote to Seward of the "good gleaning ground." Throughout the following week, Union troops set out from Washington toward Manassas, Virginia, and Bull Run creek, ready for a fight. On Sunday morning,

July 21, capital caterers filled picnic baskets for the eager sightseers who set off into the Virginia countryside to watch the battle, confident of victory. Russell got up at dawn, put on an outfit from his days in India, packed a revolver, flasks, ham and sausage sandwiches, and crossed over the Long Bridge as well. All day long, the faint boom of artillery thirty miles away could be heard in the capital.[33]

Toward evening, the first panicked sightseers made it back into town with news that the battle was lost, the army in retreat. Through the night and into the next day, exhausted soldiers straggled back, bringing the first casualties with them. Walt Whitman, a new government clerk, wrote of the sorry parade:

> The men appear, at first sparsely and shame-faced enough, then thicker. . . . Side-walks . . . crowded, jammed with citizens, darkies, clerks, everybody, lookers-on; swarms of dirt-covered returned soldiers there (will they never end?) move by; but nothing said, no comments; (half our lookers-on secesh [secessionists] of the most venomous kind—they say nothing; but the devil snickers in their faces). . . . Mean-time, among the great persons and their entourage, a mixture of awful consterna-tion, uncertainty, rage, shame, helplessness, and stupefying disappointment.[34]

Russell, back from the battlefield, watched "the beaten, foot-sore, spongy-looking soldiers, officers and all the *debris* of the army filing through mud and rain." When his vivid, first-hand account of the rout of the confused Federals, published in the *London Times*, made its way back to the States, Russell became *persona non grata* throughout the North. He received anonymous death threats and experienced cold shoulders in drawing rooms where before he had been warmly welcomed. As Russell's friend, Sam was tarred with the same brush, which only boosted his standing among the Southerners at the New York Hotel. For Russell, however, with his contacts falling silent, his usefulness to the *Times* as a reporter from America was at an end, and he sailed home to England.[35]

After Bull Run, Sam's letters to the State Department took on a new urgency. It might indeed, as Sam had predicted, be a long war, and he felt that any bit of information could prove useful. That fall and winter, the news he passed on in longer and longer letters often concerned attitudes toward the Union in England, France, and Italy, as well as events in the South. His information came from letters sent to him from contacts in Europe and letters to others that were shown to him, as well as from conversations and hearsay. He explained to Seward that his method of "gleaning" was "to evince no curiosity when told the most in-credible things."[36]

At one point, Sam feared that his letters had been intercepted. He worried that he would be exposed and his usefulness would end, but he pegged on. News that he regarded as too sensitive to trust to the mails Sam took straight to Washington and conveyed to Seward himself. "Something is transpiring in New York," he would write, "which I should like to compare notes with you about. I will call at your residence and should feel obliged by your leaving word at what hour I can have the pleasure of seeing you."[37]

Why did Sam make himself so anxious and risk exposure at the New York Hotel? Why had he risked much worse by traveling to the very heart of the Confederacy? What was Sam's stake in these risky undertakings? Probably not money, which so often had motivated him. During his swing through the South, his expenses seem to have been covered by the *Times* on Russell's expense account, and, in New York, Sam paid his own bills. Sam's letters to Barlow from his trips to Washington suggest that he was still watching out for Barlow's interests, and still being paid by him while reconnoitering for Seward.[38]

Patriotism? Although Sam loved all things European, he was an ardent American. Perhaps he thought of his family's long tradition of service to the nation, of his beloved grandfather Colonel Samuel Ward, who had fought with Washington, and he wanted to do his part. If so, even if his missions were secret, it was uncharacteristic of Sam not to brag about his exploits, or at least to drop hints to prove to Julia that he was as much a Union man as Samuel Gridley Howe, or to let Longfellow know that he was an active player in the drama. But there were few letters from Sam to any of his sisters during these months and few to Longfellow, except for heart-felt letters of condolence and commiseration after his wife's horrible death on July 10, 1861.

Fanny Appleton Longfellow, who had kept Longfellow waiting for so long and with whom he was finally so happy, was in the Craigie House library, melting wax to seal envelopes containing locks of her children's hair. Somehow her dress caught fire. Hysterical, she ran through the house until Longfellow caught her and tried to smother the flames with a rug, only to receive terrible burns on his hands and face. Fanny died from severe burns the next day. After her death, because shaving was painful on his scarred face, Longfellow would grow the beard that has defined his appearance since. When news of the accident reached Sam, he wrote immediately: "I, who used to associate your name with perfect bliss, never think of it now without speechless sorrow."[39]

Was it the element of intrigue that motivated Sam? Sam clearly delighted in his secret missions to Europe and Central and South America and in alluding to them in cryptic letters to Julia and "Longo." He had used pseudonyms before in his secret communications with President López; he had written under the name of "Midas, Jr." and invoked the Masonic symbolism for secrecy often.

Or did Sam want to curry favor with Seward? Having previously been on the State Department's payroll, Sam fancied himself a born diplomat. With his command of several languages, knowledge of Europe and Latin America, elegant manners, and glib tongue, he was, in fact, more qualified than many of the political hacks awarded diplomatic positions. An appointment as the first U.S. minister to Paraguay, following ratification of the treaty that he had helped negotiate, would have been the perfect plum for Sam. But if he thought his qualifications for such jobs made him the obvious candidate, he was wrong. When, in the spring of 1861, Seward awarded that plum to Charles A. Washburn, whom Sam had disliked ever since their days as '49ers in San Francisco, he was disappointed. Upon learning of the appointment, while he was deep in the South courting danger on Seward's behalf, or so he saw it, he wrote the secretary, "I am sorry you have given away the Paraguay mission, which is useless to the incumbent."[40]

Sam was barking up the wrong tree. Even if Seward had wanted to reward Sam for his services, he could hardly have done so without raising eyebrows. Sam was a Democrat. His good friends—Barlow, Manton Marble, who was publisher of the *New York World*, and William Henry Hurlbert, a brilliant eccentric whose recent escapades behind enemy lines had made him suspect in both North and South—were all prominent Democrats and enemies of Republicans, who would never swallow Sam's appointment to a position that could have rewarded one of their own. On top of that, no matter how pure his motives, when Sam was in New York, he was constantly in the company of Southern sympathizers. Surely Sam was savvy enough to realize the tight spot Seward was in—there is no evidence that Seward intentionally strung Sam along—but he apparently had remained ever hopeful.[41]

Perhaps a combination of all of these factors spurred Sam on in his risky business. Whatever his motivation, he kept sending a steady stream of information, major and minor, to Washington. He continued to include his own opinions, too, and he weighed in on the military men, many of whom he had known out West, who were being elevated to important commands: Frémont was a "pigmy"; Henry Halleck, "cold, heartless, cruel, and avaricious"; and Ben Butler of Massachusetts, a former Democrat in the process of turning himself into a Radical Republican, whom Sam positively could not stomach, was becoming a "loathing stock" as military commander in New Orleans.[42]

As the summer and fall of 1861 wore on, Sam's purse must have been growing thin. He needed a job or at least some sort of temporary paying assignment. Salted among the tidbits of information in his letters to Seward was lobbying for himself. Lowering his sights considerably from a ministerial position, Sam asked about an open clerk's position in the diplomatic division: "Will not Dr. [James] Mackie's temporary absence create a vacuum in your department which I might help to lessen? I only suggest this in case I might be of service." While it is clear that Seward himself or his son Frederick replied to at least some of Sam's letters, neither seems to have responded to this one.[43]

Ever-hopeful, Sam was to be ever-disappointed. In October 1861, he wrote Seward with what he considered a brilliant idea. Destroy the South's monopoly on growing cotton and the Confederacy would collapse, Sam argued. Given how much cotton had recently been harvested in Texas, why not investigate the cotton-growing capacity of Central and South America? And who better to take on that mission than he: "It strikes me that this object is one of great political importance, and that familiar as I am with the people and languages of South America I might accomplish it, and that you might dispatch me on this secret service, allowing me the customary *per diem* of such traveling agents. I should feel gratified to add this feather to your political cap and proud of the confidence it would betoken." This time, Seward did acknowledge the plan's potential and Sam's hopes briefly soared, but there were too many military defeats and other crises besetting the government that fall for Sam's project to get off the ground.[44]

Never too poor to forego presents, Sam sent Frederick Seward a saddle of venison at Christmas time in 1861, and he began the new year by trying again to interest either or both Sewards in his new ideas and angling for a job: "If you set one-tenth the store by my tact and persuasive skill that they who know me do, you would turn me to good account in London or Paris, where as a savant and man of letters I may say without vanity that I hold a desirable position." In February, he wrote to Frederick Seward: "I am thinking of taking a run over to Europe. In Paris I might be useful. Why not suggest this to the official mind?"[45]

Sam tried again in the spring, proposing that Seward send him to Mexico to report back on unfolding events as the Emperor Napoleon tried to install a puppet emperor there: "My opportunities for observation would be unequalled," Sam promised, alluding to his friends in high places in Mexico City. This time, Sam went to Washington, stayed for several weeks, and met with Seward many times to push his project, but, again, nothing materialized.[46]

Exasperated, Sam composed a last-ditch appeal to Seward in April 1862 and marked it "PRIVATE":

Some six weeks ago, I put in a suggestion that I might be of service in Mexico, and I recently saw that you had sent Mr. Plumb on an errand I should have been glad to have performed [Seward had just named E. L. Plumb secretary of legation at Mexico

City]. . . . I am loath to think that my experience and tact, coupled with some acknowledged ability, will continue to suffer neglect because I have neither bored nor importuned my friend. . . . I am a man of letters, and my zeal and capacities would make me grateful for employment. Try and keep this in view when anything offers in my line. Excepting Russian, Turkish, Chinese, and Manchurian, I believe that I speak and write all the languages of the governments at which you have missions. How many of your envoys know any other tongue than our own?"[47]

Hearing nothing by July, Sam finally got fed up and sat down to write one of his last letters to the secretary of state. He expressed his "mortification, tempered by humility, that the writer, who volunteered nothing that he would not have tripled in his performance, was not deemed worthy to serve his country in his capacity of linguist, diplomat, poet, and philosopher." He closed: "In any new combination for the future, I trust to enjoy more of the private than I have of the public confidence of the secretary, who, if my correspondence has been of service, will owe me a certificate that it had been disinterested; although I have felt at times no little mortification at his having ignored—not my claims—but my zeal and ability. Pray do not leave my letters at the State Department." Perhaps Seward had developed other sources of information; perhaps he worried that corresponding with Sam, if found out, would embarrass him; but, like Sam's other recent letters, this one received no reply. And, despite Sam's request, Seward saved it in his files, as he did all the others.[48]

Down on his luck and feeling unappreciated, Sam holed up at the New York Hotel through the end of 1862 and into 1863, making only occasional trips to Washington on errands for Barlow. Although he had never completely ceased his letter writing to friends while reconnoitering for Seward, he now had more time for his correspondence. "Sambo" and "Longo" once more wrote to each other with the intimacy and frequency they had enjoyed in the early 1840s when they were young widowers. Both old friends had lost their second wives: Longfellow's Fanny to a hideous accident, Sam's Medora to Europe, where she had taken their two boys, ages eighteen and fifteen. Sam was estranged from all three, although he was paying for the boys' educations. He wrote to Longfellow about anything he could think of—wine, books, street scenes—to distract him that summer: "You are lonely and I drop in upon you with a letter as if I lived on the next street."[49]

Sam and Russell, who was home in London, corresponded regularly, exchanging gossip about mutual friends and news about the war. Sam encouraged letters from the lonely old poet, Fitz-Greene Halleck, his father's friend. He and Julia reconciled, and they wrote to each other often. He was extremely proud of the

"Old Bird's" *Battle Hymn of the Republic*, penned in Washington at dawn one morning at the Willard Hotel in the fall of 1861 after a day of listening to Union soldiers singing endless rounds of "John Brown's Body," providing stirring new words to their old tune. In the *Battle Hymn*, Sam recognized the grim God of their father, who seemed, at least for the duration of the war, to have replaced the God of love that Julia had embraced as a young woman.[50]

Sam spent a delightful few weeks with Julia and her children in Newport, Rhode Island, in August 1862, arriving with a basket of ripe peaches. He happily reported to Longfellow that he had seen nineteen members of his extended family there—Greenes, Rays, Francises, and McAllisters, including his cousin Ward, who was busy climbing the social ladder in New York.[51]

Sam even seemed on better terms with Samuel Gridley Howe and with Charles Sumner. His relationship with his daughter, however, improved very little. Maddie was now a young wife and mother, married to a sober and respectable lawyer, John Winthrop Chanler. Sam had hoped to see more of her when he was living in New York, but Maddie's grandmother Astor had done such a thorough job of defaming Sam that neither Maddie nor her husband, even though he had gone to Columbia, studied in Heidelberg, and was a New York Democrat just like Sam, showed any interest in knowing him better. The effort was all Sam's. When Chanler was elected to Congress for the first of three terms in 1862 and took his family to Washington, Sam hoped to help them get settled in the capital; but his efforts, as well as his invitations, were almost all politely rebuffed.

While Sam wrote to Julia and Longfellow of his frustration over Maddie's aloofness, it was only to Barlow that Sam confided his financial woes. Barlow had small projects for Sam in Washington and New York that were keeping him afloat, but, in the fall of 1863, Barlow and some business partners had a big job that required someone with the skills of a diplomat, who spoke Spanish, knew his way around Central and South America, had a good knowledge of mining and a well-oiled tongue, liked adventure, and did not mind roughing it. Sam was their man.

Since 1857, when William Walker, an American adventurer who had gotten himself elected president of Nicaragua, was ousted from office, relations between the United States and Nicaragua had been rocky. The transit route across Nicaragua had been closed. Barlow and his partners in a new shipping combination wanted Sam to negotiate its reopening and inspect some inland gold and silver mines. If the ore was rich enough, plentiful enough, and could be brought to a harbor cheaply enough, it would furnish important freight for their steamship line.[52]

With a handsome retainer, the promise of future riches, and a detailed letter of instruction from Barlow signed, "Wishing you complete success, a speedy return, and all beside that you desire and deserve," Sam was ready for anything and eager to get away. After leaving his sapphire ring with Mrs. Barlow for safekeeping and a quick trip to Boston to say goodbye to Julia and Longfellow, Sam set sail for Panama in early December 1863, with little more money to his name than when he had first made the same trip fourteen years earlier.[53]

Sam sent back a constant stream of letters, some buoyant, some pensive. Longfellow's *Wayside Lyrics* was the "solace of my voyage," Sam reported to the poet from Panama on December 15. His favorite poem in the collection was "The Birds of Killingworth." In the same letter, taking stock of his life, he mused, "My life has vibrated between the zenith of wealth and the nadir of poverty, and yet . . . I am happier than when my note was worth $50,000."[54] Three days after Christmas, he wrote teasingly to Barlow that he was rocking in a hammock in the shade, eating bananas, papayas, and mangoes, and drinking "perfect coffee," all brought to his side by attendants, but Sam soon got down to business.[55]

On January 27, he wrote Barlow from Managua that, with negotiations for the renewed transit permit successfully wrapped up, he was about to set off for the interior to see for himself the rumored riches there: "I . . . do not doubt that, were I twenty years younger, I could bag a million in five years. . . . But I am fifty years old today,—entering upon the Sahara of age and infirmity, and probably unfit for the privations and toils of discovery." Sam was clearly intrigued by the stories of gold for the taking. A few lines later he added, "If I go a little beyond my depth and can see a prospect of a *seguro* [a sure thing], I shall draw upon you for my contingent remainder."[56]

Two weeks later, Sam wrote to Barlow with disappointing news. Not only were there no lakes of gold, but there was little chance that mining in the region could turn a profit for Barlow's group. The ore would have to be transported by canoes down the Coco River, which was only navigable three or four months of the year; it would need to be portaged around rapids the other eight or nine months. His report filed and his business finished, Sam was ready to head home. "I shall come jumping in some Sunday P.M.," he wrote Barlow, "with a load of coffee and chocolate to remind you that I have been in the land of the citrons and myrtle."[57]

Six months after he had sailed from New York, Sam was back to retrieve his ring. True to his word, with him came huge burlap sacks of coffee beans for the Barlows, Julia, and many friends. Julia's daughter Maud Howe Elliott recalled, "Not all our cooks had the art or the patience to roast green coffee beans, and I remember those enormous sacks in our storeroom for many seasons."[58]

Sam pocketed at least $10,000 from his Nicaraguan adventure. He had just

begun to enjoy his new riches when, on June 9, 1864, while scanning the obituaries in the *New York World*, his heart was lanced by the last entry: "Ward—On
May the 26th, at Luxembourg (Grand Duchy of Luxembourg), John Randolph
Ward, son of Medora Ward and grandson of the late John Randolph Grymes of
Louisiana." Sam's youngest son, "my poor bright little Randolph," had been dead
for two weeks, and Medora had not wired him. That he was not even listed as the
boy's father hurt him deeply. When he found out that the omission was not a
mistake but intentional—he went to the *World's* offices and saw for himself the
announcement written "in Mrs. Ward's sharpest hand"—he wrote in disbelief,
anguish, and anger to Longfellow, "What think you of the bitterness that could
brandish a hatchet at the father over his boy's corpse?"[59]

Sam's sons had been studying in Luxembourg with his old friend from his
own days in Europe, Charles Mersch. Sam was paying for their education and
room and board. A few days after the obituary appeared, a long letter arrived from
Mersch with the sad details of Randolph's death: just after Medora had taken
Wardie to study at the School of Mines in Freiburg, Randolph had fallen ill, and he
had died within thirty-six hours.[60]

Sam never saw Medora again, although he heard reports of her hedonistic life,
paid for and shared by her mother, on the Riviera at the center of the fast set. Two
years after Randolph's death, Sam's other son, Wardie, died in Paris; and, shortly
after that, in 1867, the still-beautiful Medora died in Europe as well. Looking back
from the mid-1870s, a newspaper article recounted Medora's demise: "Some
years since, and during the most dazzling period of the empire, Mrs. Ward went
to Europe for the purpose of educating her two sons. For a period in Paris, she was
a conspicuous feature of all the court entertainments and was an especial favorite
with both Napoleon III and Eugenie. While upon the eve of her departure for this
country, she suddenly sickened and after a short illness died."[61]

Sam made no reference to either loss in any surviving letters and did not
mention Medora again until years later, when he looked back on their first years
together with tenderness. He blamed the unbridgeable rift between them not on
himself, and not on Medora, but on Suzette Grymes. Even though he had been
unlucky at love, Sam remained a romantic at heart. In January 1860, after Sam
had visited the Thackerays in London, their daughter Anne, who was 22, wrote in
her diary, "Sam Ward [Sam was 46] said he hoped to get a divorce shortly and I
should hear from him." In March 1863, Sam wrote Longfellow that he had had
"the misfortune to fall in love the other day. . . . I now discover that I am not as old
as I ought to be. Of course, there are no bars to my carrying the caprice to the altar,

save poverty, my fifty years, my hair (or no hair) and teeth; and, easiest to over-look, the participation in my fancy by its object." Despite Sam's flirtations and infatuations—he was famous within the family for flirting with his nieces' pretty friends and making their plain friends feel beautiful—he and Medora were mar-ried to the end. If either ever contemplated divorce, neither left a record of it. Nor is there any suggestion that Sam ever truly fell in love again.[62]

By the end of that sad summer of 1864, Sam had come to financial grief as well. He may not have been duped by tales of lakes of gold in Nicaragua, but he still believed that gold and silver, this time from Nevada's Comstock Lode, were his ticket to quick riches. He invested almost all of his earnings from his Central American adventure in the Gould and Curry mine, and, for a few months, re-ceived handsome dividend checks. Then the vein gave out, and the value of Sam's stock plummeted to next to nothing. Credulous as ever, Sam wrote Barlow, "I had only just got a letter speaking in glorious terms of the duration of the mine and its paying dividends for years to come. Damn the world—it is all turning topsy-turvey!"[63]

The next months found Sam scrambling, "working for bread." He was push-ing the Central American Transit Company, a Nicaraguan shipping line that was just about his only remaining asset, playing the stock market, doing odd jobs for Barlow in Washington, but getting nowhere. What, at this low point, did Sam decide to do? He published a book of his poems. He had written poetry when he was young, and he had begun again in earnest when he returned from Paraguay. He had mentioned his renewed interest and sent a few samples to "Longo," who was always a kind critic: "I am still pursued by Euterpe and have done nothing of profit since we parted save boiling my old bones down to the glue of rhythm. But, I find peace in the pursuit, though I follow it as awkwardly as he who should resolve to learn the mazurka at fifty."[64]

He gathered together his favorite poems into a small volume he called *Lyrical Recreations*, and Barlow financed its publication. Sam thanked him profusely in the preface and dedicated poems to Julia, Maddie, cousins, nieces, uncles, old teachers, and his friends Hurlbert and Halleck. The first poem, "The King of the Troubadours," was for Longfellow. Some of Sam's poems were breezy and light, some were saccharine, and some maudlin. None were completely dreadful, but few were very good. He wrote of love, loss, beauty, friendship, and the passing of time. Whether he felt patriotism obligatory in the midst of war or was genuinely moved by the conflict, there was a little of that, too, as in these lines from "The Widow of Worcester":

"We hoped it was a nightmare, til the news
was brought from town
That the horde of Charleston maniacs had torn
our banner down.

In my bitter grief and anguish keen I felt the
ancient ire
Of Bunker Hill and Lexington course through
my veins like fire. . . ."[65]

Lyrical Recreations appeared in January 1865. While Sam claimed indifference to its reception, he was far from blasé. He reveled in the good notices and was stung by the bad. Fitz-Greene Halleck effusively swore that Sam was a better poet than Tennyson. Tennyson himself, whom Sam knew and to whom he had sent a volume, wrote "a long and kind letter," Sam happily informed Longfellow, and added, "[William Cullen] Bryant has written to compliment me upon the grace and brilliance of my treatment of my themes." Julia, a published poet herself, sent only mild approval, but Maddie wrote him a letter of warm praise that he treasured. Although James Russell Lowell might have thought he was doing Sam a kindness by not reviewing *Lyrical Recreations*, Sam was hurt by the omission.[66]

That spring, Sam's preoccupation with his book of poems crowded out talk in his letters about his money woes, the war, and nearly everything else. April began with news of Lee's surrender at Appomattox, which he noted with relief. Sam had not taken an active part in the November elections—General George McClellan, the Democratic candidate, had not excited him. When April 15 brought news of Lincoln's assassination, Sam mourned the slain president. "I have shed as many tears for Mr. Lincoln as for any sorrow since my brother Marion's death," he confided to Longfellow.[67]

In this and in his next letters, Sam pondered what the future held for the nation. He was certain big changes were to come. As for him, he was broke. "All my bank accounts are overdrawn," he wrote "Dearest Dudie," Julia. "I have to go back to Washington . . . to get some money."[68]

CHAPTER FOUR

The coals hot and ready for the "Great Barbecue"; Sam takes his place at the table; the means to his ends—noctes ambrosianae; the king's reign begins

AM'S TIMING was perfect. There *was* a new era dawning. The changes coming had been visible on the horizon in the 1850s. Some had been stymied, and some were nudged onward by the war, but the combination of old and new forces guaranteed that a man with Sam's unusual skills could indeed "get some money" in postwar Washington. Just how Sam went about spinning charm into gold, and the milieu that made this feat possible, are the subjects of this chapter.

Physically, the capital to which Sam returned was a mess. The receding tide of soldiers, mediums, prostitutes, and embalmers rushed out as quickly as it had surged in four years earlier, leaving all sorts of flotsam and jetsam behind. The rotting carcasses of mules piled high behind splintering military stables on the Mall gave off a terrible stench. Thousands of freedmen and women seeking the federal government's protection were packed into squalid slums bearing apt names like "Murder Bay." Tree stumps jutted out of the ground everywhere; cold troops who had camped in town over four winters had chopped down the trees for firewood.[1]

"The rents are high, the food is bad, the dust is disgusting, the mud is deep, and the morals are deplorable," Horace Greeley grumbled about the postwar capital.[2] Even one of the few improvements completed during the war, the new wings and dome of the Capitol (with Crawford's sculpture on top), came in for criticism. The huge white structure sat "enthroned on its hill like a disgraced minister exiled to his estates," groused a visiting Frenchman.[3] While a sarcastic Frenchman could be dismissed, Greeley and several other observers who commanded more attention had diagnosed postwar Washington as a hopeless mire and were calling for relocation of the capital closer to the center of the country; St. Louis, Cincinnati, and Chicago all had their supporters. This alarming suggestion, fatal to their livelihoods if adopted, galvanized District businessmen into action. The result, a beautiful "New Washington," emerged with amazing speed (and with amazing corruption) in the early 1870s to squash all talk of removal.[4]

Benjamin Brown French was one of those who had hoped that, after the armies and hangers-on left town, the capital would relapse into "its old jog trot way of life," but he and the others looking backward were left in the dust raised by the creators of the New Washington. Those old days were gone for good. The sleepy Southern antebellum town was no more. "The war," noted Dr. John B. Ellis, a keen observer of Washington, "changed everything." While just a few years earlier in Washington, "New England civilization was sneered at, as made up of strong-minded women and weak-minded men," Ohio reporter and satirist Donn Piatt opined, now "the old Southern ways, tastes, and enthusiasms are driven into the keeping of the few old families. . . . New England civilization has come in, with short-haired women and long-haired men. . . . It freezes and snows and storms, even like a Northern town."[5]

Piatt exaggerated, but not by much. While Washington had hardly become Boston on the Potomac—it still took (and takes) only a few inches of snow to cause bedlam—it was a different city. Gone were the Gwins and the other Southern Democrats who had led official society. Virginia Clay came back to Washington in 1865, but not to entertain. She was in town to plead for her husband's release from Fortress Monroe. Postbellum official society would be predominately Northern, Midwestern, and Republican. The town's old Southern families would no longer call the tune to which local society would dance. Their numbers, fortunes, and reputations had been seriously eroded. Although William Corcoran, returned from Europe, where he had sat out the war, resumed entertaining with little stigma, few of the other homes of Southern sympathizers that had sparkled before the war reopened after it.[6]

Although the changes in appearance and in the make-up of society in the postwar capital—changes they could see and count—felt dramatic enough to old Washington hands like French, they were nothing compared with the even bigger changes occurring in the federal government and in the nation. Thirty-year-old Henry Adams, returning to the United States after seven years in England as his father's secretary at the American legation, observed of the Washington they encountered in 1868, "Had [we] been Tyrian traders of the B.C. 1000, landing from a galley fresh from Gibraltar, [we] could hardly have been stranger on the shore of a world, so changed from what it had been ten years before."[7]

While a wonderful image, surely at least Henry's father, Charles Francis Adams, was not as taken by surprise as a Tyrian trader long at sea by the changes he saw. After all, before he left for Great Britain, he had been a member of the House of Representatives and served as chairman of the Committee on Manufacturers. He knew a thing or two, or should have, about the advances in industry and technology and the nationalization of businesses that had already been driving changes in the nation and its government before the war. Railroads, which would make another of his sons, Charles Francis Adams, Jr., a rich man, were a good example of these trends: state boundaries meant little to railroads laying track across miles and miles of America; technological innovation was constantly improving rail's potential and profitability; and the demand for rails and railcars, plus railroad ties, coal, picks, and shovels, was stoking a growth spurt in heavy industry.[8]

Other forces at work before the war were immigration and westward settlement. There were nearly fifteen million more people in the United States in 1876 than in 1861, and among them were more than four million new immigrants. The nation's population had nearly doubled from 1850 to 1870. Many of the millions lived in cities in the East, but many were pushing west, where the population tripled between 1860 and 1880. Nine new territories were organized, and seven new states were admitted to the Union between 1850 and 1870. Together, these changes spelled skyrocketing demands for the post offices, law enforcement, courts, internal improvements, and revenue, land, customs and pension agents that citizens looked to the federal government to provide.[9]

Then there were the changes wrought by the war itself that had important implications for the future. Only a more centralized government could have provided the leadership and organization that the war effort had ultimately demanded. The success of that effort created a new awareness of the potential of federal governance, and, once the war was over, those who embraced that lesson would put it into practice in unprecedented ways.[10] Although they might not approve, it was clear to French and Piatt and to many Americans that, while postwar Washington was still a one-crop town, with only government to export to the rest of the nation, that crop had changed dramatically. A strong, new hybrid was taking root.

In the early part of the nineteenth century, many Americans felt the presence of the federal government in their lives only when their mail was delivered, but in the years just after the war, they could not help but feel it nearly every day, through pensions, railroad policy, patronage, patents, claims, schools, even free seeds from the new Department of Agriculture. The Departments of Agriculture (1862) and Justice (1870), and the new National Academy of Sciences, Commissioner of Immigration, Bureau of Statistics, Bureau of Education, United States Weather Bureau, and Office of the Commissioner of Fish and Fisheries all helped to extend the federal government's presence in citizens' lives. Noting the changes since the prewar years, Edward Winslow Martin in 1873 explained to readers of his popular *Behind the Scenes in Washington:* "Washington is not only the seat of government, but it is the centre from which radiate the varied influences which affect every citizen of the Republic from the millionaire to the man dependent on his daily earnings."[11]

There were several yardsticks by which to measure the growth of the federal government. One was the burgeoning number of clerks required to keep it running. In 1802, there had been fewer than 300 government employees in Washington; in 1829, there were 625, and that included not only clerks, but congressmen, the president, and the Supreme Court justices. By 1861, there were 2,199 civilian employees of the federal government working in the capital; by 1871, the number would grow to 6,222, and by 1881, to 14,124.[12]

Another measure of the new vigor and scope of the federal government was the sheer increase in lawmaking by Congress. Between 1855 and 1865, an average of 1,700 bills and resolutions was introduced in each Congress, about 430 of which became law. During the next ten years, from 1865 to 1875, the average number of bills and resolutions introduced mushroomed to 4,800, and the average that passed to 824. Additional testament to the new responsibilities Congress was shouldering was the host of new committees established in the decade after the war: among them Coinage, Weights and Measures (1864), Mines and Mining (1865), Pacific Railroads (1865), Education and Labor (1867), Revision of the Laws (1868), War Claims (1873), Levees and Improvements of the Mississippi River (1875).[13]

A spate of new guidebooks promising to help newcomers negotiate the postwar federal bureaucracy also testified to its growing complexity. For comprehensiveness, none could hold a candle to George W. Raff's *The War Claimant's Guide. A Manual of Laws, Regulations, Instructions, Forms, and Official Decisions, Relating to Pensions, Bounty, Pay, Prize Money, Salvage, Applications for Artificial Limbs, Compensation for Steamboats, Cars, Horses, Clothing, Slaves, and Other Property Lost or Damaged, Commutation of Rations, Travel, etc., and the Prosecution of All Claims*

Against the Government Growing Out of the War of 1861–1865, published in 1866. Other guide books quickly followed: William B. Wedgwood, *Wedgwood's Government and Laws of the United States* (1868); Ransom H. Gillet's *The Federal Government: Its Officers and Their Duties* (1872); and William H. Barnes's three-volume *The American Government* (1875–76).[14]

The physical changes to the city that was its home were more tangible evidence of the changes in the federal government. Surveying the shabby capital just after the war, in 1867, Englishman John Walter predicted: "As the political centre of the Union [Washington] . . . typifies exactly the weakness and incoherence of the Federal Government, as it existed before the war. Perhaps, now that the Congress is assuming higher functions and the influence of the several States is proportionately declining, Washington itself may acquire a more solid and business like tone."[15] Within a few short years, Walter's prediction came to pass. The "New Washington" that emerged in the early 1870s, brought about by a partnership between panicked local businessmen and a receptive Congress that held the purse strings, literally made concrete the newly powerful federal government. While the slovenly, sparsely built antebellum town had embodied the relative insignificance of the central government, the broad, paved, tree-lined avenues, handsome new buildings, and landscaped public parks of the New Washington symbolized the Great Republic reborn by fire and the new power concentrated in its capital.[16]

Not everyone had been happy about the growing concentration of power in Washington during the war, and many hoped for a reduction in scale as quickly as possible after it ended. But many others, especially young intellectuals, initially embraced the new state as an agent for good and looked forward to playing a role in what seemed a beckoning new era. Although at seventy-four Harvard law professor Joel Parker felt too old to join in, he did envy those just starting their careers: "There is, or is to be a new epoch. . . . The opinions of men *under thirty* are to be the ruling opinions. They were educated by the war, and have lived a *deeper life* than falls to the lot of ordinary sluggish generations."[17]

E. L. Godkin, a young Irishman who had adopted America as his home, and founded *The Nation* in 1865 when he was thirty-four in hopes of influencing postwar culture, wrote to Frederick Law Olmsted, who had taken leave from designing Central Park to work as executive secretary of the U.S. Sanitary Commission during the war, "I am duly thanking Heaven that I live here and in this age." Even Henry Adams, hardly noted for his optimism in later life, shared in the hopefulness, writing to a friend in 1865, "We want a national set of young men

like ourselves or better, to start new influences not only in politics, but in litera-
ture, in law, in society, and throughout the whole social organism of the country—
a national school of our own generation."[18]

Some of these men and women were members of a host of reform groups that
flocked to the postwar capital hoping to channel the new powers there toward the
betterment of society. As a Japanese visitor to Washington in 1871 observed, the
time seemed right: "It is claimed, indeed, by the best thinkers, that the American
Government was never more powerful and influential for good than it is at the
present time." The war and reconstruction had schooled reformers in the uses of
federal power to effect social change. If the federal government could abolish
slavery, surely it could right other wrongs. Problems that had formerly been
considered largely private and best solved by moral suasion, now became candidates for government solutions. Spokesmen for the poor and the sick, for crimi-
nals, for temperance and education, for civil service reform, for the abolition of
capital punishment, for civil rights for Negroes, for justice for American Indians,
for women's suffrage, and for fair treatment of laborers converged on Washington
to plead their cases before the new agencies, committees, and departments.[19]

While the potential to do good that lay within the newly powerful federal
government attracted idealists to Washington, other inducements drew a more
cynical crowd. The potential to make millions of dollars by exploiting a number of
factors that coalesced after the war—the lucrative new areas coming under the
federal government's purview, an overworked and overwhelmed Congress, and a
lack of strong party leadership among them—was the bait that lured this group to
the capital. The war had schooled them as well. George Townsend, a reporter who
covered Washington in the late 1860s, noted in 1873: "The opportunities for gain
at the public and general expense had been too vast during the war to be suddenly
relinquished at the peace. . . . The harpies who had studied the government to take
advantage of it . . . continued their work."[20]

Conditions were ripe to spawn a ruthless era in which special interests, spoilsmen, and corruption seemed to ooze out the doors of every government office.
There was, in fact, nothing new about the essential elements at work in Washington that gave rise to these unseemly years. The "lousy combings and born
freedom stealers of the earth," as Whitman had called the evils threatening good
government in the 1850s, predated even his generation. But the confluence of so
many factors encouraging corruption, the scale and audacity of the ensuing scandals, the extravagant sordidness of the decade to come, those *were* new.[21]

The coals were hot and ready for an unprecedented feeding frenzy in Washington—what came to be called "the Great Barbecue." The most sought-after dishes at the feast were railroad charters and land. Between 1862 and 1872, the government granted 128 million acres of land from the public domain and about the same number of dollars in bonds and loans to new, federally chartered railroads. Business interests eyed tariff schedules and patent rights hungrily. Others coveted mail routes, mining and timber rights, Indian trading posts, and military contracts for everything from boots to beef. Describing the crowd descending on Washington after the war, one reporter identified "gentlemen in the Mining Interests, Railroad Interests, Banking Interests; Harbor, Shipbuilding, Express and River Interests; Cotton, Whiskey, Army, Manufacturing, Iron and Tobacco Interests—gentlemen in every conceivable Interest, except the Interests of the People."[22]

One of these gentlemen, of course, was Sam Ward. He was just as hungry as the others for fortune and, while most of his colleagues favored some degree of anonymity, he was not averse to fame. His friends in high places, his *savoir faire*, his trove of anecdotes and recipes, and his talents for diplomacy and friendship augured well for success on both fronts. Along the way, he would also add a new dimension to what it meant to lobby in Washington.

Sam's entrée into the postwar Johnson administration was Secretary of the Treasury Hugh McCulloch. McCulloch, a conservative Indiana banker, had come to Washington in 1862 to protest Secretary of the Treasury Salmon Chase's pending national banking bill. Although Sam's experience in banking was far less happy than that of sober McCulloch, who had risen slowly from cashier, to manager, and finally to bank president over twenty years, the two became friends. It helped that, although McCulloch was a Republican, he was a tepid one, and his views on reconstruction—both men disliked the stridency of the Radicals—aligned closely with Sam's own. Chase had recognized in McCulloch an expert on currency with great credibility among the states and had convinced him to stay on in Washington as the first comptroller of the currency. When President Lincoln named Chase chief justice in 1865, he elevated McCulloch to Chase's place at Treasury, and President Johnson continued his appointment.[23]

McCulloch faced a colossal task of financial reconstruction. He set out to tackle head-on the nation's indebtedness, which had reached $2,800,000,000 by October 1865, and wartime inflation, caused in part by the issuing of greenbacks. In his first report to Congress, he presented a plan for the retirement of the greenbacks or legal tenders and the resumption of the gold standard. It was not a popular recommendation, and convincing Congress to support it would not,

McCulloch knew, be easy. One of those to whom he turned for help was Sam, who could both talk the talk of finance and, more importantly, bring together men of opposing views to air their differences.[24]

Sam was happy to oblige. From his new headquarters at 1406 E Street, Sam set out to win for McCulloch via cookery his goal of currency contraction—with the Treasury defraying the cost. Sam was delighted when reporters later placed the cost of his efforts for the Secretary of the Treasury at $12,000. Soon the key senators and representatives on both sides of the currency debate—James G. Blaine of Maine, Robert Schenck of Ohio, William Stewart of Nevada, John Henderson of Missouri, Timothy Howe of Wisconsin, William Pitt Fessenden of Maine, James Garfield of Ohio—began showing up on Sam's guest lists.

McCulloch's greenback retirement plan quickly passed the House, only to be killed in the Senate. During the next session, however, a diluted version of the plan passed both houses, despite strong opposition. Although disappointed that he had not gotten all he wanted (he would soon lose even these modest gains), McCulloch was not disappointed in Sam, who, whether justly or not, claimed credit for the partial victory. Years later, when Sam looked back over his career in Washington, he listed his three greatest achievements in chronological order. At the top of the list were his efforts "for contraction of the currency by M. McCulloch."[25]

Thanks to his work for McCulloch and a string of successes for Barlow, the British banking house of Baring Brothers, and other clients (including, Sam hinted, John Morrissey, the bare-knuckle Irish prizefighter and Tammany Hall stalwart who owned a string of gambling houses), Sam's star was rising. To Julia, he boasted that he was a sort of Figaro: "*Tutti mie chiedono, tutti mi vogliono*" (Everybody calls me, everybody wants me).[26]

But what exactly did everyone want from Sam? What did he do for those who called his name? In a letter to Barlow, his friend as well as one of his most important clients, about work he was doing for him in Washington, Sam wrote: "It has taken me a week to corral my Congressional elephants and I am at length able to write you favorably touching both your projects. I can get the furniture bill passed any day." How did Sam corral his "Congressional elephants"?[27]

Although in-depth details laying out exactly how Sam went about his work are frustratingly few among Sam's papers and those of his colleagues in the lobby and their clients, there are more hints among Sam's than most. It is clear, for example, that Sam knew a recipe for success when he tasted it. Merely tinkering with the ingredients that had showed such promise when he first began to blend them just before the war intervened, Sam used dinners and diplomacy as his preferred means to his ends. When Sam told Julia that *"tutti mi vogliono,"* what most of them really wanted was a seat at one of Sam's dinners. Sam's note to Barlow about his "Congressional elephants" ended, "call at the New York Hotel on Monday at 10 a.m., when you will find me at breakfast, and I will unfold to you my *plan de campagne.*" Sam's special *plan de campagne* often began with *pâté de campagne* and champagne, with Barlow or another client footing the bill.

Sam's sought-after dinners took place against a backdrop of change in the food middle- and upper-class Americans in cities were eating and the way they were eating it in the late 1860s. Another change wrought by the Civil War was what went into American stomachs. Like the changes already mentioned—immigration, industrialization, corruption—many of the food-related changes had gotten under way before the war, becoming clearer after it. Innovations in the cutting, transporting, and storing of ice, for example, led to improvements in refrigeration, which meant that dairy products and delicate crops like lettuce could keep longer and be transported further. More miles of railroad tracks meant that more food, especially meat from new packing plants next to rail yards, could be shipped greater distances, thanks to refrigerated cars; faster ships brought delicate bananas and pineapples to more markets; new canning methods (tin cans, vacuum sealing) allowed foods like peaches and tomatoes to be available out of season. More reliable baking powder, the first commercially available yeast, and greater availability of white flour and refined sugar made a big difference in layer cakes and breads.[28]

For those who could afford it, fancy food, *haute cuisine,* was changing, too. For one thing, by the late 1860s, it was almost always French, with more courses, more wines, and more vegetables, thanks in part to the cachet of Delmonico's. For another, it might be enjoyed not only in private homes employing some of the first private chefs, but in restaurants, which had proliferated after the success of Delmonico's in the 1830s. Polite society's dinner time had moved from five o'clock to six o'clock or later, and now, at whatever time an important dinner was served, it was most likely *service à la russe,* in which each dish was offered in turn by servants, rather than *service à l'americaine,* in which all of the dishes were placed on the table or sideboard at once. When Sam's father's friend and neighbor Philip Hone, a great diner-out, first encountered *service à la russe,* he thoroughly disliked it: "The table covered with confectionery and gew-gaws . . . but not an eatable thing. The dishes were all handed around. . . . One does not know how to choose, because you are ignorant of what is coming next, or whether anything more is coming. Your conversation is interrupted every minute by greasy dishes thrust between your head and that of your next neighbor." Despite such objections, the new method caught on among style setters.[29]

Greater attention was paid to décor and details—the linens, the crystal, the flowers, the party favors—and an explosion of domestic manuals offered detailed instructions for starching the napkins and polishing the silver. In 1872, Mrs. E. F. Ellet's *The New Cyclopedia of Domestic Economy, and Practical Housekeeper* admonished: "*Plate* should be well-cleaned, and have a bright polish; few things look worse than to see a greasy-looking épergne and streaky spoons. . . . *Glass* should be well rubbed with a wash-leather, dipped in a solution of fine whiting and stone-blue, and then dried; afterwards it should be polished with an old silk handkerchief." One could, of course, get carried away with the "gew gaws," and reporters of extravagant affairs claimed that sometimes more money was spent on details than on "eatables"; but yet to come was the era of the truly over-the-top event, at which after-dinner cigars came rolled in $100 bills, swans swam on a lake in the middle of the banquet table, and each oyster came garnished with a lustrous black pearl.[30]

No profusion of orchids, multiplication of courses, or exotic fruit, however, could guarantee dinners of good taste that tasted good or could assure a good time, a fact born out by society in the nation's capital in the late 1860s. The uniqueness of Sam's special evenings is shown off best when contrasted with what passed for socializing, entertainment, and *haute cuisine* elsewhere in post-war Washington.

A new caterer, Maillard's of New York, favored by Mrs. Lincoln, had briefly established a Washington outpost and edged out Gautier's as the preferred maker of spun-sugar frigates, but Maillard's faded away after the war. The Grant White House showed some culinary promise under the direction of "the incomparable Melah," the pretentious Italian steward who favored meals of as many as twenty-nine courses; but journalist Ben Perley Poore, known as "Perley," described the grim, all-too-common ritual of all-too-many official dinners in the late 1860s. Night after night, "a watery compound called vegetable soup was invariably served, followed by boiled fish, overdone roast beef or mutton, roast fowl or game in season, and a great variety of puddings, pies, cakes, and ice creams." "Torture" was society reporter Emily Briggs's word for these graceless dinners. "Is it strange," she asked rhetorically of Sam, "that this man became an idol to the public men whose constitutions were impaired by the dyspeptic dinners of 'high society'?"[31]

There were also official receptions, often overcrowded and rarely conducive to conversation or digestion. Lillie Greenough de Hegermann-Lindencrone of Boston, wife of the genial Danish minister, who wrote odes to Sam and his dinners each time she and her husband dined with him, described several unpleasant evenings like this raucous one at the Mexican legation in 1875: "There was no question of getting into [supper]; only prize-fighters and professional athletes could elbow their way through the crowd. . . . The chairs intended for guests were utilized as tables on which to put unfinished food and half-empty glasses. Everything that was not spilled on the floor was spilled on the table. . . . Gentlemen (?) broke the champagne-bottles by knocking them on the table, sending the contents flying across the room. The lady guests drew out the silver skewers which ornamented the *plats montés* and stuck them in their hair as mementos of this memorable evening."[32]

Neither overdone roasts nor jam-packed rooms were ever part of Sam's entertainments. When in New York, Sam always favored Delmonico's, with its French cuisine *non pareil* and fifty-seven wines. He worshipped Delmonico's young chef, Charles Ranhofer, who was said to allow no other outsider to conjure up a sauce in his kitchen but Sam. In Washington, Sam rotated his larger lobbying dinners, rarely for more than a dozen guests, among Wormley's Hotel, the Metropolitan Club, and occasionally John Chamberlain's new club. But when it came to special dinners, for no more than seven or eight guests, only Welcher's restaurant, on 15th Street near the Treasury Building, would do.[33]

After the war, John Welcher, a Belgian who reportedly had come to the capital as a steward to the elite Seventh New York Regiment, bought out Gautier's and renamed the elegant eatery. Welcher's could seat a hundred guests in a handsome large dining room, but it also had adjustable screens that could create intimate rooms that were better suited to Sam's needs. Some idea of how Sam's dinner bills must have run comes from one of the restaurant's admirers. He noted that Welcher's prices were slightly "less than those of the Fourteenth Street Delmonico's. . . . the most expensive dinners he [Welcher] has ever given have cost $20 a plate. Fine dinners cost from $10 to $12 per plate, and breakfast from $5 to $8 per plate." Giving the nod both to the superiority of Welcher's kitchen and to Sam as the city's arbiter of *haute cuisine*, this same devotee claimed that Welcher's "sauces can please even Mr. Sam Ward."[34]

As he had done when lobbying for President López and Paraguay before the war, Sam gave his most select dinners in the privacy of his own home, now on E Street. There he had a two-man staff: his chef and his loyal valet and secretary, Irishman Jerry Valentine, a horse handicapper who was Sam's second set of eyes and ears around town and whose job it was to make sure that the glassware was polished and the plate shined. No delicacy, claimed one reporter, was too costly or rare for Sam Ward's table in his snug home. Sam shopped for his own terrapin and canvasback ducks at the city's markets, imported his own teas, and blended his own coffee.[35]

Sam's kitchen was his laboratory, in which he invented culinary rules and recipes, sometimes in verse: "To roast spring chickens is to spoil 'em / Just split 'em up the back and broil 'em." Until his friend Hurlbert, the *New York World*'s editor, began to tinker with his meters, "Uncle Sam's Culinary Rhymes" ran in the newspaper. "How Sam Ward Cooks a Ham," in which he claimed to disclose the secrets of one of his most popular dishes, appeared in the *Chicago Daily Tribune* in 1875: "I soak it for four days in water, changing it four times a day; then boil it five hours in cider, with a wisp of new hay; then I baste it with brandy, sherry, or claret, according to the weather; and when they have tasted a slice of that ham, why, they will pass anything I want in Congress."[36]

Sam happily shared his knowledge of cookery and offered advice on menus for all sorts of occasions. When Longfellow wrote in the summer of 1873 that Sumner was coming to visit him at Nahant, Sam sent back menu suggestions for the week to keep Sumner "tranquil:" "Monday—Ducklings dressed with orange marmalade; Tuesday Suckling pig à la Viennoise; Wednesday, chickens roasted à la Parisienne; Thursday, gosling à l'Anglaise; Friday—clam chowder; Saturday, knuckle of veal with boiled English bacon; and Sunday, tripe pudding with stewed tomatoes."[37]

Although, in his 1890 memoir, Ward McAllister claimed decisive and superior knowledge of all things culinary, he was man enough to admit that it was his older cousin who had taught him everything he knew about fine dining. He described Sam's technique for bringing out the best in a restaurant's most temperamental chef to achieve the perfect balance of courses. First, Sam would emphasize the importance of the evening at hand, the prominence of the guests, their discriminating tastes, the fame sure to come to any chef that could please them. Then he would "bury his head in his hands and (seemingly to the chef) rack his brain, seeking inspiration, fearing lest the fatal mistake should occur of letting two white or two brown sauces follow each other in succession, or truffles appear twice in the dinner. The distress that his countenance wore as he repeatedly looked up at the *chef*, as if for advice and assistance, would have its intended effect on the culinary artist, and *his* brain would at once act in sympathy."[38]

Whether in consultation with Welcher's chef or his own, Sam took great care in composing his lobby dinners. After all, the menu was "the plan of campaign, dependent upon the numbers of the enemy who will be reduced to capitulation by the projected banquet." Each course must be exquisite but small. "Sam Ward," wrote Briggs, "managed that his guests should never be satiated. The oyster patties, like a little woman, would be so perfect, though small, that the next course would be anxiously awaited." When it came to selecting wines for the meal, Sam asked for help from no one. He prided himself on his knowledge of European vintages and favored Rhine wines and Burgundies.[39]

At Sam's most intimate dinners, guests simply awaited in innocent expectation whatever fruits of Sam's planning came from the kitchen or bottle. For the large banquets he sometimes orchestrated, menus were engraved on heavy cream stock, often decorated with lovely watercolors. For dinners somewhere in between, Sam sometimes wrote out the menu in his own hand; here is one for a dinner the date of which is unknown:

Menu
Huîtres
Potage
Sheepshead Hollandaise
Salade de concombres
Pommes de terre de Bermuda
Agneau de printemps
Champignons Pommes de terre frites
Riz de veau à la sauce tomate
Croquettes de volaille
Choux-fleurs
Sorbet au kirsch
Canvasback duck
Gelée de groseille
Salade de laitue
Fromage de Camembert et de Roquefort
Mousse aux macarons
De la glace
Fruits
Vins

Xérès Amontillado	Château La Rose
Scharluckberger	Pommery
Bauenshalerberg	Clos de Vougeot[40]

While Sam chose the menu, he deferred to his client, whether it was the Secretary of the Treasury, Barlow, European financiers, men with mining interests in Latin America, or the heads of railroads or steamship lines, when drawing up the guest lists for his lobbying dinners. If the client's interests were financial, Sam would make sure that key members of the appropriate House and Senate committees received invitations. Mining and mineral rights? That was another group of players. In composing his guest list, Sam considered which members' constituents would howl if they voted for or against certain measures and whose had little stake in certain issues, and he would court the latter. Everything Sam knew, or could find out, about potentially important players involved with the issues he followed came into play. Which members were alone in Washington and lonely? Who was most persuasive and who most easily persuaded? Who was leaning one way and who another? Who might like to sit next to whom? All of these factors went into the mix when selecting guests.

Once he had determined his tablemates, Sam concentrated on orchestrating the talk around the table. Good conversation was as essential as good food and wine, Sam believed, to the success of the evening: "It is with the succession of courses as with the sparkling wit that enlivens the repast. The airy nothings, the *mots*, the repartees and spontaneous flashes of wit and humor that crackle like so many electric sparks, are as unrecoverable as the lost patterns of a kaleidoscope." Sam was full of *mots* and flashes of wit. He used stories from his variegated life like condiments at his table. He could salt dinner conversation with all sorts of anecdotes: one of his favorites was about the time he improvised a weir to catch salmon on the Merced River.[41] "Nothing was ever served on Sam's table," claimed Emily Briggs, "that was half as delicious as himself." After one pleasant evening at Sam's house, Lillie de Lindencrone-Hegermann wrote to her mother that Sam Ward was the "diner-out *par excellence* . . . the King of the Lobby *par preference* . . . and the most delightful talker, full of anecdotes."[42]

The results of Sam's great care in composing and conducting his dinners? "*Noctes ambrosianae!*" gushed one guest. An evening at Sam's was, enthused another, "the climax of civilization."[43] But how did these ambrosial nights serve Sam's, and more importantly his clients', ends? Subtly, slowly, and congenially—and therein lies what set Sam apart as a lobbyist.

Sam's methods were as discrete as he was charming. He claimed that he never talked directly about a "project" over dinner, and—perhaps it was because of his excellent wines—his guests left with the impression that he never outright asked anyone for anything. Illinois Republican "Uncle Joe" Cannon, a frequent guest at Sam's house in the 1870s, made no mention of all the other lobbyists swarming the capital but recalled Sam fondly years later when he retired from a long career that included nearly a decade as Speaker of the House: "Years ago Sam Ward was the only so-called lobbyist here. He gave dinners and entertainments: he always had plenty of food and drinks and never asked any one to help him out." While Sam probably never actually found his job quite so easy, one reporter wrote that guests at these evenings confirmed that "Samuel Ward never asked a man about a measure in which he was interested at his dinner table. . . . but he treated his friends so well that they were always anxious to do something for him and usually asked how they could help."[44]

Sometimes for a fee, sometimes as a favor, Sam brought guests together around his table and let a good dinner, good wine, and good company educate, convince, launch schemes or nip them in the bud, or overcome obstacles. Nudged by Sam's careful steering of the conversation, his guests, all chosen with a purpose, might find to their surprise that they had common interests or much to learn from each other. A client might find himself sitting next to a congressman who was wavering on an issue of importance to him and have a chance to talk to him casually away from his Senate or House office.

Sam also used his dinners to mend fences. He had, declared Ben Perley Poore, "an unusual power of reconciling people who were at variance with each other, and the dinners at which he presided furnished occasions to bring face to face political opponents accustomed to avoid each other, but unable to resist the *bon homie* which sought to make them better friends."[45] Sam liked to call himself "the gastronomic pacificator." In one instance of "pacificating," some of his Republican friends asked him to step in as a favor and heal the breech between two important party men, both of whom Sam knew and liked. Sam was happy to help, and the story of his efforts was often recounted, and not only by him:

> A bitter feud between Generals [James A.] Garfield and [Robert C.] Schenck [both congressmen from Ohio at the time] terminated at one of the small, elegantly-appointed, exquisitely dished dinners which were Sam's specialty. "Uncle Sam" . . . invited the two hostile politicians to dinner without letting either know of the other's presence. He allowed them to meet in his hallway and exchange glowers for a few moments before he made his urbane entrance. Seating them, he held their attention with anecdotes until his excellent imported vintages could take hold. And when Sam's exotic foods were melting in their mouths, Garfield the former towpath boy, had beamed upon Schenck, and Schenck, forgetting the hardtack he had eaten in the war, smiled upon Garfield. Late that night the two guests departed, leaving their hatchets buried in the dinner debris.[46]

Dinners were not Sam's only means to his ends. He used other methods as well. He spent many of his days visiting members' offices on Capitol Hill and the cabinet departments clustered around the White House. Like some other lobbyists, Sam traded in information, providing facts and figures to anyone he could buttonhole, to bolster his clients' cases. Many commented on Sam's prodigious memory. With the data he memorized about mining, or steam travel, or rail rates, coupled with amusing anecdotes and nuggets from his trove of trivia, he could hold his listeners' attention while persuasively arguing for whatever measures he was being paid to push. And like some other lobbyists, Sam gave gifts to government officials, although his were more likely to be thoughtful tokens, based on his knowledge of the individual's tastes, rather than expensive but more generic ones: a bushel of Chesapeake oysters for someone who loved them; a choice Burgundy to a wine aficionado; a rare book for a collector.

Nowhere—not in contemporary newspaper accounts, obituaries, congressional testimony, Sam's own letters, or those of his clients and contacts—was there any hint that Sam ever took a bribe, offered a bribe, engaged in blackmail, or used any other such methods to win his ends. Sam was very proud of that. When he listed the three achievements of his Washington career of which he was most proud, his reputation as a lobbyist who did not lie, cheat, steal, or resort to vices to seduce other men came right after his work for Secretary of the Treasury Mc-Culloch and his role in preventing the impeachment of President Johnson, described below.

The sums Sam named for his work for Barlow, the best documented of his clients, while handsome, were too small to allow for bribery—congressmen did not come that cheap and Sam's services were expensive. The most heavy-handed follow-up to one of his delightful evenings, one reporter claimed, might be that, on the day a measure came up for a vote, a witty note in Sam's unmistakable handwriting would be delivered to a congressman's desk: "This is my little lamb. Be good. Sam Ward."[47]

Only once did Sam himself tell of using unorthodox methods. On one of the few occasions that he shared details of his professional life in Washington with Longfellow, Sam told him a story that he said was too good to keep to himself. It was about "a client, eager to prevent the arrival at the committee of a certain member before it should adjourn at noon, who offered me $5,000 to accomplish his purpose, which I did by having his boots mislaid, while I smoked a cigar and condoled with him until they could be found at 11:45! I had the satisfaction of a good laugh, a good fee in my pocket, and of having prevented a conspiracy!"[48]

This is not to say that Sam stood alone as a paragon of virtue or a beacon of civility in the lobby or that all other lobbyists were bribers and blackmailers. Among his fellow lobbyists at the "Great Barbecue," some were blatant and some were gross. Some were both, but many were neither. It is to say that Sam stood out from the rest because, while he used other methods in the lobbyists' bag of tricks, he alone employed entertaining so deftly and so often to win his ends. True, rich Philadelphia businessmen had wined and dined members of the early congresses in hopes of influencing their votes, and men like Samuel Colt and Thurlow Weed had bought their share of food and drink for congressmen. But Sam enlisted the combination of delicious food, fine wines, sparkling conversation, and a keen knowledge of his guests in a systematic and central way that set him apart.

Sam's style of lobbying required patience and *savoir faire*. While he had not exhibited the former earlier in his life, he possessed both in spades in the late 1860s. He often gave dinners seemingly for no reason at all save to bring together interesting men and women for evenings of lively conversation and mutual enjoyment. Urbane, genial, from an old respected family, a college classmate of some, a sister's dance partner of others, Sam was the equal of the most patrician politicians, and he seems generally to have been viewed as their peer. He would seat freshmen members of Congress and new foreign ministers between his old friends from the diplomatic community and the long-time Washington hands around his table. At these evenings, Sam cast seeds that might not bear fruit for several years, but new friendships developed, old ones were cemented, and Sam's list of men upon whom he could drop in for a chat and of houses or legations where his card would be welcomed lengthened. Although not yet given a name by the press—that would not come until the 1880s—in Sam's methods were all the hallmarks of what reporters would dub the "social lobby."

Once, when Longfellow probed for details about what exactly Sam did in Washington and how he did it, Sam had coyly promised: "The mystery of my Washington work shall entertain you some evening, with a bottle of Burgundy and two glasses between us, when, if the spirit moves me, I will take off my jacket and tell you the story." If Sam and Longfellow ever had that conversation, neither alluded to it. Sam put almost nothing in writing to his best friend about the specifics of his "Washington work"—the story of the misplaced boots was the rare exception. Barlow, however, Sam's most reliable client, had secretaries who saved every incoming letter and copies of many outgoing ones. From their correspondence, from Sam's letters saved by others, and from the vivid impressions he made on men and women who wrote them down, details about how and for whom Sam conducted his "Washington work" emerge.[49]

These sources suggest that, from that first secret agreement with President López in 1859 to lobby for Paraguay, the list of Sam's clients expanded to include insurance companies, telegraph companies, steamship lines, railroads, banking interests, mining interests, manufacturers, investors, and businesses and indi-

viduals with claims of all sorts. When Congress adjourned, Sam would sail for
Europe to meet with his foreign clients, most notably Baring Brothers, involved in
shipping, finance, and mines and railroads in the American West, Mexico, and
Brazil. For all of them, Sam put to work his dinners, his knowledge of the federal
bureaucracy, his friendships with key players of both parties, his divining of
officials' preferences—who would most enjoy a case of red wine and who white,
who smoked cigars and who did not—to slide certain bills through Congress,
sidetrack others, and guide claims through government bureaus.

Samuel Latham Mitchill Barlow had many business interests, both foreign
and domestic. His personal interests were as varied as Sam's. He raised blooded
cattle, show dogs, and tropical plants, collected paintings and books, and played
an expert game of whist. He prized good wine and food. Sam often stayed with the
Barlows when he was in New York, where Mrs. Barlow always made a fuss over
him, just as Julia did. When Sam and Barlow were apart, their correspondence
enriched them both, literally and figuratively. Letters between them, which often
began "For Your Eyes Only," "PRIVATE," or with the Masonic □ for utmost secrecy,
included puns, recipes, the prices of rare books, and invitations to Christmas
dinners, in between the candid discussions of client and lobbyist. From Barlow
came legislation, regulations, subsidies, nominations, and claims that he wanted
pushed or killed; the names of men Sam might profitably contact; requests and
thanks for political gossip; annoyance and commiseration when one of his efforts
failed, but more often congratulations when one succeeded.[50]

From Sam came requests for more detailed information to boost his arguments; updates on whose offices he had visited and whom he had invited to
dinner (and what he had served); the names of men who might appreciate a
personal note from Barlow; who was leaning one way, who the other; insider
information about pending fiscal policy; gleanings about Republican strategy;
names of those to whom he had sent baskets of perfect peaches; news of either
victory or defeat; and, no matter which outcome had resulted, a bill.

Barlow made clear that Sam was not his only agent in Washington, although
none of the others was his personal friend. When it served his purpose, Barlow
used the services of other lobbyists, among them, in the 1870s, Richard Taylor,
son of President Zachary Taylor and a Confederate veteran with influence among
Southern Democrats. For his part, Sam made sure to write his letters to Barlow on
the most prestigious stationery he could lay his hands on. Letterhead of the
Department of the Treasury, the Office of Internal Revenue, the House of Representatives, and the House Committee on Ways and Means was at his disposal
when he stopped by to visit, and he helped himself. Sam also dropped names

continually, mentioning private conversations with Secretary McCulloch and a string of other men in high places. Access, Sam knew, was (and still is) all-important to a lobbyist, and Sam drove home his impressive connections to his chief client every chance he got by any method he could. He did not need to exaggerate. The *New York Times*'s "Gossip From Washington" column on October 11, 1868, half of which was devoted to Sam's activities, was just one of several reputable sources acknowledging that Sam Ward had *"entrée* everywhere."[51]

Sam made Barlow's interests his. In March 1868, Barlow wanted banks, and then he wanted government deposits in those banks. Writing with the assurance of a man used to getting his way, Barlow spelled out his wishes: "I want to establish a bank under U.S. law in Savannah and another in Charleston. Nominally, the number allowed by law has already been reached, but in some way this difficulty can be overcome. I think the Secretary [McCulloch] would do whatever lies in his power to aid us in this attempt to circulate *loyal* paper in the South and if you can help me I will pay you well."[52]

Sam set to work. Two, sometimes three, telegrams a day flew between Washington and New York. Four days later, Sam thought he had just about wrapped up the deal. Pleased, Barlow wrote, "Much obliged for your friendship!" and promised "I think you will be satisfied with my treatment of you if everything goes through as you seem certain." Three days later, Sam reported that a fly had appeared in the ointment. Barlow wrote Sam, "I begin to see that the cool $5,000 which I thought was already in your pocket . . . has practically vanished. If you see any way in which this can be rescued I shall be happy." In this case, Sam could not. The charters were not the problem, he wrote, but getting the government to deposit currency in the new banks would be and that problem Sam apparently could not surmount.[53]

A year and several successful projects later, the Transatlantic Cable Company, in which Barlow had an interest, wanted a certain bill passed. Never shy about emphasizing the amount of work he was doing or the stiff odds he was facing, Sam sent frequent reports about the horde of "anti-cable" lobbyists in town. Nevertheless, he was confident, and he was "using some of my best cards."[54] This time his confidence was not misplaced. The bill passed, and, in his next letter, Sam was looking for a check from Barlow for $250. "If you desire to retain me for work next session best make it $500," Sam told him.[55]

Sam was never squeamish about naming a fee for a job. While he sometimes named a specific price for a specific job (the $250 for the Transatlantic Cable project was at the low end of Sam's scale, which, by the mid-1870s, reached up into the thousands for difficult jobs), for the on-going work of keeping an eye out for anything that came up that might concern his client, Sam's fee started out at $250 but quickly jumped to $500 per company per session of Congress, *plus* expenses. By 1875, from Barlow and his business associates alone, Sam had five or six retainers, for a minimum of about $3,000 per session, not including reimbursements for dinners. Barlow never balked at Sam's bills. "I like to win," he wrote Sam; "That is what I chiefly care for." In Sam, he had a winner.[56]

Not all of Sam's jobs were big ones. He often did small favors for friends. Barlow thanked him for theater tickets, cigars, and rare books in notes usually closing, "You shall be remembered." When one of Barlow's other agents was going to Mexico and needed documents quickly, Sam used his connections at the State Department to get them in twenty-four hours, a service for which a grateful Barlow wrote, "I send you a check for $25 with many thanks."[57]

From February through August 1868, banking and everything else took a back seat to politics for Barlow and Sam. Their letters were consumed first by the impeachment, trial, and acquittal of President Andrew Johnson and then by the Democratic convention and campaign. Both men approved of Johnson's conciliatory stance toward the defeated South and viewed the impeachment effort as pure vindictiveness on the part of the Radical Republicans, men like Ben Butler, whom they detested. The second of what Sam regarded as his three greatest accomplishments in Washington took place that spring: "I am prouder of the part I took in defeating the impeachment of Andrew Johnson than of any of my grand and lofty tumults." While Sam almost certainly embellished his role, he had indeed played a part, and when telling the drama he began, "It was on Washington's birthday, 1868 . . . ."[58]

Sam was at Welcher's with a group of leading Democrats, canvassing prospects for that summer's nominating convention, when word reached them that Radical Republicans in the House were at that moment pushing to a vote their motion to impeach the president. "It was I who first carried the tidings to Secretary McCulloch," Sam wrote, "and took a card from him to the President, whom I did not know. He was entertaining the *Corps Diplomatique* at dinner, and I had an hour to spare which I consumed in seeing Chief Justice Chase, to whom the news was a surprise. It was also news to the President, when I found him at ten o'clock, and told him to secure the ablest counsel, half Democrats and half Republicans."[59]

On the advice of many besides Sam, whom he had never before met, Johnson did choose bipartisan counsel that included another of Sam's Republican friends, William M. Evarts. When the impeachment trial began in the Senate less than two weeks later, Ben Butler, whom Sam called "the Great Unscrupulous," was among the House managers. Because conviction would require a two-thirds vote of all senators, the pressure was immediately on both sides to line up the necessary votes and the lobbying grew more intense with each week leading up to the vote. Sam was in the thick of it.[60]

The odds in the betting parlors swung back and forth, as did Sam's mood. At first, he was pessimistic; on February 25 he wrote to Barlow, who had money riding on the outcome, "Make your calculations upon having Ben Wade [president *pro tempore* of the Senate and next in line for the presidency] President by the 30th March." On February 27, he was more hopeful: "The chances since yesterday are rather favoring the President." He went back and forth between optimism and despair right up until May 16, the day of the vote, when his early-morning prediction of acquittal by one, not more than two, votes proved accurate.[61]

The drama was not over yet for Sam. Bitter and licking his wounds, Butler demanded a House inquiry into "the raising of money to be used in the impeachment." He had quietly been offering hefty rewards for information about behind-the-scenes maneuvering. Sam's name cropped up as one of many men who had been raising money and exerting influence for one side or the other. Butler's chief informant, George Wilkes, who had taken over as editor of *Porter's Spirit of the Times*, turning it into *Wilkes' Spirit of the Times*, went so far as to write Butler that his sources vouched that it was Sam who had delivered payoff money of $12,000, raised from a variety of wealthy men, to freshman Kansas senator Edmund Ross to cast what turned out to be the deciding vote against impeachment, a calumny against both Sam and Ross that was never proven. Butler, who felt as strongly about Sam as Sam did about him, was intrigued and summoned him to appear before a special House committee investigating the impeachment process.[62]

Butler, finding some of Wilkes's most inflammatory charges unconvincing, focused instead on some cryptic telegrams between Sam and a cousin on Wall Street which strongly suggested that heavy bets rode on the trial's outcome. What interested him most, however, was a dinner at Welcher's on the night before the Senate voted. Butler was certain that Sam had arranged it. He knew that Sam and Evarts were there, as well as other Johnson supporters and odds makers, and he knew that it would have been just like Sam to bring together a variety of sympathetic factions over dinner.[63]

When Sam appeared to give his testimony, Butler claimed that some of those present that night were betting two to one on Johnson's acquittal, and he argued that proof "that the dinner was to bring together those principally engaged in procuring it is apparent from the card of invitation issued to Mr. Evarts by Sam Ward, under the feigned name of 'Horace.'" Butler had one of the actual invitations in his hand and gave it to Sam to inspect. Sam agreed that it did appear to be his handwriting, but his storied memory, which could recall hundreds of lines of Horace's poetry, suddenly failed him. Imperturbable, Sam swore that he could recall nothing about the invitation or the evening, and nothing Butler could do could shake his story.[64]

Although he appeared placid when testifying, Sam had actually been quite nervous that something else that he was hiding—possibly the extent of not only his bets but those of Barlow and other New Yorkers—would come out. He railed to Barlow about "that d——d strabismal inquisition" (Butler suffered from strabismus, which made his eyes appear hooded and leering) and confessed that he "trembled about that d——d telegram . . . but it has escaped his notice."[65]

While Sam was testifying in June, Barlow, August Belmont, Samuel Tilden, and Manton Marble, all leaders of New York's Democrats, were busy trying to consolidate their power before the party nominating convention at Tammany Hall in July. After the convention nominated former New York governor Horatio Seymour for president, they turned to plotting his victory in the fall elections. Sam was a second- or third-tier power broker, but he was one of the best-connected Democrats-without-portfolio on the ground in Washington, privy to all sorts of gossip and eager to feel like an insider. He began sending off letters to Barlow and Marble, editor of the *New York World* until 1876, a Democratic mouthpiece owned by Barlow, with news about how the Republicans planned to wage their campaign for Ulysses S. Grant and suggestions for how the Democrats should wage theirs for Seymour.[66]

Sam deplored the negative tenor of the Democrat's campaign and was certain that they had got it all wrong. Writing to "My Dear Marble" on House of Representatives stationery on July 31, Sam called their campaign "attacking and offensive," "not constructive": "We propose to blacken the Republicans so deeply that white men must vote with us, and say to the people 'try us' because the Radicals are such d——d Rascals. We have no *vision* to provoke enthusiasm at the sight of his [Seymour's] name." Instead, Sam proposed: "Let us have some glimpses of a future promised land. Formulate this view so as to give us a *positive* cry and an attractive motto, instead of a negative and a vindictive defense."[67]

Sam wrote several more letters to Marble in the same vein, all of which he felt were ignored. Miffed, and sweltering in Washington's wretched August heat, he grumbled: "I'll be d——d if I will take the trouble to *write* and take much useless and gratuitous trouble on myself, unless inspired by the hope of doing some good for the cause." Somewhat mollified by a long, complimentary letter from Marble a few days later, Sam continued sending along Washington gossip, but, as he came to regard the Democrats' hope for taking the presidency in November as hopeless, his letters trailed off, and he turned his attention back to the lobby.[68]

Seymour did lose to Grant, and, with Ben Wade, Ben Butler, and the other Radicals in charge of Congress, Sam's access to Capitol Hill offices was trimmed back. With McCulloch replaced by George Boutwell, whom Sam did not know well, his run of the Treasury Department was also somewhat curtailed. But Sam still had plenty of good contacts in Washington and plenty of Republican friends. Fellow admirer of Horace and friend James A. Garfield was a rising Republican star. James G. Blaine, with whom Sam was on very good terms, became Speaker of the House when the 41st Congress convened. Hamilton Fish, an old family friend, was the new secretary of state. And Evarts, although temporarily without an office, was very much a figure to be reckoned with. There was also a respectable Democratic minority in the Congress, many of whom owed their seats to support from Barlow and his friends.

As the Grant administration settled in, Sam was busier than ever. He had handsome retainers from a number of clients and several more nibbling on his line. So flush was Sam in the months after Grant's inauguration that he made his will, most uncharacteristically planning for the future. He felt that his sisters Annie and Louisa were provided for but that Julia was both financially hard-pressed and, Sam sensed, oppressed by Howe.[69]

The Howe marriage was a stormy one. Samuel Gridley Howe never ceased to pressure Julia to give up what he regarded as her unseemly pretensions to a literary career and conform to the canons of domesticity. And Julia, despite the birth of six children, refused to abandon her writing. While more candid in letters to her sisters, Julia had alluded to her unhappiness in letters to Sam, and he, keenly attuned to nuances, was good at reading between the lines. He took Julia's part against Howe.[70]

Sam shared the news of his will with Julia in May 1869: "My dear Old Bird, Having recently resumed my frequent carrier pigeon trips to and from . . . Washington, and feeling by the gradual subsidence of the battalion of Veteran contemporaries that age [he was 55] as well as the possibility of accident make it prudent for me to put my affairs in order, I yesterday executed in Washington a will in your favor, which I will send to you under Granny Sumner's [Senator Charles Sumner] frank. . . . It is now in the safe of John Welcher, the restaurant at which you graced those two charming dinners."[71]

While he was in the chips, Sam also designed his own distinctive stationery. Business correspondence would continue to go out on Treasury, House of Representatives, or some other letterhead intended to impress, but his personal letters to family and friends were written on heavy cream-colored notepaper engraved with a compass rose, sometimes in gold or red, purple or green, with its needle pointing to SW.

Henry Adams, who had come to Washington eager to be a part of the new day dawning at the beginning of the Grant years, soon decamped for Harvard in disgust. The nation was indeed changing but not as he had hoped. Later, Adams sniped that, during Grant's two administrations, government became the detail and waltzing the profession in Washington. For Sam, who was an exceptionally good dancer and who brought with him no such high-minded goals, the next eight years were some of his busiest and most fruitful.

Sam seemed to be in constant motion, traveling between the capital, Boston, New York, and the South, to England, Switzerland, Germany, Italy, and France, in the course of his "Washington work." Wanted by everyone, as he had bragged to Julia, during this period Sam would exert the most influence and get the most recognition that he would ever enjoy. A brief note in *Every Saturday*, a weekly news, society, and gossip compilation, in 1870 testified to Sam's travels, but, more important, to his name recognition. In between news about the Empress Eugénie, the Prefect of Leon, and the Emperor of the Brazils was this notice: "Sam. Ward . . . who is too multifarious a character to be described by a personal word, is in London."[72]

Sam did not get his name in the newspapers because he excelled in the fields he had once dreamed of conquering as a young man—not in letters, or mathematics, or languages. He had made a name for himself in a field unknown to him and his friends in their youth, using the same skills he had honed in those heady days. Once a young prince of New York, Sam had become the "King of the Lobby" in Washington.

Sam Ward, by Carl Christian Vogel von Vogelstein, Dresden, 1836. Sam's four years in Europe were almost at an end when he sat for this elegant portrait by a court painter. Shown with him is one of the expensive acquisitions that his father lamented, a Newfoundland dog named Rover. (Courtesy Mrs. William Mailliard. Photograph from the Frick Art Reference Library, New York.) ᴥ

Bridal portrait of Sam Ward and Emily Astor Ward by Ann Hall. Sam had hoped that Emily would wear orange blossoms in her hair at their wedding on January 25, 1838, but she chose instead a diamond parure, a gift from her grandfather. When Ann Hall, a relative of Sam by marriage, painted their bridal portrait, he got his wish: Emily wears the jewelry but he holds the flowers over her head. (Courtesy J. Winthrop Aldrich, Astor family archives, Rokeby, Barrytown-on-Hudson, New York.) ✆

Medora Grymes Ward, engraving by E. B. Hall after a drawing by Charles Martin. Sam married Medora Grymes of New Orleans on September 20, 1843. Described by one artist as "the incarnation of Aphrodite," she was chosen by Caroline Kirkland as one of the most beautiful women in America, and this picture of Medora was among the illustrations in Kirkland's 1852 book on the subject. (Caroline Kirkland, *The Book of Home Beauty* [New York: Putnam, 1852].) ⤫

Sam Ward, circa 1851. After his recklessness caused the smash-up of Prime, Ward, and King in 1847, Sam headed west to the California gold fields with the '49ers. During this period, Sam briefly abandoned his carefully clipped Van Dyke beard for a more rugged look. (Courtesy New York Public Library, New York.) ⤫

Henry Wadsworth Longfellow, 1858. Sam and Longfellow, fifty-two years of age in this photograph, met in 1836 and began a friendship that lasted nearly five decades. Longfellow would adopt his iconic bushy beard and mustache after suffering facial burns while trying to save his wife Fanny, who died after a fire in their home in 1861. (Courtesy National Park Service, Longfellow National Historic Site, Cambridge, Massachusetts.) ⌒⌒

Opposite, above. East front of the Capitol looking southwest, 1862. When Sam arrived in Washington in 1859, the original squat dome of the Capitol had been removed to make way for a better-proportioned replacement. In this photograph, scaffolding marks the outlines of the new dome that would be crowned with the statue "Freedom," sculpted by Sam's brother-in-law Thomas Crawford. (Courtesy Office of the Architect of the Capitol, Washington, D.C.) ⌒⌒

Julia Ward Howe, circa 1865–70. A reformer and the author of the *Battle Hymn of the Republic*, Julia Ward Howe disapproved of "Bro. Sam's" lifestyle, but she loved him deeply and reproached herself after his death, in 1884, for not better appreciating his good qualities. Sam's "Dear Old Bird" mentioned him often in her diary until her own death, in 1910. (Courtesy Schlesinger Library, Radcliffe Institute, Harvard University.)

The Mendacious Club and guest, 1875. Sam, perhaps in his capacity as president of the exclusive (three-member) Mendacious Club, offers a mock benediction to the youngest member, Archibald Philip Primrose, the Earl of Rosebery. Although spidery writing on the back of the photo identifies the gentleman on the left as the club's only other member, William Henry Hurlbert, it looks little like him. Lord Houghton, the poet Monckton Milnes, looks on. (Courtesy J. Winthrop Aldrich, Astor family archives, Rokeby, Barrytown-on-Hudson, New York.) ⧼⧽

Samuel Latham Mitchill Barlow, circa 1889.
Samuel Barlow, a wealthy and powerful
New York Democrat, was one of Sam's best
friends and best clients. The two shared a
passion for good food and fine wine, and
their letters mixed recipes with legislation
that Barlow wanted passed and Sam's plans
to make that happen. (*Harper's Weekly*,
1889, vol. 3.) ஒ

Collis P. Huntington, circa 1890. Collis
Huntington headed west with the '49ers, like
Sam, as a merchant. He invested his profits in
railroads and battled ferociously in Washington for federal funds for his lines. One
reporter called Huntington, who looks quite
respectable in this image, the "great, huge
devil-fish" of the lobby. (Courtesy Library of
Congress, Prints and Photographs Division.)
ஒ

Grenville Dodge, circa 1911. Grenville Dodge's passion was railroads. He surveyed them, built them, lobbied for them, over a long career served as chief engineer and president of dozens of them, and was made rich by them. With his command of facts and figures, Dodge was a formidable lobbyist for the Union Pacific and other lines. (Courtesy Library of Congress, Prints and Photographs Division.) ∽

William E. Chandler, circa 1870–80. William Chandler was at the top of his game when this photograph was taken. His career as a successful lobbyist, while well known, did not stand in the way of his advancement in government: Chandler served as secretary of the navy under President Arthur and as a senator from New Hampshire from 1887 to 1901. (Courtesy Library of Congress, Prints and Photographs Division.) ∽

Uriah Painter, Charles Batchelor, and Thomas A. Edison, 1878. Investigations into several lobbying scandals exposed the devious work of reporter Uriah Painter, but he still realized his goal of becoming a rich man when he invested in the work of young Thomas Edison. In 1878, Painter *(left)* introduced Edison *(seated)*, his assistant Charles Batchelor, and their phonograph to Washington. (Courtesy National Park Service, Edison National Historic Site, West Orange, New Jersey.) ∽

"The Spider-Lobbyist at Home." Reporters devoted quarts of ink to the "lobbyesses" at work in Washington after the Civil War. "Spider-lobbyists" enticed congressmen with "iced champagne and Burgundy at blood heat" and with their "velvet, feathers, and laces prove[d] what a railroad can do when its funds are applied in the proper direction." (Benjamin Perley Poore, *Perley's Reminiscences of Sixty Years in the National Metropolis* [Philadelphia: Hubbard Brothers, 1886].) ∼

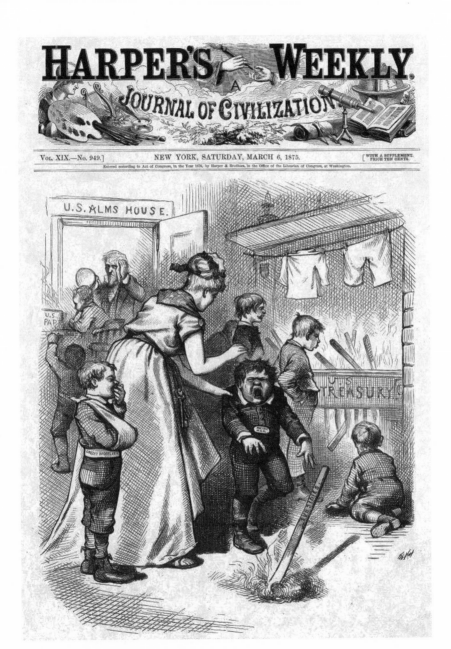

"Any Thing But A 'Pacific Mail,'" 1875. After the Pacific Mail Steamship Company hearings, Thomas Nast criticized federal subsidies in a cartoon for *Harper's Weekly*. Dame Columbia, matron of the U.S. Alms House (Congress), chastises bad boys labeled "Credit Mobilier" and "Pacific Mail" for grabbing subsidy irons from the U.S. Treasury fireplace. (*Harper's Weekly*, March 6, 1875.) ❧

"Uncle Sam Ward," 1876. After lecturing the House Ways and Means Committee on the hazards of lobbying and the importance of dining well, Sam told a parable about a clever cook, the king of Spain, and a meal with an unusual ingredient. In this newspaper cartoon, Sam cooks up a pot of $1,000 pigs' ears himself. (*New York Daily Graphic*, December 20, 1876.)

"Our Congressmen," lithograph by Mayer, Merkel & Ottmann, New York, 1882. This vivid depiction contrasts the changing demands on a congressman's time. In the "past," the member offered impassioned speeches on lofty themes like liberty and freedom. In the "present," he is besieged by lobbyists demanding anything and everything. One petitioner's succinct sign reads, "I want a post office." (Courtesy Library of Congress, Prints and Photographs Division.)

Sam Ward, caricature by "Spy," 1880. After his visit to England in 1880, the London *Vanity Fair* ran a glowing article about Sam, complete with a caricature by "Spy," the *nom de crayon* of Sir Leslie Ward (no relation). Dubbed "the Prince of good livers," Sam was portrayed as a man who "often controlled legislation and decided the fate of important measures." (*Vanity Fair*, January 10, 1880.) ∝‿○

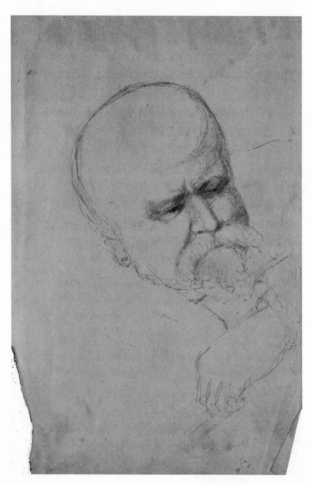

Unattributed pencil sketch of Sam Ward, circa 1882. The
identity of the artist who sketched an older, pensive Sam is
unknown. The drawing is among the contents of eight thin
boxes of Sam's papers at the New York Public Library, all that
are left of the "several large chests" of his documents described
in 1903, before Julia burned them. (Courtesy New York Public
Library, New York.)

W. & D. DOWNEY
PHOTOGRAPHERS

57 & 61, EBURY STREET.
LONDON, S.W.

COPYRIGHT

Sam Ward, W. & D. Downey Photographers, London, 1883. One of
the last photographs of Sam, this one was taken in London, where
he had fled to escape creditors. "Not a word about my whereabouts," he had warned Julia upon departing the United States,
but when he became the lion of the social season, seen everywhere
with the British elite, the secret was out. (Courtesy J. Winthrop
Aldrich, Astor family archives, Rokeby, Barrytown-on-Hudson,
New York.)

"Nidden"
23ᵈ Feb 1872

My dear Don Tomas,

I am excessively sorry that a despatch from Bob Randall should summon me to Philadelphia on important business early tomorrow a.m. I will be with you in spirit and you will have more spirit in my absence,

Mr. Mrs. T. Bayard U. S. S.

I am affectionately
Uncle Sam

In the late 1860s, Sam designed his own distinctive monogram and stationery. The compass rose engraved on heavy cream-colored notepaper might be red, gold, purple, or green, but the needle always pointed to SW. In February 1872, Sam signed this jaunty note to "My Dear Don Tomas" (Delaware senator Thomas Bayard) with his customary "Yours affectionately, Uncle Sam." (Courtesy Library of Congress, Manuscripts Division.) ✑

CHAPTER FIVE

Sam looks, acts, and loves the part of Rex Vestiari; "this huge, scaly serpent of the lobby"; new lobbyists in the postwar realm: "spider women" and reporters

BY THE END of the first Grant administration, when Sam's name appeared, as it frequently did, in one of the growing number of "news from Washington" newspaper columns, it was likely to be followed by "King of the Lobby." Even at a time when the press was portraying lobbyists as the most reviled of men, Sam's honorific never had the ring of an epithet. Even unfriendly reporters seemed to toss the phrase into their articles only to identify Sam's pride of place within the Washington hierarchy, not to deride him. Sam, who delighted in hobnobbing with European royalty, loved his title. So proud was he of it, and so little stigma seemed attached to it, that Sam could give a dinner in honor of James G. Blaine and present the powerful Speaker of the House with a silver loving cup inscribed from *"Rex Vestiari"* without embarrassing either of them. As the first Grant years unfolded and the "Great Barbecue" got under way, Sam was a busy man, and his realm was growing and changing, in part thanks to him.[1]

Fifty-five years old when Grant first took office in 1869, Sam was taking on a rich patina as he aged. He gave dinners befitting his potentate title and he looked the part. "Short and stout, he had a noble head, twinkling eyes, and a snow-white imperial beard which gave him the appearance of a French count," wrote reporter Frank Carpenter, whose richly colored columns captured the essence of Washington for his many readers during these years. "Always dressed in the best of clothes and the whitest of linen, he habitually wore a rose in his buttonhole and diamond studs in his shirt. Wherever he went he stood out above the crowd as a distinguished character." Sam's niece Maud Howe, accustomed to strict economy at home, was in awe of everything about her Uncle Sam, including his clothes: "checked trousers, superb waistcoats, an overcoat of pale gray box cloth with large white pearl buttons, unmistakably from London."[2]

Sam was always dapper and always busy during these years, as his correspondence with Barlow makes clear. In addition to the clients already in his stable, he was acquiring new ones, often by referral. In one letter, Sam thanked Barlow for steering to him one client who was paying him $750 and another who gave him $500 and "only wants four votes and even two will answer."[3]

Writing to Barlow on House Ways and Means Committee stationery in 1873, Sam shared news about several projects on which he was working and described an encounter with an unnamed congressman: "I met him yesterday at the Capitol and had a long intelligent talk. I then perceived that he has a tantalizing way of unbuttoning and buttoning up again the right side pocket of his trousers. Several times I fancied that, like other pilgrims in peril, he hoped open sesame would produce a check or a pungent greenback." The congressman went away disappointed. That was not how Sam operated.[4] In another letter, after Barlow had outlined a measure that he wanted passed, Sam replied, "To accomplish such a result will cost some money and dinners—not more than I am giving of the latter, but more of the former than I have to spend."[5]

Sam wrote to Barlow about claims—cotton claims, tobacco claims, claims involving Peruvian guano, and claims arising from the Gadsden treaty—that he was pushing for Barlow and his friends. After Sam had worked out a happy resolution to various Mexican claims for some of Barlow's friends, who apparently had balked at his high fee, Sam urged Barlow to "reconcile the triumvirate to the large charges of last year which—*entre nous*—I justified by the immense and successful labor of getting all settled."[6] Railroad business began to take up more of Barlow's, and thus Sam's, time. After James Fisk's murder in 1872 by a rival for his mistress's affection, Barlow and his associates fought a long, and ultimately successful, battle to wrest control of the Erie Railroad away from Jay Gould, and Sam was one of his soldiers. When Barlow's interests turned to mining—coal, iron ore, gold, silver—so did Sam's.

Sam dashed off letters from wherever his business took him, which, in addition to Boston, New York, Philadelphia, and Washington, included Richmond, Mobile, New Orleans, London, Geneva, Zurich, Basel, and, in 1871, Rome and Florence. Sam was representing British investors interested in railroads in Brazil, and he learned that Dom Pedro, the emperor of Brazil, was traveling in Italy. Louisa's daughter, Mary Crawford, recalled throwing open the door of her family's apartment in Rome to be scooped up by her Uncle Sam, wearing a shepherd's-plaid suit, a dark-red scarf, and, on his right hand, his sapphire ring. After a quick visit, he set off to Florence, where Julia's daughter Laura and her husband lived and where the emperor was staying incognito.[7]

Laura recounted what happened next, as she heard it from Sam:

> Uncle Sam had come to Florence on a singular errand. Dom Pedro, Emperor of Brazil, was there, and Sam came from Washington on some political errand. He told us with glee how he had been refused admission. The Emperor saw no one except the members of his party. . . . But, the King of the Lobby had brought him a presentation copy of Longfellow's latest work—"Evangeline" perhaps, I don't remember—which he sent to the Emperor, begging his acceptance of the book with his compliments. Presto! The door flew open. Dom Pedro would be delighted to see Mr. Ward. They became intimates in an hour.[8]

Another window onto Sam's busy life, this one from the perspective of a frequent dinner guest and friend, is afforded by the diary and letters of James A. Garfield. Sam, a Democrat from a prominent New York family, and Garfield, a Republican born in a log cabin in Ohio and seventeen years his junior, met in 1865 during Garfield's second term in the House. The glue that cemented their friendship was their mutual love of Classical studies. Sam was rarely without a volume of Horace in his pocket; Garfield had been a professor of ancient languages at Hiram College in Ohio before enlisting in the army in 1861. The two often corresponded in Latin, calling each other Quintus, Horatius, or Flaccus, all parts of Horace's Roman name.

Garfield was a rising star among Republicans. He was fiscally conservative and supported McCulloch's and subsequent efforts to withdraw greenbacks and resume specie payments. His committee assignments included the House Ways and Means Committee, the Banking and Currency Committee, and the Appropriations Committee, all important for Sam's clients. Some of Sam's American clients wished that Garfield were more of a high-tariff man, but, for Sam's European clients, his stance was just right.

Amiable, moderate, a Republican insider, *and* a lover of Horace, with a wife and children back home in Ohio, Garfield was a perfect candidate for Sam's guest list. His presence lent prestige and credibility to Sam's dinner table and, in return, as his diary makes clear, he enjoyed these evenings of good food, cigars, and conversation, as well as the flattering deference due an up-and-coming congressman. Sam could count on Garfield to explain to any of his wavering colleagues the importance of hard money and to listen to the concerns of the bankers and insurance executives paying the dinner bills.

Garfield was not naïve. He knew that Sam was called the King of the Lobby, and still he was happy to dine with him, sometimes three times a week, at Welcher's and Wormley's and in private at 1406 E Street. So, Garfield's diary and letters make plain, were dozens of other Republicans and Democrats, Senate and House members, cabinet members, and foreign ministers. It is equally telling of Sam's unusual position in the capital that these men reciprocated Sam's hospitality. Garfield ran into Sam all over town at dinners and receptions to which they had both been invited.

In winter and spring of 1872, when Garfield was harassed with Appropriations Committee work, he looked forward to dinners with Sam. The other guests present on the nights that Garfield dined at Sam's made an impressive bipartisan roster. Among them were Representatives Nathaniel Banks of Massachusetts, a Republican and chairman of the Committee on Foreign Affairs; Samuel "Sunset" Cox, one of the most powerful Democrats in the House and an expert on banking and currency; Horatio Burchard, a Republican from Illinois interested in finance who, a few years later, became head of the U.S. Mint; Michael Kerr, a Democrat from Indiana, who would become Speaker when the Democrats took the House in the 44th Congress; Union major general Henry Slocum, another Democrat from New York; Oliver Dickey, another Union army veteran and a Republican from Pennsylvania; and William Frye, a Republican from Maine. Senators included Republican president pro tempore of the Senate Henry Bowen Anthony of Rhode Island; Allen Thurman, a Democrat from Ohio soon to become president pro tempore and chairman of the Committee on Private Land Claims; and Eugene Casserly, a Democrat from California, who sat on the Committee on Pacific Railroads. Others included economist David Wells, a free trade advocate and a close friend of Garfield's who counseled him on tariff matters; William McFarland, a New York lawyer; and Walter Dorsey Davidge, a prominent Washington lawyer, who represented clients with claims before the government. Sometimes dinner was just the beginning of the evening. After Garfield dined with Sam and Wells on February 28, 1872, all three called on Freeman Clarke, a Republican congressman from New York, at his home, "where we had a conference . . . on questions of currency and exchange."[9]

When Garfield came back to Washington for the third session of the 42nd Congress the next winter, frequent dinners with Sam resumed. A memorable one, on January 21, 1873, included Harvard professor Louis Agassiz and Joseph Henry of the Smithsonian Institution, plus Republican representative Eugene

Hale of Maine, Republican William Boyd Allison of Iowa, whose long Senate career would begin shortly and who was very interested in monetary policy, and Samuel Hooper, a Republican from Massachusetts who sat on both the powerful Committee on Banking and Currency and the Committee on Coinage, Weights, and Measures.[10]

On December 3, 1873, Garfield noted in his diary that Sam had introduced him to his good friend "the Earl of Westbury," "a very bright young Englishman." Garfield had misunderstood. It was actually the young Earl of Rosebery, Archibald Philip Primrose, visiting America for the first time, whose letters of introduction had brought him to Sam's door and whose charm made these two kindred spirits fast friends, despite an age difference of more than thirty years. Garfield had been set straight by the next evening, when he wrote, "Dined at Welcher's with the Earl of Rosebery, at a dinner given by Ward. There were present Senators Conkling [Roscoe Conkling, Republican of New York], Anthony, Bayard [Thomas Bayard, Democrat from Delaware], Representatives Hale [Robert Hale, Republican] of New York, Frye and myself, Secretary Robeson [Secretary of the Navy George Robeson] and Attorney General Williams [George Williams]. A very pleasant party."[11]

The following week, Garfield was embroiled in the turmoil over repeal of what had been quickly dubbed the "Salary Grab," an odious bill spearheaded by Ben Butler and passed on the last day of the 42nd Congress that not only raised congressmen's salaries by 50 percent but made the increase retroactive for two years. Dining with Sam for the third time in five days, Garfield noted on December 8 that, after a grueling day of floor debate, he "dined with William Orton, David A. Wells and Ward and discussed a number of public questions." Orton, president of Western Union, was often in Washington to oppose the government's getting into the telegraph business. A frequent guest at Sam's dinners, Orton likely paid for many of them.[12]

Two months later, after another frustrating day, Garfield noted that both he and Sam had been invited to the secretary of state's house for dinner: "At seven o'clock PM dined at Sec'y Fish's with Admiral Polo [de Bernabé, the Spanish minister], Caleb Cushing [former congressman from Massachusetts and newly appointed minister to Spain], Orth [Godlove Orth, Republican congressman from Indiana], Bancroft Davis [assistant secretary of state], General Butler [Sam's nemesis, Ben Butler], Ben Perley Poore, Sam'l Ward."[13]

That summer, Garfield and his young son Jimmie set out from Ohio on an adventure to New York. As soon as they got off the train, they headed for Sam's rooms at the Brevoort House. Proving correct his nieces' and nephews' claim that their Uncle Sam always knew just what children wanted, Sam "took charge of Jimmie by sending him to see Barnum's Hippodrome" in the care of his valet Jerry. That evening, Garfield "dined with Ward and Hurlbut." Garfield could be forgiven for misspelling the quirky Hurlbert's name. Born William Henry Hurlbut, he so enjoyed a printer's error on his calling cards while at Harvard that he decided to adopt the spelling.[14]

Letters between Sam and Senator Thomas Bayard offer another perspective on Sam's activities during these years. Although the two men had long known one another from Democratic politics, their friendship blossomed when Bayard, fourteen years Sam's junior, came to Washington as Delaware's junior senator in 1869. He and Sam shared a distaste for Radical Reconstruction but little else in terms of policy: Bayard consistently condemned subsidies for shipbuilders, high protective tariffs, and land grants to railroads. They did agree, however, on fine food and wines, especially on the superiority of diamond-back terrapin, a subject on which both men were experts. While some found Bayard austere, he and Sam exchanged warm, light-hearted letters full of puns and news of Bayard's children.[15]

Although the two disagreed on many topics, Bayard seemed happy to help out with what he dubbed Sam's "mysterious work" when he could, and Sam returned the favors. Bayard suggested colleagues important to Sam's clients who might enjoy receiving a case of Rhine wine and relayed inside information from committee meetings about who spoke in favor of a measure and who against. Sam went out of his way to suggest friendly cosponsors for Bayard's pet projects and shared with him tidbits of information that he picked up on visits to government agencies. Sam lightheartedly tweaked Bayard for not supporting him on a bill related to tea and coffee, but, in the same letter, invited him to dinner at Welcher's that night. Bayard accepted many such invitations and extended many to Sam to dine at his Washington home and vacation with his family in Wilmington.[16]

Their letters were filled with gossip about other men in public life, and, as Bayard considered a run for the presidency in 1876, speculation about how other Democrats might lean. In March 1872, Sam wrote Bayard about the "startling sight" of Daniel Sickles, back in Washington: "I saw him . . . with his young wife very coolly and smilingly by the spot where on a bright day like this 13 years ago he murdered the lover of his old one."[17]

Correspondence between Sam and William Evarts fills in more details about Sam's "Washington work" during these years. Sam had known Evarts since the late 1850s, when Evarts and Seward were deeply involved in Republican politics in New York. While Sam's regard for Seward diminished as a result of perceived slights, his respect for Evarts grew when he served as President Johnson's counsel during his impeachment trial and, afterwards, as Johnson's attorney general. Reporter Frank Carpenter described a man who looked very unlike Sam—"He [Evarts] is by all odds the ugliest man known to fame. Thin and bony, with slightly stooping shoulders . . . a big rough nose"—but he touched on one source of kinship between the two: "There is no man in Washington who enjoys a good dinner more than Senator Evarts. He is one of the highest livers in the capital."[18]

When Evarts was named one of the counsel for the arbitration of American claims against Great Britain in Geneva in 1871, he was in a position to affect an outcome in which Sam was intensely interested. Sam had clients deeply invested in what were collectively known as the *Alabama* claims, claims made by the United States government against Great Britain for damage inflicted on Northern merchant ships during the Civil War by the *Alabama* and other Confederate cruisers built by British shipyards. Millions of dollars were at stake, and Sam traveled from New York to Washington to London and Geneva to keep an eye on the proceedings.[19]

At first, Sam mentioned the claims in only the most disinterested way in letters to Evarts. He brought Evarts together with Robert Schenck, the newly appointed U.S. minister to Great Britain, over dinner at his home, with the purpose, he told Longfellow, of their exchanging "points and details of value" about the upcoming discussions, but kept his distance.[20] When negotiations concluded in 1872, however, and the arbiters awarded the United States $15.5 million in damages to be divided up among the aggrieved parties, the tone of Sam's letters to Evarts shifted. Sam began to push his clients' cases. Evarts pushed back. For a time, a chill entered their correspondence.[21]

During the winter of 1873–74, Evarts invited Sam to visit him several times to discuss the claims. Evarts himself was working for several insurance companies, pursuing their claims for a share of the money, but he promised to see what he could do for Sam's clients and urged Sam, "Write me any facts that it is important for me to know." Sam did, sending off so many letters filled with the particulars of the cases that by spring his persistence was grating on Evarts. The two did not see eye to eye: "I know your views about the *business*," Evarts wrote, "but they are not mine as I have often told you as to this particular matter." Nonetheless, the next day, Evarts invited Sam to a private dinner that he was convening to bring together the principals in the matter, among them Secretary of State Fish, Speaker Blaine, and Minister Schenck.[22]

A few days after the dinner, Evarts teased Sam about his continuing deluge of letters: "I am much obliged by your letters and telegrams, tho' your latest one perhaps exceeds the rule of stating facts only." Within a few weeks, the matters

were settled; Sam alluded to pocketing a sizeable fee; and their next letters resumed their old, cordial tone. Evarts thanked Sam for a case of Burgundy, asked
Sam how to obtain one hundred boxes of cigars, wondered what champagnes
Sam would recommend for his daughter's wedding, and urged him to save the
date so he could join them for the nuptials.[23]

Although Sam told Longfellow that he was so busy that "thought has no more
chance to crystallize than the taker of tickets at Barnum's Hippodrome has to
remember the 119th Psalm," he was never too busy to do favors for friends or for
the friends of friends, as was the case with scientist Louis Agassiz, a good friend
of both Julia and Longfellow.[24] After visiting Agassiz's "wonderful museum" at
Harvard, and learning how much the scientist had to pay for highly taxed alcohol
to preserve his specimens, Sam set to work. A few months later, he told Longfellow that he had run into one of Agassiz's colleagues and "received his gushing
thanks for having drawn and passed for him a bill to exempt the Agassiz alcohol
from duty."[25]

Sam also found time to act as literary agent for Longfellow again. While, years
before, Sam had worked hard to place the young poet's poems for $15 each, by the
1870s, Longfellow was world famous and his work commanded high sums. Even
so, Sam pulled off a remarkable coup. In December 1873, after Longfellow had let
him read his latest poem, "The Hanging of the Crane," Sam had asked Longfellow's permission to see what Sam's friend Robert Bonner, publisher of the *New
York Ledger,* would pay for it. On February 22, 1874, Longfellow wrote in his
journal: "Sam Ward came to lunch. He has negotiated with Bonner for the 'Hanging of the Crane.' I am to have three thousand dollars. It is a great sum. It was
not my asking, but his offer." In fact, it was an even greater sum. Sam had actually negotiated for $4,000—$3.16 a word, then the highest price ever paid for a
poem—and kept $1,000 as his commission.[26]

Sam found time for gift giving to family, friends, even strangers, too. He sent
off crates of melons and boxes of cigars to Longfellow; books and spending
money to his nephew Marion Crawford, Louisa's son; a large pearl to his niece
Mary; and baskets of peaches and bottles of sherry to Julia. After writer Mary
Abigail Dodge, whose pen name was Gail Hamilton, had a "delightful conversation" with Sam at the Capitol, she was startled when "he pressed a banana into my
hand at parting, and the next morning came up a box of candied fruit." Years after
the fact, a woman recounted to Sam's niece Maud Howe Elliott how her father
had once sat next to Sam at a dinner in New York where they discussed sauces
and spices. Weeks later, a wooden box containing twelve bottles of McIlhenny's
Tabasco Sauce had arrived on their doorstep.[27]

While Sam's generosity never wavered, the scale of his largesse depended on whether his purse was fat or thin. Sam entertained in Washington on a grand scale, but with other men's money. For things like pearls for nieces, he had to use his own. In lobbying, Sam found ways to put not only bread—and very good bread—but exquisite wines and foods on his table, but his fortunes fluctuated wildly all his life. Julia was not surprised to learn, in May 1870, that the inheritance Sam had promised her just a year before had evaporated—how was not clear, even to Sam.[28]

Sam was, as he wrote Barlow, "as busy as a blacksmith shoeing other peoples' horses at a fair," but he was hardly the only busy lobbyist in Washington during these years.[29] The growing number of lobbyists that had so worried James Buchanan in 1852 was nothing compared to the surge in their ranks after the war. The expanding, industrializing nation was drawing all sorts of diners to Washington to jockey for the juiciest joints at the "Great Barbecue's" buffet of federal largesse.

The Washington guidebooks that listed the new agencies of the growing federal bureaucracy were joined by another genre of books about the capital that took note of these newcomers. Written by Washington insiders, they were short on facts and long on fulmination and purported to reveal how scoundrels were exploiting the federal government. Dr. John B. Ellis's *The Sights and Secrets of the National Capital* (1869) and *Washington, Outside and Inside* (1874), by reporter George Alfred Townsend, who wrote as "Gath" and "Laertes" for the *Chicago Tribune* and *New York Graphic*, were two of them. The subtitle of a third, Edward Winslow Martin's *Behind the Scenes in Washington* (1873), left no ambiguity about his point of view: "*Being a complete and graphic account of the Credit Mobilier investigation, the congressional rings, political intrigues, workings of the lobbies, etc. giving the secret history of our national government, in all its various branches, and showing how the public money is squandered, how votes are obtained. etc., with sketches of the leading senators, congressmen, government officials, etc., and an accurate description of the splendid public buildings of the federal capital.*" All of these exposés devoted at least one chapter to the lobby.

With a few exceptions, while the lobby was growing, it was the names and number of the lobbyists, not the types, that had changed since 1859, when Sam first arrived in the capital. Samuel Colt, the munitions magnate, had died in 1862; Thurlow Weed, the smooth lobbyist for hire, was losing touch with his party and retreating to Albany; and Benjamin Brown French, the claims agent who played for smaller stakes, had been stripped of even his minor clerk's position at the Treasury Department before his death in 1870. As the first Grant administration got under way, new men took their places in each of these categories.

Society reporter Emily Briggs made no secret of her low opinion of the lobby in general and of specific members in particular: "Winding in and out through the long, devious basement passage, crawling through the corridors, trailing its slimy length from gallery to committee room at last it lies stretched at full length on the floor of Congress—this dazzling reptile, this huge, scaly serpent of the lobby."[30] She described two of Colt's successors, rich men who came to lobby for themselves and their businesses. It was no accident that both were railroad men: the fortunes of railroads laying thousands of miles of track in all directions rose and fell on government subsidies. No industry employed more lobbyists, Sam among them, or fought more ferociously for its interests. Briggs described one of the most single-minded combatants, Collis Huntington:

> Floating in Congressional waters . . . at all hours of the legislative day may be seen the burly form of Huntington, the great, huge devil-fish of the railroad combination. . . . He ploughs the Congressional main, a shark in voracity of plunder, a devil-fish in tenacity of grip; for once caught in the toils of the monster for the helpless victim there is no escape. At the beginning of every session, this representative of the great Central Pacific comes to Washington as certain as a member of either branch of Congress; secures his parlors at Willards, which soon swarm with his recruits, both male and female. . . . Every weakness of a Congressman is noted, whilst the wily Huntington decides whether the attack shall be made with weapon of the male or female kind.[31]

Like Sam, Huntington had gone West with the '49ers to make money as a trader, not a miner. He invested his profits in railroads, chiefly the Central Pacific, and he had been coming to Washington each year since 1863, it was rumored, with a trunk full of cash with which to buy the votes he needed to crush his competitors. There was nothing subtle about the man or his methods. To the Central Pacific's other officers, he wrote of spreading around $200,000 to push a single bill through Congress and of paying Republican Congressman Ignatius Donnelly of Minnesota, a member of the House railroad and land committees, who later became a Democrat, then a Populist, and a foe of the railroads, $5,000 for his support. At times, Huntington sounded as busy as Sam, only less eloquent: "I went to Washington Wednesday night, rode all night in the cars, was at work in Washington until three o'clock in the morning Thursday and returned [to New York] Friday night, and am about as near used up today as I ever was in my life."[32]

Briggs found Sidney Dillon of the Union Pacific Railroad quite different but equally repellent: "What a princely presence and distinguished bearing, towering far above the average of his sex in height, with features as classic and clear cut as a cameo gem. In action, the embodiment of an Achilles, and in repose as graceful as the statue of the Greek slave. . . . As he stands mentally playing with a Senator, he might easily be mistaken for something more than human, yet neither horns nor tail are visible."[33]

Dillon and Huntington were just two among many powerful railroad men in Washington fighting tooth and nail for government support. The list included Jay Gould of the Erie Railroad, Jay Cooke of the Northern Pacific, Thomas Durant of the Union Pacific, and Tom Scott, whose pitched battled against Huntington in 1874 for control of the Texas Pacific was rumored to have cost as much as $4,000,000.[34]

Jay Cooke had his fingers in several lucrative pies—finance, shipping, insurance—in addition to railroads. His brother Henry served as his eyes and ears in the capital. While Henry Cooke liked to think of himself as his brother's equal, he was really his lobbyist, and a good one, and as such he was part of a select group of men that included Sam, who followed in Thurlow Weed's footsteps and made up the very top tier of the hired lobby at the start of the Gilded Age.

Henry Cooke was an Ohio newspaper man who had backed Salmon Chase, John Sherman, and Robert Schenck for office and rode their coattails to Washington. He made his brother's banks useful to them, and they made him privy to useful information from the Treasury Department and Senate and House committees dealing with finance. The Cooke brothers' successful efforts to renew and expand the government subsidy for the Northern Pacific in 1870 was one of their most important collaborations. Henry was in charge of buying favorable publicity in newspapers when possible and buying silence when it was not, by passing out stock certificates and railroad passes to editors and reporters. As a third brother, Pitt Cooke, noted, "It is only a question of [the] *price* you will pay whether these Editors will lie *for* or *against* you."[35]

Henry Cooke also did many favors for President Grant and members of his family, and the two men had become good friends. When the new and short-lived Territory of the District of Columbia was created in 1871, the president named Cooke its first governor. Via kickbacks and insider knowledge, Cooke milked the position for all it was worth, which turned out to be several hundred thousand dollars. By midsummer 1873, the exposure of rampant corruption and mismanagement brought down the territorial government and Henry Cooke with it. Jay Cooke had helped his brother out of scrapes before, but not this time. He had worries of his own. In September came the astonishing failure of the banking house of Jay Cooke and Company, which precipitated the Panic of 1873 and the beginning of a nationwide depression.[36]

Another member of the very top tier of hired lobbyists was Robert J. Walker, whose career in Washington was ending just as Sam's was beginning. Urbane, well-educated, often living beyond his means, an aspiring writer, and a Democrat, Walker had much in common with Sam. The son of a Pennsylvania judge, he had moved to Mississippi in 1826 and got caught up in land and cotton speculation and politics. He was elected to the Senate in 1836 and served as secretary of the treasury under President Polk and briefly as governor of the Kansas Territory under President Buchanan. Between stints of federal service, Walker had stayed on in Washington to practice law and make money by lobbying for the new railroads. When war came, he supported the Union, and Chase sent him to Europe to bolster confidence in the financial stability of the United States. To get the attention of Londoners, Walker personally showered them with pro-Union leaflets from a hot-air balloon.[37]

Walker believed in the nation's manifest destiny. He had lobbied for the annexation of Texas and for acquiring all of Mexico, supported Seward's acquisition of St. Thomas and St. John and urged him to go after Greenland and Iceland, too, and backed every other expansionist plan that was floated. An experienced lobbyist with access to the Senate floor, a friend of Secretary of State Seward, a persuasive speaker and writer with close ties to the press, and very enthusiastic about the acquisition of Alaska, Walker was perfect for the job of shepherding the Alaska Purchase, called "Seward's Folly" and "Seward's Icebox" by opponents, across pitfalls to passage, and Russian Minister Edouard de Stoeckl knew it. Stoeckl hired him as counsel to the Russian legation, and Walker set to work. Just what Walker did to smooth out any wrinkles holding up the Alaska Purchase became the topic of a congressional investigation, examined below.[38]

Two other premier lobbyists, Grenville M. Dodge and William E. Chandler, had careers that began about the same time as Sam's. Both men were successful; both played above board; both made a great deal of money (both also hung onto more of it than Sam ever did); but neither had Sam's flash and dash nor did they aspire to it.

The early career of pioneer, engineer, Civil War general, Indian fighter, congressman, and author Grenville M. Dodge rivaled Sam's for variety, even if his sober, single-minded personality was the opposite of Sam's. Born in poverty in Massachusetts in 1831, Dodge became a civil engineer, headed West, hired on as a surveyor for several railroads, and then became their lobbyist in state capitals and in Washington, where he was known for overwhelming legislators under an avalanche of statistics. He also lobbied for himself, winning a commission as a colonel in the United States Volunteers.[39]

Throughout the Civil War and the Indian campaigns that followed, Dodge kept up his contacts with railroad men. As he told it, while escaping from a war party in the Black Hills in 1865, he realized that he had discovered a pass through the mountains perfect for a railroad. In short order, he resigned from the military and became chief engineer and chief lobbyist for the Union Pacific, starting at a salary of $10,000 a year. While retaining both of those positions, Dodge got elected to the House of Representatives as a Republican from Iowa and looked out for the Union Pacific's interest and those of several smaller railroads from inside Congress. He chose to serve only one term, but that was all it took to be accorded floor privileges for life.[40]

Dodge's job as the Union Pacific's chief engineer was to plan its route and devise solutions to any obstacles encountered. That was his job as a lobbyist for the railroad, too, and he was very good at both. Highly respected as a surveyor, he was recognized as one of the most knowledgeable and most successful of the railroad lobbyists in Washington. He continued to lobby for the Union Pacific and for the many other lines he helped to develop into the early 1880s, when, having made several million dollars, he opened offices in New York and hired lobbyists of his own.[41]

Where Dodge was a specialist—railroads were his passion—William E. Chandler, like Sam, was a generalist. He was key to the efforts of Jay Cooke, several railroads, and a host of other business interests. Chandler was born into an old New Hampshire family in 1835 and went to Harvard law school. He got deeply involved in Republican politics and worked for Lincoln's election, for which he was rewarded with a position as solicitor and judge advocate general in the Navy Department. President Johnson appointed him Assistant Secretary of the Treasury under Secretary McCulloch, which is how Sam came to know him.[42]

At the Treasury, one of Chandler's responsibilities was to handle claims, so every lobbyist and congressman with an eager client or constituent came to see him. Sam was among them. He expressed his appreciation for kindness Chandler had showed toward one of his clients in his unique style: "I entreat the acceptance of a sparkling though effervescent token of my remembrance of your unvarying courtesy and kindness. *Dulce est desipere in loco* [It's sometimes pleasant to play the fool] and trust that you will find in the Saratoga Club Champagne a source of gaiety by the limpid waters of Silver Spring."[43]

When Chandler left the Treasury Department in 1867 and opened a law practice in the capital, he promised not to take on any claims that he had dealt with in office, and he was true to his word. Over the next fifteen years, however, he did take on just about every other kind of job and made successes of most of them. Before he had even left the Treasury, the Union Pacific was offering him $5,000 a year to work exclusively for the line as its counsel and agent in Washington, where he would work next to the line's chief lobbyist, Grenville Dodge. Chandler declined. It was not working with Dodge that gave him pause. He did not want to be tied to any one client: "As I wish to connect myself with important cases outside your matters," he explained, "I would not wish to agree for any salary to absorb myself entirely, to the neglect of all other businesses, in any plan of obtaining legislation before Congress. . . . I know how hard, tiresome, absorbing and vexatious is lobbying around Congress and, while I shall be willing to advise and assist in relation to measures of legislation, I am not willing to agree beforehand to devote myself, body and soul, to such business."[44]

Throughout his career as a lobbyist, Chandler always preferred to be paid by the job or the session. When one of the Union Pacific's directors protested his high fees and refused to pay them in full, Chandler switched allegiance to a direct competitor, bringing the Union Pacific back to him on its knees. "They cannot get along in Washington without you," Dodge wrote him. Chandler made no secret of his work for other concerns. He lobbied for Western Union Telegraph, the National Life Insurance Company, Cyrus Field's Atlantic Cable Company, Adams Express, and, when tariff reductions threatened their product, the Plate Iron Manufacturing Association.[45]

These high-end clients made Chandler a rich man. He lived well in Washington and made no secret of his profession. In 1882, President Arthur had no qualms about naming Chandler Secretary of the Navy, and, in 1887 he was elected to the Senate from New Hampshire and served in that capacity for almost thirteen years.

Beneath the men at the very top of their game like Sam, Dodge, and Chandler, an array of lesser lobbyists spread out and down. At the upper end were men not quite in the same league as these three, but mostly capable and honest. Some had once held office or worked a government job; a few still did. They might have one client or a few—a handful of lesser railroads, for example. They played for smaller stakes and made less money. Three of these men, the heirs of Benjamin Brown French, were Richard Franchot, J. Sterling Morton, and, thanks to the notoriety he obtained, almost in a class by himself, Oakes Ames.

Briggs had pictured Huntington mulling over which of his army of lobbyists to send out for a particular job. If the task was important, most likely he tapped his right-hand man Richard Franchot. The two had been friends since their shop-keeping days in New York. Franchot, a Republican, had served one term in Congress in 1861 and was brevetted a brigadier general during the Civil War. During the decade after the war, he was Huntington's chief lobbyist for the Central Pacific and the other railroads in which Huntington had an interest, getting paid $25,000 in Central Pacific stock, plus expenses, each year.[46]

Franchot led Huntington's forces in the battle against Tom Scott, whose forces were led by Dodge, over the Texas and Pacific. When Franchot died at a critical juncture in the fight, Huntington wrote a colleague, "We have lost a good man. . . . I do not know his equal." Huntington was right—in this case, Franchot had no equal. Huntington found another lobbyist, Charles Sherrill, who had been working in the capital for several years, but the battle was lost.[47]

J. Sterling Morton, later secretary of agriculture under President Cleveland and cofounder of Arbor Day, was another railroad man. Morton, who was born in New York and raised in Michigan, went West, settled in Nebraska territory, and became a newspaper editor, using his editorials to promote railroads and agriculture. The Burlington and Missouri River Railroad sent him to Washington to lobby for its interests, and, by the early 1870s, he was also working for the Atchison, Topeka and Santa Fe Railroad, and the Chicago, Burlington and Quincy Railroad.[48]

Morton never really liked the capital. The food made him sick, he confided to his diary, and the heat was horrible. Once, he had hurried home with a bad case of diarrhea as soon as he thought his bill's passage was certain, eager, he told his wife, "to escape from this deluge of damphools [damn fools]." Leaving before passage was a mistake other lobbyists had made before him. Without him there as watchdog, Morton's bill died. The next session, despite the food and the humidity, Morton stayed in Washington to shore up support for his bills and watch the vote.[49]

Plenty of former members of Congress like Walker, Dodge, and Franchot used their lifetime floor privileges to lobby sitting members at their desks. That sitting members were themselves lobbyists became clear when the Credit Mobilier scandal cracked open in 1872, exposing Massachusetts congressman Oakes Ames at its core. Ames was even more specialized than Dodge. He did not lobby solely for railroads; he lobbied for just *one* railroad, the Union Pacific. For a time, Ames became the face of all that was dangerous about the lobby.

Elected to Congress as a Republican in 1862, Ames, who had made millions manufacturing shovels, was a burly, closed-mouth man, who rarely made a speech or introduced legislation. He had invested heavily in the Union Pacific and, through the Union Pacific, in Credit Mobilier, a dummy corporation with a fancy title (taken from a French company noted for its financial prowess), set up in 1864 with the goal of, according to its friends, building the railroad or, according to its foes, looting the Treasury. Credit Mobilier had immediately begun paying huge dividends, mostly, as it turned out, from funds put up by the federal government.[50]

Rumors had circulated about Credit Mobilier as early as 1868, but the story did not make headlines until the summer of 1872. Testimony at the congressional investigation that followed, plus a "smoking gun"—the dog-eared memorandum book in which Ames had recorded all of his transactions—revealed how he had operated as Credit Mobilier's insider lobbyist. Ames boasted to his business partners that he was distributing Credit Mobilier stock "where it will produce the most good to us," namely among his colleagues in Congress, who voted to keep money pouring into its coffers. He offered them Credit Mobilier stock far below its market value. Buyers did not need to pay any money down; they could credit dividends against the purchase price; Ames guaranteed the stock against loss; and he promised that if anyone was unhappy with his purchase, he could get a full refund.[51]

Many of his colleagues had taken Ames up on his generous terms. In January 1873, the *Nation* offered a preliminary assessment of the damages: "Total loss, one Senator; badly damaged and not serviceable for future political use, two Vice Presidents and eight Congressmen. The condition of Ames' reputation language is inadequate to describe."[52] The senator was James Patterson, a Republican from New Hampshire; the vice presidents, Schuyler Colfax and Henry Wilson. Damaged representatives included Henry L. Dawes of Massachusetts, Garfield, Blaine, Allison, George Boutwell of Massachusetts, who was secretary of the treasury by the time the scandal broke, House Judiciary Committee chairman John Bingham of Ohio, William "Pig Iron" Kelly of Pennsylvania, James Harlan of Iowa, and Glenni Scofield of Pennsylvania, all Republicans, and James Brooks of New York, the lone Democrat.

Many had excuses. Some pleaded forgetfulness; some stupidity. Not surprisingly, none said they considered the stock to be a bribe to buy their votes but, rather, as Ames swore it was, Ames' attempt to let his colleagues in on a good deal. Only two individuals, Ames and Brooks, were formally censured. The *Nation* was wrong in thinking that all of those tarred by Credit Mobilier were finished. In December 1873, newly reelected Speaker of the House James G. Blaine called the 43rd Congress into session. Allison was not there because he had been elected to the Senate. Ames and Brooks were not there because both had died— Brooks in April, Ames in May.[53]

Moving downwards through the layers of the lobby, next came the small-time and the part-time lobbyists, many of whom were "locals." John Ellis complained, "Every man, woman, and child in Washington is a politician," or even a lobbyist, for he claimed that "[they] talk and think of but little else" than their "influence . . . real or fancied."[54] At the bottom of the lobbying barrel was a thick sediment of opportunists, charlatans, and "hopeless cases" pushing hopeless causes. They ran the gamut from crippled veterans pressing for their pensions to low-lifes willing to do any kind of dirty work for a fee. Grasping, two-bit claims agents were the most numerous. Mrs. Senator John A. Logan described how some of them worked: "These people burrow in the records of the government for possible claimants who might not otherwise give their claims a thought." Others preyed on widows, orphans, and aged parents who had lost husbands, fathers, and sons in the war, promising compensation from the government, which, if it came at all, was quickly eaten up by the agents' accumulated fees.[55]

Most types of lobbyists pulling up chairs at the "Great Barbecue"—the industrialist/financier/merchant, the premium lobbyist, the middling lobbyist, the two-bit claims agent—had counterparts in the smaller antebellum capital, but there were some new types of lobbyists among the postbellum crowd. Some of them were women, whose presence was a postwar phenomenon and one upon which nearly every observer of the postwar Washington scene commented.

Women were hardly new to wielding influence in the capital. From the federal government's earliest days in Washington, women like Margaret Bayard Smith, wife of Samuel Harrison Smith, publisher of the *National Intelligencer,* and Dolley Madison had used their access to prominent men to secure patronage positions, relief measures, and other favors for family and friends.[56] In the 1850s, Samuel Colt had showered the wives and daughters of congressmen with gloves and other trinkets in hopes that they would nudge their menfolk to look favorably on his rifles.

New in the Gilded Age were the women who came to Washington with the intent to lobby, pure and simple, and not for lofty goals like justice, civil rights, equal rights, or any of the other abstract principles like those that had brought women abolitionists and would continue to bring advocates for women's suffrage to Washington. These new women were after pensions, contracts, compensation, land, subsidies, and patents. Some were advocating for their own claims, but some pushed the claims of others for money—a commission, a salary, living expenses. They acquired a name during these years: reporters called them "lobbyesses."

Grenville Dodge, who knew the prewar capital well, noticed the lobbyesses right away when he returned in 1867. Shortly after arriving in Washington for his first and only term in Congress, he wrote home to his wife, Anne, about "the lobby . . . you have heard so much about." It consisted, he told her, of "unscrupulous thieves" and "pretty women with flashing diamonds," who knew how "to handle and influence men." Dodge hastened to add that he had "not met any of them" but had "had them pointed out to me as breakers to steer clear of."[57]

About the same time, Emily Briggs described one of the new lobbyesses working for Collis Huntington and Jay Gould as "a luscious, mellow banana; a juicy, melting peach; a golden pippin, ripened to the very core. From India's coral strand comes the two-thousand-dollar cashmere wrap that snuggles close to her fair shoulders. Diamonds, brilliant as the stars in Orion's jeweled belt, adorn her dainty ears, whilst silk, satin, velvet, feathers, and laces prove what a railroad can do when its funds are applied in the proper direction."[58]

Although reporters lavished quarts of ink on the diamond-studded "melting peaches," almost certainly out of proportion to their actual number, the dazzlers were just one type of lobbyess. Like their male counterparts, they came in several varieties. In 1873, Mary Clemmer Ames, who wrote for the *New York Independent*, used the device of a glance around the Senate lobby to describe three women who stood in for three subgroups of lobbyesses. One was the self-assured "beauty," one of Briggs's "golden pippins," who "tunes her tongue to honeyed accents, and lights up her eyelids to lead men down to death." But the other two were far less glamorous:

> The dejected looking woman on the sofa opposite is a widow, with numerous small children. You may be certain by the unhopeful expression of her face that it is her own claim which, almost unaided and alone, she is trying to "work through" Congress. Her home is far distant. She borrowed money to come here, she borrows money to support her children, money to pay her own board; borrows money to pay the exorbitant fees of the claim agent, who, constantly fanning the flame of "great expectations," assures her every day that Congress will pay her the thousands which she demands for her losses.
>
> See that sharp-faced woman, with darting, prying eyes. She rushes in one door and out of another. She hurries back. She meets a senator, and "buttonholes him," after the fashion of men, and begins conversing in the most importunate manner. . . .

This woman not only has one claim in Congress, she has many, and not one her own. She is a claim-agent, an office-brokeress. She buys claims, and speculates in them as so much stock. She takes claims on commission, deluding many a poor victim into the belief that "my influence" and "my friends, Senator So-and-So and Secretary P. Policy," will insure it a triumphant passage and remunerative end.[59]

Despite the attention the "beauties" received, the drab, sad widow represented by far the most numerous of the lobbyesses. Correspondent Olive Logan, who wrote for the *New York Daily Graphic* and came to the capital expecting to see bevies of gorgeous lobbyesses in velvet and jewels, was disappointed to find many more "impecuniosities, clad in faded, undraped merinos and battered bonnets and finger-holed gloves, anxiously hanging about with hands full of papers, and trying to buttonhole a Senator as he is returning to the floor."[60]

Reporter George Townsend suggested that there was a fourth type of lobbyess —the woman who traded sex for a vote for a claim or patent or land grant—and he offered titillating details about three of them. One, he claimed, was known as "Comanche," because she represented the builders of a celebrated iron-clad ship by that name. "She was large, voluptuous. . . . It was not very plain that she possessed other than bodily endowments, and the presumption has not been contradicted that she had only one manner of accommodation, which was pretty sure to make an obligation." Another he called Mrs. General "Straitor," confident, he said, that readers would know whom he meant. She had lived in a little Southern town and had caught the eye of a hard-drinking Union general who married her and died. "His army companions brought her on to Washington where she was put forward to influence the Interior Department in the matter of Indian contracts." "No woman of her period was more notable in Washington," Townsend said of his third lobbyess, than Mrs. Lucy Cobb, although her name has showed up nowhere else. "She was remarkably handsome, and inclined to volup-tuousness. Her eyes were dark, and her form just over the limits of decency. . . . At this time, the procuring of pardons for officials in the late rebellion was quite an avocation, and the rumor gained ground that Mrs. Cobb could get a pardon where anybody else would fail."[61]

While other reporters wrote of senators making fools of themselves over a beautiful lobbyess, and there were other veiled allusions to seductresses, using sex as a lobby tactic was extremely risky and almost certainly rare.[62] Instead, while poor widows hoped for pity from congressmen and the persistent claims-agent lobbyess hoped to wear them down with her persistence, "insinuation and fas-cination" that stopped short of violating the "limits of decency," many reporters suggested, were the powers that recommended beautiful women to their employers. Charming women, John Ellis noted, "cannot be shaken off rudely." As Mark Twain's character Harry Brierly explained in *The Gilded Age*, "petitions are referred somewhere, and that's the last of them; you can't refer a handsome woman so easily."[63]

Ben Perley Poore agreed and described the social rather than sexual allure that the "spider-lobbyists," often the "widows of officers of the army or navy, others the daughters of Congressmen of a past generation," employed to entrap hapless congressmen:

> They have pleasant parlors, with works of art and bric-a-brac. . . . Every evening they receive, and in the winter their blazing wood fires are often surrounded by a distinguished circle. Some treat favored guests to a game of euchre, and as midnight approaches there is always an adjournment to the dining-room, where a choice supper is served . . . with iced champagne or Burgundy at blood heat. Who can blame a Congressman for leaving the bad cooking of his hotel or boarding-house, with the absence of all home comforts, to walk into the parlor web which the cunning spider-lobbyist weaves for him?[64]

"Many members," another reporter noted, "come from homely homes, the ladies of which have expended their vivacity and beauty in that American phrase of 'the struggle for life.' . . . Such members, when they find themselves in a drawing-room next to a lady who expends *her* vivacity in entertaining them, and arrays *her* beauty in all the charms of novel costume and bewitching decoration, are only too apt to surrender to the fascinating influence."[65]

Reading about these golden pippins and spiderwomen must have been fascinating, but also quite threatening to all of those women who had expended their vivacity on "the struggle for life." Perhaps it was frightening, too, to the congressman who might find himself in a lobbyess's sights. It was certainly proof positive for all those handwringers certain that the nation was going to hell in a handbasket.

All reporters agreed that, no matter how charming a lobbyess might be, these delightful beauties, and certainly women like "Comanche," were part of the city's demimonde. Theirs was no respectable profession for a lady. Sam might dine with one secretary of state and attend the family weddings of another, and William Chandler and J. Sterling Morton might go on to hold cabinet posts, but no "melting banana" could hope to hobnob with the crème of official society. Except for one. Some reporters claimed, slyly at first and then boldly, that one genuine lobbyess could be found within official society itself.

Until 1867, Oregon senator George Williams, a widower, had had an undistinguished career and was seldom seen in Washington society. All that changed when he married widow Kate George, described by the *Oregon State Journal* as a "tall, shapely, handsome, brilliant brunette." The newlyweds took an expensive suite at the National Hotel, and, rather than waiting for the wives of her husband's colleagues to call on her, as was customary, Mrs. Williams held elaborate receptions to introduce herself to official society.[66]

Mrs. Williams also drew attention to herself in a variety of other ways. After the entire Oregon congressional delegation had unsuccessfully appealed to President Grant to pardon a convicted Oregon official, "Mrs. Senator Williams," claimed the *Journal,* "visited the White House . . . and the fair diplomatist . . . had more influence with the stubborn President and a cold and calculating Attorney General than could have been exercised by a score of members of Congress." The official was pardoned, and Mrs. Williams bragged of her success.[67]

After George Williams lost his Senate seat in 1870, President Grant named him attorney general, despite his lack of qualifications. Soon Mrs. Williams was seen driving about in a very expensive landau, attended by liveried servants. Such ostentation was unseemly, but her next move was, to official society matrons, outrageous: Mrs. Williams let it be known that, henceforth, contrary to longstanding protocol, Senate wives' first call should be upon her. A former Senate wife herself, she should have known better. No group guarded their social prerogatives more jealously. In her memoir, Mrs. Senator John A. Logan scornfully noted that Mrs. Williams's "elevation from obscurity on the frontier" had gone to her head.[68]

Nasty gossip began to circulate about the Williamses. It was rumored that both took "presents" from individuals with business before the Justice Department and that Mrs. Williams lobbied on behalf of appointment seekers in return for "gifts." Mrs. Williams's past became grist for the rumor mill, with the most salacious stories suggesting that her first marriage had been hasty because she was about to bear the man's child and that her second husband's tavern had really been a brothel with her as its main attraction.[69]

After Chief Justice Chase died in 1873, President Grant nominated Attorney General Williams to take his place over a howl of objections from the press, bar associations, and law reviews, all of which cited his mediocrity and rumors of malfeasance in office. Equally strong objections were raised in Washington's drawing rooms. Writing of Williams's nomination, C. H. Hill of the Justice Department referred to the "animus" of the Senate wives and noted that "the fair sex are to a man (or to a woman) opposed to the appointment." When Williams's nomination came before the Senate Judiciary Committee, specific accusations replaced gossip: Williams had blocked potentially embarrassing investigations; both he and his wife accepted bribes; he misused public funds to pay for their lavish lifestyle. Groaned Hill, "that unfortunate carriage and horses ($2,350) has of course attracted attention."[70]

Seeking to help her husband's case, Mrs. Williams spread spiteful gossip about members of the Judiciary Committee. She told it to Mrs. Hamilton Fish, who immediately told Secretary Fish, who told the President, who was furious. Perhaps President Grant had already heard the rumors, apparently groundless, linking him to Mrs. Williams. *New York Sun* reporter Jerome Stillson had shared the supercharged gossip with his editor, Charles A. Dana:

> Williams' appointment . . . is more horrible perhaps than even you know it to be. He, Williams, has said within two days that *his wife* knew of Grant's purpose to nominate him on Saturday night—that he did not learn of it till Monday morning. . . . The old Senators and Representatives who "know" things in Washington believe that Kate "screwed" her husband into the Attorney Generalship—One of the shrewdest of the old Senators said yesterday in conversation about this appointment—"Mrs. W. has the most profitable c—t that has been brought to Washington in my day." By Jupiter it is horrible.[71]

Williams's position was hopeless, and he withdrew his name from consideration. He remained attorney general until concrete evidence surfaced indicating that both husband and wife had demanded money from individuals in exchange for appointments and from businesses to drop suits before the Justice Department. Threatened with impeachment, Williams resigned in the spring of 1875, and the couple moved back to Oregon.[72]

Lobbyesses, from the glamorous to the shabby, made up one group new to the postwar lobby. Some of the very people who devoted so many colorful words to describing these women were members of another new lobbying type: reporters. There had been journalists in Washington ever since the government had moved in, and by the 1850s a recognizable press corps had evolved. The same 1854 investigation into Colt's lobbying that turned up the Parisian gloves revealed that reporters were already lobbying, too:

> The evidence shows another important fact, that the letter-writers for the daily press who have been admitted to desks on the floor of the House are very generally regarded as the most efficient agents who can be employed by those who have measures to advance. Although these letter-writers, before they can obtain a seat within the House, are required to give a personal pledge of honor that they are not

"employed as agents to prosecute any claim pending before Congress," yet we find
that, in utter disregard of this pledge and its spirit, they have been employed in many
of the railroad, patent, and other schemes which have engaged the attention of
Congress during the present session.[73]

What was new after the war was the greater numbers of reporters, their increasing power, and, because of changes in the government, new opportunities to
turn access and insider information to a profit. With the coming of war came a
flood of hard-driving correspondents; when the war was over, many of them
stayed on in the capital to cover the federal government, which promised to be
much more interesting than before. They were mostly ambitious, young, well-
educated, white men, although the number of female journalists was growing.
Some reporters, like Ben Perley Poore of the *Boston Journal*, a veteran correspondent from before the war, and Uriah Painter of the *Philadelphia Inquirer*, were
from well-to-do families. Most made their headquarters on Newspaper Row, a
stretch of buildings along Pennsylvania Avenue anchored by the Willard and
Ebbitt hotels at either end.[74]

Many of these reporters saw themselves as part of a new group of professionals
bent not only on covering government, politics, and all that went on behind the
scenes, but on having a hand in shaping them, too. Many journalists who wanted
to shape events were honest and adhered to a self-imposed code of personal
ethics. Some were not and did not. Reporter James Parton, examining Congress
in 1869, declared that there were only five or six truly corrupt men among the
approximately sixty correspondents covering the capital, and he may have been
right about the number who were genuinely venal, but there were several journalists who walked a fine line between integrity and corruption, occasionally straying
onto the dark side. Some correspondents traded insider information, held patronage jobs, accepted and performed favors, drafted speeches for and managed
the campaigns of politicians, blackmailed, lobbied for measures by writing "puff"
pieces, assassinated characters, and pushed or killed stories.[75]

In 1875, one of their own, Henry Van Ness Boynton of the *Cincinnati Gazette*,
claimed: "I know—everybody knows—that there are professional correspondents
in this city who attack projects that are before Congress for no other purpose than
to get paid for silence in the future. I believe—everybody believes—that there are
agents of newspapers here who bargain for the opinions of the journals they
represent."[76]

Some reporters undoubtedly enjoyed exercising some degree of power over the
men they covered, and some may have found it useful to have an important politi-

cian indebted to them, but Poore, who pushed his own share of measures, spoke for many of his colleagues when he claimed that it was often about the money. Reporters, he argued, were "so scantily paid by the journals with which they are connected that they are forced to prostitute their pens" to make ends meet. Washington correspondents were only paid by their papers for those months when Congress was in session. During long recesses, reporters had to scramble to make ends meet, and a job as a committee clerk, or as secretary to a congressman, or as a lobbyist was often just the ticket to tide them over until Congress returned.[77]

The savvy businessman knew the value of reporters as lobbyists and knew that they could almost always use additional funds. Henry Cooke, a newspaperman himself, made it a point of making friends with the press corps. He had hired reporters like Samuel Wilkeson of the *New York Tribune* to sell his brother's bonds during the war. A decade later, when Jay Cooke had to sell the nation on the virtues of his Northern Pacific Railroad, Wilkeson and other reporters obliged, for a fee, with puff pieces touting the wonderful sights and salmon of the Northwest in more than four hundred newspapers. The campaign was expensive, but Henry assured Jay that it was worth it: "It will cost something, but I know of no *cheaper* advertising, and none, on the whole, so efficient."[78]

Reporters struck a variety of deals. Lorenzo Crounse, who wrote for the *New York Times*, took a monthly retainer from the Cookes to lobby for their projects in his columns. Donn Piatt, who wrote for the *Cincinnati Commercial* and edited the *Sunday Capital*, boasted that he would expose corruption wherever he found it, but he was himself on the payroll of the New India Mining Company. For a fee, Piatt also helped the firm of Cowles and Brega win a large contract to mothproof army uniforms. When the company refused his demands for more money, Piatt wrote an exposé claiming that the chemicals that Cowles and Brega used were worthless.[79]

Uriah Painter was among the most grasping of the correspondents. Hardly a rock of scandal was upturned during the Grant years that did not reveal him underneath. He had seemed destined for better things when he arrived in Washington in 1861 as an earnest young reporter for the *Philadelphia Inquirer*. Although he ended up on the wrong side of several congressional investigations, Painter started out as one of the investigators. He thought he smelled a rat when the Alaska Purchase treaty was sent to the Senate in 1867 and was quickly ratified. He had fanned rumors about the roles of three men, Robert J. Walker, former Tennessee congressman and lobbyist Frederick Stanton, and Russian minister Edouard de Stoeckl, in securing the $7,200,000 appropriation, suggesting that they had paid reporters for favorable stories about the Alaska deal and given cash to congressmen for their votes, until Congress finally called for an investigation. Painter crowed that he had gotten hold of the "biggest lobby swindle ever put up in Washington."[80]

Walker was the chief witness before the Committee on Public Expenditures. He pointed out that he had long been an aggressive advocate for purchasing Alaska and took umbrage at the suggestion that he was "pushing" the project for the money alone. Nevertheless, he and Stanton both acknowledged that they had been hired by Stoeckl to secure the treaty's ratification. Walker testified that he had received $26,000 for his services, which included writing newspaper articles touting the glories of Alaska. He also acknowledged using his floor privileges to stop by the desks of wavering members to tell them in person of Alaska's splendor.[81]

After adamantly denying paying off a single reporter or congressman, Walker and Stanton turned the tables and leveled accusations of their own at Painter, who, they claimed, had actually tried to blackmail *them* for a cut of the Alaska money. Charges and countercharges flew back and forth, as Painter protested that he had been misunderstood. The investigation ended without anyone's being charged with anything, but Painter's credibility had been undermined and that of the whole press corps had been tarnished by association. In its final report, the committee pointedly condemned the "loose morality" of the press, "which for sensational purposes, or to cater to a morbid curiosity, couples names of public men or private citizens with clandestine receipt of large sums of money in connection with votes or influence."[82]

Painter was undeterred. Like many other reporters, he held a second job. He was clerk of the House Committee on Post Offices, which not only gave him floor privileges and made him privy to information valuable to a variety of businessmen but gave him a berth inside Congress from which to lobby. Both Jay Gould and Jay Cooke paid Painter for advance news of Congress's intentions. Railroad men Jim Fisk and Tom Scott and shipbuilder John Roach retained him. William Chandler and Grenville Dodge both subcontracted lobbying work to him, and, on his own, he lobbied for real estate deals, patents, Western Union, insurance companies, and for and against nominations.[83]

Painter's blatant lobbying made some of his colleagues up in the press gallery, from which they could plainly see him on the House floor below buttonholing members, uneasy and perhaps jealous. His colleague George Townsend put his poor opinion of Painter into a long poem he called "The Striker." A "striker" was the lowest of the low, a feared and despised lobbyist-in-reverse—a man, Townsend explained, "who hears of a claim, grant, or bill of value, about to pass Congress, and who opposes it in order to be bought up." A few unsubtle verses leave no doubt about his disdain for Painter:

Slouched, and surly, and sallow-faced,
With a look as if something were sore misplaced,
The young man Striker was seen to stride
Up the Capitol stairs at high noontide,
And as though at the head of a viewless mob—
Who could look in his eyes and mistrust it?—
He quoth: "They must let me into that job,
      Or I'll bust it!"

What it was that troubled him so
How shall we innocent visitors know?
Perhaps a scheme of subsidy great,
Or perhaps a mightier project of state;
A plot, perhaps, some widow to rob—
Whatever, whoever discussed it,
Unless Mr. Striker was "let into the job,"
      He would "bust it."

Striker! in thee no specie rare
We see ascending the Capitol stair.
All the ages and States of eld
Some similar hound or highwayman held;
Some Herod, who 'ere Heaven's babe might throb,
In the cradle would strangle or thrust it,
And, unless he were "let in" the holiest "job,"
      He would "bust it."[84]

Townsend's low opinion was confirmed at the Credit Mobilier hearings. Painter had first gotten the scent of the Credit Mobilier scandal in 1868, but instead of scooping his fellow reporters, Painter went to the Credit Mobilier directors and demanded to be cut into the deal. When they promised him fifty shares but it turned out that Oakes Ames had only thirty left to give away, he was furious, or, as Ames testified, "quite indignant." Painter did, however, keep his mouth shut. When the Credit Mobilier scandal finally broke open in 1872, after sleuthing by other reporters, Painter was the only non-congressman in Ames's list of stock recipients.[85]

The Credit Mobilier hearings wrapped up in 1873. As 1874 came to an end, still another congressional investigation into still another scandal loomed, and, like the earlier hearings, this one would reveal something of the lobby's inner workings. Dozens of lobbyists, including Huntington, Dillon, the Cookes, Dodge, Painter, and Piatt, were implicated, and this time so was Sam. He had thus far managed to steer clear of scandals, but his subpoena to testify arrived with the new year.

CHAPTER SIX

Sam defends his profession and his dinners before Congress; amid fears of rampant corruption, panicked pundits blame the lobby; fledgling attempts at regulation

OT RAILROADS this time but shipping lines lay at the heart of the investigation by the House Ways and Means Committee that got underway in January 1875. Rumors had been circulating for months in several newspapers, asserting that the Pacific Mail Steamship Company had spent fantastic sums of money, as much as a million dollars, in 1872 to renew and expand its federal subsidy to carry the mail to the Orient in iron ships built in the United States. The company, whose survival was at stake, had been caught in a bitter struggle for government support that pitted against one another rail, finance, shipping, and shipbuilding magnates Collis Huntington, Jay Gould, Sidney Dillon, and John Roach, among others.[1]

For the high-stakes lobbying campaign which the renewal fight had required, shipbuilder Roach, whose regular lobbyist in Washington was William Chandler, had also hired Uriah Painter, perfectly placed to help, being clerk of the House Committee on Post Offices and Post Roads. The hearings revealed that Painter once again was playing a double game, secretly taking money from Grenville Dodge to lobby for Gould against Roach. The House Ways and Means Committee's efforts to untangle the complex mess would fill 632 pages without coming to any real conclusions or punishing any of those implicated.[2]

Before Sam arrived to testify, a variety of lobbyists had squirmed under the committee's examination. It emerged that the man doling out the money for the Pacific Mail Steamship Company had been Colonel Richard B. Irwin, "a gentleman who knows Washington as well as his own pocket, who has been on the inside of three or four Administrations, and who is hardly the sort of person to throw a whole prize beef to a cur who would be made happy with a shin bone." The beef referred to was the $4,500 and $11,000 that Irwin had given to two House doorkeepers in connection with the renewal of Pacific Mail's subsidy. What was expected in return was never made clear. Both doorkeepers testified that they thought the money was simply a tip![3]

One of Irwin's lieutenants produced a list of men who, he claimed, had received a total of $120,000 to lobby for the Pacific Mail subsidy. On it were editors and reporters, former government employees, and House officers. William B. Shaw, who wrote as "Nestor" in the *Boston Transcript*, was down for $15,000 and Donn Piatt for $5,000. Also mentioned were the former mayor of Washington, James G. Berrett, and Sam.[4]

The witnesses who preceded Sam came reluctantly and stammered out their versions of the affair. Not Sam. He strode into the hearing room with, wrote the *Chicago Daily Tribune's* reporter, "his eyes twinkling, his face beaming with good humor." When Representative John Kasson, a Republican from Iowa who had once been assistant postmaster general and was genuinely interested in the postal service, asked him to state his connection with the Pacific Mail subsidy, Sam got right down to details:

> I think it was after the first failure of the measure in the House that Mr. Berrett called at my rooms one afternoon, and said that he had been requested to see if I would accept a retainer to help this subsidy along. I asked him how much? He said five hundred dollars and five thousand contingent on success. I said, "All right." He sent me that afternoon or next morning a check for five hundred dollars, signed by a gentleman I had never seen, Mr. R. B. Irwin; and some days after Congress adjourned I was agreeably waited upon by Mr. Berrett, who said to me: "They have cut us down three thousand dollars, and there is seven thousand paid; shall we insist on more?" I said, "No; let us take what we can get. It is all right." He handed me $3,500 in bills.[5]

"I suppose," Kasson followed up, "it is unnecessary to ask you if you retained all of that sum and applied it to your own use?" "I did," Sam replied, and added, "I must say that it was a very liberal compensation for the moderate amount of work which that subsidy seemed to require."

"And the nature of that work?" asked Kasson. "Simply stating on all occasions, where it was proper to do so, that I was in favor of the measure; that I thought it a good measure," Sam replied, explaining that he knew the Pacific Mail Steamship Company well:

As an old Californian, having sailed often on those steamers, I had a sort of friendship for them. I thought well of the line; I thought that it was a national undertaking;
that our ship-building was going to the dogs, and that if those ships were to be built
in this country it would give an impetus to iron ship-building. I thought that a
subsidy to the Pacific Mail Steamship Company was a proper thing, particularly as
the Cunard Steamship Company had a subsidy from the English government, and
had attained a colossal success. I wanted to see the American flag flying again on the
seas, and I would have helped the Pacific Mail Steamship Company subsidy without
one penny of compensation.

Did he know of money being paid to others to lobby for the subsidy? "Not a
penny," Sam said. Did he know of money being paid to any member, officer, or
employee of Congress in connection with the subsidy? "No, sir," Sam answered.

Then Representative James Beck, a Democrat from Kentucky, interrupted, a
bit off topic but still about lobbying: "I have heard it suggested that you had
remarked that there was a great deal of difficulty in a gentleman living in Washington on the oxygen of the atmosphere, and that a gentleman was obligated to do
something." Beck had struck a nerve. Sam launched into a description of the
lobbyists' difficult life:

This business of lobbying, as it is called, is as precarious as fishing in the Hebrides.
You get all ready, your boats go out—suddenly there comes a storm, and away you are
driven. Everybody who knows anything about Washington, knows that ten times, ay,
fifty times, more measures are lost than are carried; but once in a while a pleasant
little windfall of this kind recompenses us, who are always toiling here, for the disappointments of the session. I am not at all ashamed—I do not say I am proud, but I am
not at all ashamed—of the occupation. It is a very useful one. In England it is a separate branch of the legal profession. There they have parliamentary lawyers who do no
other business. There the committees sit all day to hear these lawyers and they sit in
Parliament at night, whereas here committees are only allowed to sit for an hour and a
half, and so it is very hard to get through four thousand bills in a session. The disappointments are much more numerous than the successes. I have had many a very
pleasant "contingent" knocked away [here the stenographer entered "(laughter)" into
the record] when everything appeared prosperous and certain, and I would not insure
any bill if I were paid fifty per cent to secure its passage. That is the general rule. In this
matter I think that the gentleman (Mr. Irwin) paid more money than he need have paid.

But, Representative William Niblack, a Democrat from Indiana, pointed out,
"You got much less than the others got?" " I don't know," Sam replied, "I was

retained, I suppose, because 'the King's name is a tower of strength,' and I am called the 'King of the Lobby.' But I am not the treasurer of the lobby, that is certain. If you were here for entertainment, I could entertain you with histories of well-concerted plans which all disappeared just at the crack of one member's whip; perhaps a matter of caprice, perhaps a matter of accident; you can't tell which."

Sam continued with his description of the lobbyists' plight:

We who are of the regular army know when we are whipped. But gentlemen of little experience come down here, and peg on and peg on till the end of the session, and never understand when they had better go home. To introduce a bill properly, to have it referred to the proper committee, to see that some member in that committee understands its merits, to attend to it, to watch it, to have a counsel to go and advocate it before the committee, to see that members of the committee do not oversleep themselves on the mornings of important meetings, to watch the coming in of the bill to Congress day after day, week after week, to have your men on hand a dozen times, and to have them as often disappointed; to have one of those storms which spring up in the Adriatic of Congress, until your men are worried and worn and tired, and until they say to themselves that they will not go up to the Capitol to-day, and then to have the bird suddenly flushed, and all your preparations brought to naught—these, these are some of the experiences of the lobby.

Sam was just warming up:

Another point—the question of entertainments—is spoken of. There is nothing in the world so excellent as entertainments of a refined order. Talleyrand says that diplomacy is assisted by good dinners, but at good dinners people do not "talk shop," but they give people who have a taste in that way a right, perhaps, to ask a gentleman a civil question, and to get a civil answer; to get information which his clients want, and that can be properly given. Sometimes a railroad man wants information; some-times a patentee wants his patent renewed; that is a pretty hard fight. Then a broker wants to know what the Treasury is going to do about a certain measure. Sometimes the banker is anxious about the financial movements in Congress, or a merchant about the tariff. All these things we do constantly, and we do not make any charge for them. We keep up a certain circle of friends, and once in a while an opportunity comes of getting something that is of real service, and for which compensation is due and proper. But the entertainments are proportioned to the business of the session. When the business is good, so are the entertainments, and when the busi-ness is not good, the entertainments are meager.

Sam then tossed in a long, enigmatic anecdote about a talented cook, who had whipped up a delicious dinner for the King of Spain, who had dropped in on his master unexpectedly late one night. The main ingredient? Fifty-two pigs' ears. Before his listeners had time to ponder Sam's story, Niblack, who was not amused and who apparently had never dined at Sam's table (nor, it seemed, had any of Sam's other interrogators), asked, "Is there not a great deal of money wasted on good dinners?" Sam indignantly replied, "I do not think money is ever wasted on a good dinner. If a man dines badly he forgets to say his prayers going to bed, but if he dines well he feels like a saint."

There was just one more exchange. The chairman asked Sam, "Were you aware that Mr. Berrett, in point of fact, had received $10,000, instead of $7000?" Although it was clear that Sam had been cheated by Berrett in the split, he claimed to harbor no hard feelings: "No, I did not know anything about it until I saw it mentioned in the papers. It is quite right; he probably did more work than I did. I was quite satisfied with what I got." And with that, Sam was dismissed and strode from the chamber.

The next day, the New York Sun's story, entitled "A Noted Lobbyist's Testimony," began: "Samuel Ward, famous for his grand entertainments and convivial qualities, was the most amusing and frank-spoken witness that has yet helped to enliven the proceedings of the Committee." The Chicago Daily Tribune, in its story under the headline "The King of the Lobby: His Experience as Related by Himself," noted, "Mr. Ward gave his testimony, or rather, delivered his humorous lecture, standing at the end of the table, with his . . . whole person presenting evidence of his being, not only in belief, but in practice, a disciple of the gospel of gastronomy."[6]

The New York Daily Graphic ran a cartoon of "Uncle Sam" wearing a chef's hat and dropping pigs' ears, each marked $1,000, into a simmering pot and called him "a good-natured, Pickwickian old fellow. . . . Wit, scholar, and poet, gourmand and political intriguer, he has seen about as much of the world as any man living. . . . As a lobbyist he holds that the first step towards inducing a senator or representative to vote in any desired way is to clear his judgment and vanish his prejudices by a comfortable dinner."[7]

Newspapers all across the country carried stories about Sam, his testimony, his dinners, and his riddle of the pigs' ears. Was he, some speculated, warning fifty-two congressmen that he knew of their involvement with the Pacific Mail subsidy? No other lobbyist received so much individual journalistic attention, and in no one else's case, at a time when the press was heaping condemnation on the lobby, was so much of it merely bemused.[8]

Sam lapped up the attention. To Longfellow, he sent an envelope full of press clippings and crowed that this "business which people imagined must have been unpleasant has turned out profitably." His "saucy testimony" had, he wrote, "a certain humor, which I can no more suppress than a stammerer can suppress his stuttering, and it has made me famous." He went on to tell Longfellow about all the publishers who were beating a path to his door.[9]

Sam's response to one of the congratulatory letters filling his box, the one from his friend Edmund Stedman, a Wall Street broker and successful poet, offered a more sober reflection on his profession:

> When I appeared at the short summons of the committee and gave my testimony I had no idea it would spread throughout the land. . . . I quite agree that the profession of lobbying is not commendable. But I have endeavored to make it respectable by avoiding all measures without merit. In the struggle for existence, to which I was not born, my various chances and mishaps have landed me upon that shore,—like the émigré who escapes the guillotine to make a good living by compounding salads. . . . I tried my hand at various things, but never got to the north of independence, then came to Washington, first on one errand, then on another, until finally I made this place my headquarters and Congress the theater of my employment.[10]

Sam seemed at the top of his game. He had the spotlight he craved—the "King's" name was known far and wide. His testimony was even good for business; several new clients came his way after the hearings. Prominent Republicans and Democrats, foreign ministers, Supreme Court justices, and cabinet members were still happy to share his table and to return the invitation. James Garfield, still in the House, spent many pleasant evenings with Sam in 1875. Evarts, too, was a frequent guest even after he was named secretary of state by President Rutherford B. Hayes in 1877. Sam and Blaine met frequently. Samuel "Sunset" Cox, who became chairman of the Banking and Currency Committee when the Democrats took the House in 1875, stopped in at "My Dear Uncle Sam's" home often. Sam remained Bayard's "Uncle Sam," too.[11]

Nevertheless, Sam's initial post-investigation buoyancy was short-lived. He was feeling his age—sixty-one when he testified—more keenly every year as friends died. Even though they had not been very close for years, he missed Sumner, one of "the boys," who had died the year before.[12] Although new clients sought him out, Sam hinted that the deepening nationwide depression, which had begun in 1873, was tightening the purse strings of some of his old clients—not Barlow's, but others. While he referred to them only indirectly, the scandals coming one right after the other and the unrelenting castigation of his profession in the press were taking their toll on Sam as well.

Sam's letters to Barlow began to suggest that, while he still had many powerful Republican friends, as the second Grant administration wound down he could not always work his magic. Sam was mortified when he could not pull off for Longfellow one of the few favors that friend had ever asked of him. Longfellow sought Sam's intercession with Secretary of State Hamilton Fish on behalf of a friend. With deep regret, Sam had to tell him, "No sooner did I read your letter touching Sgr. Luigi Monti than I approached the Fishing Grounds. But the *Rex Vestibuli* had no more effect on the 'school' than had Canute upon the waves. . . . I am very, very sorry."[13]

Sam was also deeply distressed by a story in the *New York Times* in March 1875 about the will of "Samuel Ward, Jr., the son of Mr. 'Sam' Ward, whose testimony about the effect of good dinners in influencing Congressional legislation recently caused much attention." Wardie had died in Paris in 1866, but his estate had just been settled. Suzette Grymes, who claimed she was alone with Wardie when he died, told the court and reporters that he had repudiated his father on his death-bed. Even with her daughter and two grandsons dead nearly a decade, Sam's harridan mother-in-law could still wound him deeply. Sam was despondent, but an even more crushing blow came just months later.[14]

After mid-December 1875, Sam's letters to Longfellow and other close friends and family were inscribed on black-bordered stationery. Maddie had died suddenly at thirty-six. Sam had never lost hope that the chill in their relationship, nurtured by the Astors all those years, would someday thaw. He longed to know his grandchildren—all ten of them—better. Now those hopes lay dashed. He poured out his grief to Longfellow: "My Dear Longo, I am alone in the world. My daughter Maddie died on Monday of pneumonia, after an illness of three days, leaving ten children, the eldest thirteen, the youngest 12 months. . . . My old heart has been seared until it has lost nearly all its perennial susceptibilities. . . . it is a lunar landscape, nothing remaining of the volcanoes but craters and fissures. . . . I . . . am beset by no end of miserables."[15]

Maddie, who had inherited about five million dollars in property and money when her grandfather, William Astor, died shortly before her, left Sam an annuity of one thousand dollars, what the Astors left to faithful servants. Her husband, who died just two years later, was terrified of jeopardizing his children's inheritance by encouraging interaction with Sam. In his will, he established a shield of guardians and trustees to protect his children, who became collectively, and incorrectly, known in the press as "the Astor orphans," from fortune hunters, and that included Sam, their grandfather, who was only allowed to see them once a year under strict supervision.[16]

Less than a month after Maddie's burial, another death touched Sam deeply. Samuel Gridley Howe, Julia's difficult husband and another of "the boys," died on January 9, 1876, after a long illness. Sam rushed to Boston to be with Julia and her children, sending ahead a letter: "My darling Dudy, . . . What shall I say to you in this sad hour so long impending and yet so cruel? . . . Memory transported me this morning back to those old days in Bond Street, musical with youthful joys and warm with thoughtful aspirations. . . . Now, you and Longo and I are the only ones that remain, save Annie and Louisa, of that happy period."[17]

After these deaths in quick succession, Sam's letters became more reflective. That spring, he opined to Longfellow, "I am no longer necessary to anyone and am tired of myself."[18] To his niece Maud he lamented, "I am working as usual against wind and tide in my old scow, to which the barnacles cling, and have hardly time for individual thought and feeling. I sometimes think of running away to recultivate my own acquaintance."[19]

Despite his disappointments and personal griefs, Sam was busy. Although he had suggested to Stedman that he was contemplating cutting back, the truth was that he could not retire or run away. At sixty-one, he was still scratching for a living. Sam was famous, but he was not rich. He lived well—very well indeed—but on other men's money. Of personal savings he had none. Although he worked hard, when it came to being provident, Sam was the grasshopper, fiddling, or in his case spending money on pearls for nieces, while the more sober ants of the lobby like Dodge and Chandler amassed small fortunes. Sam had never quite given up his dream of striking it rich and becoming a man of letters, but, in fact, he still had to work at "compounding salads" to earn his keep, like the émigré in his analogy.

Sam was hard at work in the months after his testimony. He was representing Peruvian guano interests, a wealthy Frenchman, a group of Mexican business-men, Americans with mining and transportation interests in Central and South America, the Erie Railroad, cotton claims, and individuals with claims against the British government. Barlow kept urging him to take on even more projects, appealing to Sam's vanity and his pocketbook: "You can do these [two more claims] better than anyone else. If you can do so, you will oblige me and earn a nice fee for yourself."[20]

There was no question, however, that, while working harder than ever, Sam was enjoying it less. He was growing tired and feeling pinched. Before, there had been more than a touch of braggadocio in his complaints about how busy and greatly in demand he was. Now, his weariness, even if cleverly framed, seemed genuine. It was with Longfellow that he most often shared his unhappiness. In May 1875 he grumbled: "The session that expired March 4th was a failure as a harvest and I have been obliged to grow root crops to keep the wolf from the door. . . . It is hard for a fashionable bootmaker to be compelled to take to cobbling, but, I have the health and spirit of your old blacksmith."[21]

Sam's letters to Bayard, usually so breezy, also grew discouraged. In the spring of 1876 he wrote: "I am getting weary at the weight of my . . . sisyphean task of working eternally. . . . This session has been a beggar's opera."[22] That summer, Sam, who spent a good deal of time shuttling among the various Democratic presidential contenders' camps gathering information for Barlow and Manton Marble, was deeply disappointed when Bayard did not get the nomination. In December 1876, with another birthday approaching, Sam mused to his niece, Julia Romana, about the passage of time: "At 63 one has the avalanche of years upon one's back and the flinty boulders of reality in one's path."[23]

Sam had hit his lowest point since he had slunk out of New York twenty-seven years before, but, while he was in the dumps as the Grant years ended, the lobby in general was sinking even lower. It was taking a beating in the press, in journals and political novels, in biting cartoons like those by Thomas Nast and Joseph Kepler, and, consequently, in the court of public opinion. Just as many constituents might like their own congressman but loathe the Congress, while most reporters portrayed Sam as a likeable charmer, they were leveling scathing criticism at his collective colleagues and his profession.

Lobbyists were not the only ones taking their lumps in the press. Captains of industry, especially railroad moguls, local and national politicians, the electoral system, and Congress all came in for their share of blame for the sad state of the so-recently-glorious Union. It was corruption, spiraling out of control, that was the perceived overarching villain: lobbyists, moguls, and politicians were its supporting cast. In newspapers across the country and in journals like the *Nation*, *Harper's Weekly*, *Galaxy*, the *Atlantic Monthly*, *Continental Monthly*, the *Republic*, *Century*, and the *North American Review*, the chorus of lamentation had begun to build as soon as the first scandals of the first Grant administration were exposed. As scandal after scandal unfolded—Black Friday, Credit Mobilier, the Salary Grab, the Belknap affair, the Whiskey Ring, the Sanborn contracts, the Emma Mine swindle, the Pacific Mail contract—the chorus swelled as the frightening depression deepened, and the revelations of venality continued into the mid-1870s.

Some feared that dictators would rise. Some foresaw anarchy. George Templeton Strong predicted a "general smash" if the government did not mend its sorry ways. Union general and Washington lawyer Thomas Ewing warned his fellow citizens: "We are in danger of going the way of all Republics. First freedom, then glory; when that is past, wealth, vice, corruption."[24] Almost all of the reporters, pundits, novelists, and cartoonists suggested that the corruption so visible in Washington in the 1870s was a new evil, part of the postwar world, and that the times had never before been so bad. But, of course, corruption was not new. The stink of corruption had hung especially thick over the not-so-distant 1850s: schemers had bilked the government, officials had sold contracts, lobbyists had offered bribes, and politicians had taken them.[25]

Some of those harkening back to better, purer days were looking through cataracts of disappointment that the war had cost so many lives yet not cleansed the nation for good. In 1875, poet James Russell Lowell, one of Longfellow's good friends, whose "Commemoration Ode" in 1865 had reflected the hope of that moment, encapsulated the disillusionment felt by him and his friends in a poem in the *Nation*. With the country's upcoming centennial in mind, Dame Columbia asks Brother Jonathan what she might show off to Europe that is uniquely American. He spits out his scathing suggestions, which included:

> Show your new bleaching-process, cheap and brief,
> To wit, a jury chosen by the thief;
> Show your State Legislatures; show your Rings;
> And challenge Europe to produce such things
> As high officials sitting half in sight
> To share the plunder and fix things right.
> If that don't fetch her, why, you only need
> To show your latest style in martyrs,—Tweed:
> She'll find it hard to hide her spiteful tears
> At such advance on one poor hundred years.[26]

Lowell was in an even darker mood a year later, when he wrote "An Ode for the Fourth of July, 1876," which included these bitter lines:

> Is this the country that we dreamed in youth
> Where wisdom and not numbers should have weight,
> Seed-field of simpler manners, braver truth,
> Where shams should cease to dominate
> In household, church, and state?[27]

While wrong about corruption being new, Cassandras like Lowell were on firmer ground with their second claim: the late 1860s and 1870s *were* the worst of times thus far, if measured by quantity, audacity, and scale of corruption. More important, more Americans knew it, because the gory details of freshly exposed rings, bosses, lobby deals, sell-out congressmen, and other scandals filled newspaper columns from Mobile to Cleveland. Just as the relative paucity of reporters in the capital before the war partly accounted for the general population's lack of knowledge of antebellum corruption, the plethora of reporters after the war played a role in fanning the fears in these uncertain times.[28]

A portion of the postwar panic engendered by the scandals was attributable to the corruption's increased visibility thanks to the aggressive journalists of Newspaper Row. Reporters had agendas of their own for exposing corruption. Some were out to smear a rival with a negative story; some were "strikers," lobbing word grenades every which way until paid off to stop. Uriah Painter, for example, was both. Many felt pressured to find fresh news and to scoop their rivals, and this led to far more stories coming from the capital than ever before, some of them more rumor than reality. In addition, most reporters worked for intensely partisan newspapers for whom tales of corruption could serve a variety of masters: Democrats or Republicans out to undermine opponents; nativists eager to malign Catholics and immigrants; reformers who intentionally or unwittingly exaggerated the evilness of the times for their own ends.[29]

Whether motivated by moral superiority, broken dreams, or hard-driving editors, those surveying the scene in Washington generally agreed that the whole system of government was breaking down and that corruption was to blame. Despite their certainty, however, corruption was actually not the biggest story of these years. It was just the easiest one to see. The very nature of the federal government was undergoing a profound reorientation on its way to becoming modern. Corruption, and an increase in lobbying, were the by-products of this process.[30]

While he did not like what he saw, Henry Adams was one of those who did grasp something of what was going on. In his article "The Session" in the *North American Review* in 1870, he acknowledged that "to say that the government of the United States is passing through a period of transition is one of the baldest complacencies of politics." Elaborating, he pointed out, "This system is outgrown. . . . New powers, new duties, new responsibilities, new burdens of every sort, are incessantly crowding upon the government at the very moment when it finds itself unequal to managing the limited powers it is accustomed to wield."[31]

Reformer Gamaliel Bradford agreed, but recognized that the problem was bigger still. The new challenges that the postwar nation faced were not black and white, or grandly compelling, or easily resolved by one great cataclysm. The new issues were less emotional, more complex, and called for a new type of government. In the same year of Adams's *North American Review* article, Bradford wrote, "The questions of slavery and the war were perfectly simple. The people comprehended them. In contrast, the questions which are now pressing upon us are technical, and call for the exercise of statesmanship. . . . the people do not understand the subjects."[32]

Adams and Bradford were both right. The old system was outgrown, and the new issues, like expansion, immigration, industrialization, and modernization, were difficult to grasp. New people—milllions of them—new territories, and new states were demanding their share of internal improvements. Reformers of all sorts were clamoring for the federal government to take up their causes. New sources of wealth seemed immune to old economic rules, and old local regulations could not control new national industries. As Adams noted, all of these new forces were crowding together, pushing on the federal government, which had little choice but to begin, however haltingly, to try to grapple with all of them. Much of that burden fell to Congress, which was not only disorganized but already overwhelmed by an avalanche of bills that congressmen, many of them greenhorns each session, had not a prayer of even reading, let alone studying.

While Adams and Bradford recognized that change was afoot, they did not see that the very process of transition, when so much was unsettled and with so much up for grabs, created conditions ripe for all sorts of potentially corrupt practices. While that would become visible to later generations with hindsight, many of those living through the upheaval, trying to figure out what was going wrong in their world, were certain that they had found their culprit. While venal politicians and grasping businessmen came in for their own share of condemnation, it was onto the lobby's back that the greatest share of the blame was heaped.[33]

Most observers did not see that the lobby was actually one element in Washington that could bridge the widening gulf between constituent and Congress and help to bring some order out of the chaos. Policymakers lacked the time, staff, money, and expertise to cope with the explosion of business that came with the expansion of the government's powers. Many who tried to deal with the government found only frustration, as they butted heads with what seemed like unresponsive officialdom. The old channels of communication were clogged; congressmen were overwhelmed; agencies like the Pension Office were swamped with work; constituents big and small found themselves left out in the cold. Frustrated, individuals and businesses looking to break through the logjam joined league with lobbyists, who were good at getting things done.

Lobbyists, however, seemed both blessing and curse. With so much to be gotten from the government but so many impediments in the way, there was increased demand for their services. At the same time, more people began to realize that what went on in Washington had the potential to affect their lives for good or ill, and more attention was focused on the capital. So, more lobbyists were doing more work in the capital, and there was more awareness that more lobbyists were at work there. When confronted by a government seemingly riddled with corruption, it was a short leap for worried citizens to latch onto lobbyists, newly visible and poorly understood, as the explanation for its ills.

The lobby made a perfect scapegoat for several reasons. First, there was no denying that some of its members *were* involved in some of the most noxious scandals of the era. Second, while the right to petition was protected by the Constitution, there was real unease with the idea of outside advocates-for-hire pleading not for themselves or their relatives or townspeople but for whatever special interest would pay their price. Third, while there were procedures in place for holding officials accountable, such as the ballot box and impeachment, the public felt powerless to control what seemed at best extralegal and at worst illegal agents. And fourth, by blaming lobbyists for what ailed the body politic, the public and the politicians could absolve themselves of culpability. Everyone could find a reason to point to the lobby as a corrosive alien force, outside traditional checks, seducing congressmen and cabinet members with impunity.[34]

The lobby became a potent lightning rod, attracting simplistic explanations for what was perceived to be the breakdown of government. Speaker Blaine pointed out that it had become the all-purpose response to revelations of impropriety: "That is always the cry when anything unsavory comes up, 'There is a lobby!'" Vilification of the lobby was ubiquitous during the last of the Grant years, and there was just enough truth in the charges to make them credible.[35]

No terms were too harsh to describe lobbyists. In 1869, the *Nation* defined the generic lobbyist as a man of the lowest morals, "a man whom everybody suspects; who is generally during half the year without honest means of livelihood; and whose employment by those who have bills before a legislature is only resorted to as a disagreeable necessity." The *New York Herald* claimed, "the word 'lobbyist' is justly deemed a term of reproach which no respectable man is willing to have applied to him."[36]

These were mild. Emily Briggs had portrayed the lobby as a scaly lizard slithering through the Capitol. Added to that description, lobbyists were now also "birds of prey," "leeches," "vagrants," "a portion of mankind . . . never heard mentioned in terms other than contempt and disgust," "that great army of bloodsuckers," men "destitute of patriotism" who were out to "rob the public treasury," "a swarm of adventurers," "all the arts of temptation ooze from their tongues in drops of honey, and fall from their hands in streams of gold."[37]

No method was considered beneath them—not blackmail, not bribery, not seduction—and every single crumb that the government had to give, no matter how small, was fair game. In "The Small Sins of Congress," in the *Atlantic Monthly* in November 1869, the author claimed that one lobbyist gave a congressman's wife a grand piano and got a cadetship for a client's son in return. Even artists were lobbyists. The same reporter described how one painter obtained a federal commission: he pretended "that the excellent but not beautiful wife of a member of Congress reminded him constantly of an exquisite model he once had in Rome."[38]

Popular political fiction took up the cry in the early 1870s and indicted lobbyists, as well as greedy congressmen and scheming businessmen, in tales of outrageous, and sometimes outrageously funny, corruption. Mark Twain and Charles Dudley Warner's *The Gilded Age*, published in 1873, in which the "Salt Lick Pacific Extension" stood in for the Credit Mobilier, brought heartless lobbyist "Colonel Mulberry Sellers" and beautiful lobbyess "Laura Hawkins" into the nation's parlors and, when adapted into a popular stage show, into theaters across the country.[39]

Twain, who had spent an unhappy winter in Washington in 1867 as secretary to Nevada senator William Stewart, one of the western "Bonanza Kings," and Warner, editor of the *Hartford Courant*, covered the ins and outs of corruption when Colonel Sellers explained to a naïve aspiring lobbyist, "Henry Brierly," the going rate for passage of a bill:

> A majority of the House Committee say $10,000 apiece—$40,000; a majority of the Senate Committee, the same each—say $40,000; a little extra to one or two chairmen of one or two such committees, say $10,000 each—$20,000. . . . Then, seven male lobbyists, at $3,000 each—$21,000; one female lobbyist, $10,000; a high moral Congressman or Senator here or there—the high moral ones cost more, because they give tone to a measure—say ten of these at $3,000 each, is $30,000; then a lot of small-fry country members who won't vote for anything whatever without pay—say twenty at $500 apiece, is $10,000; . . . and then comes your printed documents, . . . your advertisements in a hundred and fifty papers at ever so much a line—because you've *got* to keep the papers all right or you are gone up, you know.[40]

The dark Washington novels of John William De Forest—*Honest John Vane* (1875), *Playing the Mischief* (1875), and *Justine's Lovers* (1878)—mirrored his own pessimism. De Forest, from a wealthy Connecticut family, had come home from

Europe when war broke out, enlisted in the Union army, and fought under General Philip Sheridan in the Shenandoah Valley. His wartime experience made him bitter, as corruption seemed to take over the victory he had helped win. His novels left no doubt whom he blamed. His revolting lobbyists were in league with the devil, if they were not the devil themselves. In *Honest John Vane*, where the "Great Subfluvial Tunnel Road" greatly resembled the Credit Mobilier, lobbyist "Darius Dorman" spoke "with spasmodic twinges of cheerless gayety which resembled the 'cracked and thin laughter heard far down in Hell.' . . . Shaking all over with his dolorous mirth, his very raiment, indeed, quivering and undulating with it, so that it seemed as if there might be a twitching tail inside his trousers."[41]

Even a brand new congressman like "Honest John Vane" should have been able to pick out and steer clear of lobbyists had they matched De Forest's detailed description: "men of unwholesome skins, greasy garments, brutish manners, filthy minds, and sickening conversation; men who so reeked and drizzled with henbane tobacco and cockatrice whiskey that a moderate drinker or smoker would recoil from them as from a cesspool; men whose stupid, shameless boastings of their briberies were enough to warn away from them all but the elect of Satan." Harder for Honest John to identify and avoid were the "corruptionists whom he could not steel himself to treat rudely. These were former members of Congress whose names had been trumpeted to him by fame in his youthful days." They had become "decayed statesmen, who were now, indeed, nothing but infragrant corpses, breeding all manner of vermin and miasma, but who still had the speech of patriotism on their lips."[42]

Honest John had to watch out for other types of lobbyists as well: "pundits in constitutional law and Congressional precedent, whose deluges of political lore overflowed him like a river. . . . highly salaried and quick-witted agents of great business houses, which he, as a businessman, knew, respected, and perhaps feared. . . . a woman, audacious and clever and stylish and handsome,—an Aspasia who was willing to promise money, and able to redeem her promises in beauty."[43]

De Forest's allusion to Aspasia was apt. In fifth-century BC Greece, Aspasia was known for her sexual allure and her unseemly influence over Pericles and Athenian politics. De Forest's novels offered up several nineteenth-century Aspasias as remarkable as Twain's Laura Hawkins. While in *Honest John Vane* he took on big schemes like Credit Moblier, De Forest focused on claims agents in *Playing the Mischief*, where his readers met pretty, innocent "Josie Murray," who had come to Washington to press her family's modest claim for $20,000. Josie fell under the spell of claims broker "Simeon Allchin," very likely a stand-in for Henry Cooke. Gripped by the lobbying fever which held out the promise of riches,

Josie ended up with a hard gleam in her once-soft eye, bereft of friends, and driven to prostitution, consequences similar to those suffered by poor "Justine" in De Forest's *Justine's Lovers*.[44]

The message in both the press and fiction was clear: lobbyists were swarming over every inch of Washington, perverting the government and preventing it from serving the people. John Vane could not avoid them, no matter how hard he tried: "If a gentleman offered him a cigar, he discovered that it was scented with appropriations. If he helped a pretty woman into a streetcar, she asked him to vote for her statute or her father's claim."[45] Nonfiction and fiction also agreed that the reason lobbyists were successful was because government officials were so easily tempted. "Congress itself is a nest of lobbyists," "Congressman Drummond," who was one of them, explained to Josie Murray. "It is a game of tickle me and I'll tickle you." A seasoned lobbyist warned Josie that if he was to push her claim for her, "I shall have to pay a lot full of members, and they are extortionate as the dickens. They ask higher and higher every year."[46] Twain's famous quip that the only distinctive native American criminal class was Congress was heartfelt. He began one sentence in *The Gilded Age*, "If you were a member of Congress, (no offense) . . . ."[47]

How to set things right? The remedy seemed clear: get rid of the lobbyists. The *Republic* proposed in 1873 that "the only effective cure [is] the complete abolition of the 'third house' by the overwhelming power of organized public opinion."[48] But that was much easier said than done, and, ironically, the *Republic*'s suggestion hit on precisely the difficulty: "organized public opinion" came awfully close to being part of the third house itself, a special interest not unlike the iron manufacturers and the railroad combinations that lobbied for their own goals. Of course, neither the *Republic* nor its readers wanted to think of what they were advocating as lobbying. Lobbying, after all, was corrupting, while an effort to rid government of corrupting influences was a high-minded crusade. There was, however, no escaping the fine line between the two. One could not get rid of the lobby without throwing the baby, the system of redress guaranteed by the Constitution, out with the admittedly dirty bathwater.[49]

If the lobby could not be eliminated without trampling on constitutional rights, perhaps it could be reined in. Although more than half a century would pass before legislation to regulate the lobby would be adopted and enforced, three efforts were introduced in Congress during the second Grant administration, close on the heels of Sam's testimony, as anti-lobby hysteria was peaking. All sought to define good and bad lobbying, protect the former, and eliminate the latter.

In January 1875, Massachusetts senator George Boutwell, a Republican who had already served more than a decade in the House and as Grant's secretary of the treasury, where he had had to cope with the Black Friday financial crisis and got his fill of claims agents, introduced a bill "to provide for the organization of a bar of the two Houses of Congress." Much as Sam had lectured the House Ways and Means Committee, Boutwell told his Senate colleagues that his proposal was based on British precedent, where parliamentary lawyers or practitioners—terms that had a much nicer ring than lobbyist—were accepted as part of the recognized governmental structure. Why not, Boutwell asked, accredit similar practitioners in the United States, thereby eradicating the wicked "claims lobby"? As envisioned by Boutwell, only "respected and qualified" attorneys, who would represent petitioners before Congress and its committees, need apply, and each would be required to register. Boutwell made it clear that he did not want to end most of the lobby's activities; he just wanted the business to be above board and confined to honorable gentlemen.[50]

Boutwell's bill went nowhere. The end of the session came and went with no action, and neither Boutwell nor anyone else revived it when the 43rd Congress reconvened. Meanwhile, another, more sweeping, measure had been introduced, this time in the House, by Congressman Ellis Roberts, a Republican of New York. Roberts was a newspaper man from Utica finishing his second term. He had been defeated for reelection that fall and knew he would not be back for the 44th Congress. He was fed up with paid lobbyists, agents, counsels, and "bought" reporters, and, he told his colleagues, wanted before he left "to regulate the appearance of agents and attorneys prosecuting claims or demands before Congress and the Executive Departments of the Government."[51]

Roberts's bill required all lobbyists, although they were never called that anywhere in the proposal, to register with the House and Senate clerks and with the clerks of those committees before which their clients had business and to account for their expenditures. Not only did his bill address what so many critics condemned as one of the most noxious aspects of lobbying—the secrecy in which it was so often cloaked—but its reach went further than Boutwell's plan, including not just claims agents but all kinds of advocacy and not just on Capitol Hill but throughout the executive branch as well.

On March 3, 1875, the last day of the 43rd Congress, the House passed Roberts's bill, H.R. 4849, by a vote of 113 to 31. With no time for the Senate to act, the bill died, but not before 113 members of Congress had gone on record for the first time supporting the registration, and thereby the recognition, of lobbyists by whatever name they were called.

Barely a year later, for a short time and with a more limited scope, a call for registration of lobbyists actually did take hold, although with shallow roots and only in the House. In the spring of 1876, Massachusetts representative George Frisbie Hoar, a Republican pillar of rectitude who never hesitated to criticize members of either party for ethical lapses, was one of the managers of the House impeachment trial of former Secretary of War William Belknap. He had been listening to hours of testimony about corruption. In addition, Hoar and his colleagues on the Judiciary Committee were being bombarded by an assortment of "counsels," all claiming that they had been retained to advocate for the same issue before the committee. "Four persons," Hoar complained, "coming from different parts of the country, coming from cities and neighborhoods which the different members of the committee come from, have accosted the different members of the committee in regard to that particular measure." He and his colleagues, he said, had no idea whom to believe, suggesting that they would listen to those who truly did represent legitimate interests. "It seems to us," Hoar explained, "that it would be a great protection to members of the committee and of the House to require that any person or corporation who employs an agent to represent his or its interest here to file the name of that agent with the House, so that the House may know who is the responsible agent in such cases."[52]

With this explanation, Hoar introduced his resolution: "Ordered, that all persons or corporations employing counsel or agents to represent their interests in regard to any measure pending at any time before this House, or any committee thereof, shall cause the name and authority of such counsel or agent to be filed with the Clerk of the House; and no person whose name and authority are not so filed shall appear as counsel or agent before any committee of this House."[53]

The resolution, which passed by voice vote the same day, carried little real weight: it applied only to the House; it expired at the end of the 44th Congress, less than a year away; and it had no "teeth," no mechanism for enforcement. It did, however, mark the first time that either branch of Congress had granted quasi-official status to certain activities that could be described as lobbying.

The Hoar resolution and Boutwell's and Roberts's bills marked an important change in Congress's relationship with the lobby. All three acknowledged that lobbying, by whatever name, existed, that it was legal, and that it was not going away; and there the matter lay for decades. The public's fixation on lobbying, however, did not end with these initial attempts to corral it or with the end of the second Grant administration and the worst of the scandals. Zeroing in on the lobby was part of the larger effort to come to grips with the changes taking place within the nation and the government that would continue for years. De Forest's satanic Darius Dorman, Twain's cold Colonel Sellers, and all of the real-life lobby-ists and lobbyesses whom the press and the public saw hiding behind every pillar in the Capitol were stand-ins, a shorthand attempt to rationalize the world as the ground shifted beneath their feet and to absolve themselves from responsibility for the corruption that accompanied the on-going transition.[54]

The lobby continued to take a beating through the Hayes administration and beyond, although with lessening intensity. Sam's downward slide, however, came to an abrupt halt in 1879, when, as it had many times before, his luck changed dramatically.

CHAPTER SEVEN

The "good SAMaritan" is rewarded; the king abdicates and decamps but keeps his hand in; a final fortune evaporates; on the lam again; the king is dead

Julia got wind of the changes in Sam's circumstances all the way in Rome, where she was visiting Louisa, and wrote to him in the spring of 1878:

> Dearest Bro Sam.
>
> Do, dear, take up your quick, graphic pen and write. Jacques Rubino [a business associate of Sam's] gave us some news of you which last advices from America have confirmed—that is, that a wealthy Californian, in recognition of your great kindness and devotion, has settled upon you a certain modest but comfortable income. We all hailed this information with great joy.[1]

News had traveled fast. Although hard to believe, it was correct. A wealthy Californian, James R. Keene, had indeed just provided Sam with a modest income. Keene had immigrated to the United States from England when he was about fourteen, and he had headed for the California gold fields a year later. That was where Sam had found him, down on his luck and desperately ill in the early 1850s. Sam had nursed the young man back to health and moved on. Keene had stayed in California and moved up, becoming one of the most successful stock manipulators in the West, president of the San Francisco Stock Exchange, a thoroughbred race horse breeder, and a millionaire many times over. Through it all, he never forgot Sam's kindness.[2]

When his doctors prescribed an ocean voyage and European vacation for his health in the mid-1870s, Keene wrapped up his affairs and headed East, with a brief stop planned in New York to look up old friends, including his "good SAMaritan," before embarking. Keene was eager to meet his eastern counterparts on Wall Street, and Sam, who knew them all, was happy to oblige. Sam gave dinners in Keene's honor and made sure Keene's wife and daughter met the leaders of New York society. Wall Street fascinated Keene, and he was determined to master it, even if it meant delaying his departure. Although almost certainly exaggerated, reporters put his early profits between $8,000,000 and $13,000,000.

Business rivals found Keene ruthless and cold, but he was generous to his friends. For Sam, whose precarious finances had come to Keene's ears, he used some of his first Wall Street profits to set up a trust fund that would guarantee Sam $3,000 a year for life. It was news of this gift that had elicited the letter from Julia. But Keene did not stop there. Within the year, he went much, much further to reward his old friend. Keene manipulated a block of railroad stock that he had set aside for Sam, sold it when the time was right, and turned over the profits to him. Sam's family later learned from J. P. Morgan and Company the extent of Keene's magnanimity—$750,000.

Sam was thunderstruck. "There is nothing more certain than that I have been the object of some supernatural intervention," he wrote Longfellow. "You may have heard that after nearly half a century of the life of a galley slave I have suddenly become quite independent in my circumstances and am as free as air." Lest "Longo" worry that he might fritter away this sudden fortune, Sam hastened to add, "One good effect of my prosperity is that it has chastened me more than adversity ever did, and I feel the grave responsibility of one of the stewards of the Most High."[3]

Despite his assurances, Longfellow and all who knew Sam well knew they had good reason to worry. Sam's wise banker friend William Butler Duncan minced no words in a letter of advice: "Your generous soul is about as fit to be trusted with money as a child's. If you can't spend it yourself, you will give it away. If my hopes are well founded, won't you let me act the part of a true friend, and salt some of it quietly away for a rainy day? No one need know of this but you and me. Pardon this impertinent suggestion, and believe me it comes from your real friend."[4]

Bayard, traveling in France, heard the news about Sam's sudden wealth and was also concerned. From Paris, he wrote a more gentle letter to his old friend, commiserating about a bad fall Sam had taken and urging him to slow down and reflect, now that he had a "substantial, pecuniary independence": "Now, your tumble gave you more than five minutes to let you see a certain person of three score years with a big fine brain and much acquirement acted upon by a broad and tender heart, living a most feverish life, with no time for rest and recuperation; a bundle of odds and ends of hours and half hours and *not one he could call his own*. This time you have been laid up and compelled to rest . . . is a gift of the gods—and I so regard it—and want you to lay plans broad and deep that shall fill the remainder of your days."[5]

Sam ignored Duncan's advice, but he did heed at least part of Bayard's and laid plans for his future. With this dramatic change in his circumstances, Washington would see less of him. Although he would be a frequent visitor, host, and guest in the capital, continuing to act as "gastronomic pacificator" and advocate, the "King of the Lobby" was abdicating his crown, leaving the field to others, pulling up stakes, and decamping for New York twenty years after he first blew into town.

Sam gave up the lease on the little house on E Street, the site of so many of his Washington *noctes ambrosianae*. In New York, he moved out of his basement rooms at the Brevoort into a handsome apartment at 85 Clinton Place, a fashionable address near Washington Square, where he at last could have that hour of his own. He filled his new home with his beloved volumes, many acquired during his Heidelberg days and all long in storage. "I am very comfortably lodged, for the first time in many years. But I hardly know the faces of my lovely books after so many years of separation," he wrote Longfellow, jauntily signing off, "Adios amigo mio." Sam's nephew, Marion Crawford, described walls covered with books and pictures, "and there was not an available nook or corner unfilled with scraps of bric-a-brac, photographs, odds and ends of reminiscences, and all manner of things characteristic of the occupant." Sam, who smoked Russian cigarettes, would tramp from room to room, chatting with visitors, "leaving a trail of white smoke in his wake, like a locomotive."[6]

If Bayard thought that Sam would settle down to anything like an ordinary existence, he was mistaken. Sam's new wealth bought him freedom from "the feverish life" that had been weighing upon him more and more heavily, but that did not mean that he was ready for "rest and recuperation." Quite the contrary. His new fortune energized him. Sam was busier than ever, but on his own terms, deciding what to do based on whether it gave him or others pleasure, rather than put money in his pocket. Sam plunged into his new life with gusto.

With money to spend, Sam's gift-giving took on staggering dimensions. For his youngest sister, Annie, Sam paid off the mortgage on San Geronimo, the 10,000-acre California ranch that she loved. Annie's handsome husband, Adolph Mailliard, was charming but an erratic businessman (all three sisters married men—Louisa, two of them—very unlike their banker father), so Sam placed the property in her name. For Julia, Sam's "dear Old Bird," there was a house as well.

Since her husband's death, Julia had been struggling financially. Her writings and lectures brought in only a meager amount, and she and her youngest daughter Maud were living in Boston during the winter in two rented rooms and spending frugal summers on a small farm in Newport, Rhode Island. In 1880, while they were on the farm, Sam bought Julia a handsome townhouse at 241 Beacon Street as a surprise and spent the summer furnishing it with rugs, curtains, and sofas sent up from New York.[7]

For Louisa and her daughter Margaret, known to all as Daisy, there was a much-longed-for trip to America in 1881. Sam met their boat at the dock in New York. Daisy delighted in her "radiant uncle, and my true uncle . . . , though all the world called him Uncle Sam." Sam had been planning a wonderful surprise in great detail: swearing Annie to secrecy, he brought her east from California for a reunion of the three sisters for Julia's sixty-second birthday. It was, Sam happily wrote Barlow, "the first time in twenty-five years we four have all been united."[8]

There were sacks of coffee, crates of peaches, baskets of melons, boxes of grapes, casks of olive oil, wheels of cheese, plus cigars and books for Evarts, Barlow, Bayard, Longfellow, and Hurlbert, whom he saw much more frequently now that he was spending more time in New York. Sam took a piece of Gorgonzola cheese and a bouquet of moss roses when he dined with author Mary Sherwood; gave a bookcase to his niece Laura; a handsome check to his niece Julia Romana, for an Easter treat for the residents at the Perkins Institution, which she and her husband ran; a diamond and sapphire pendant to his niece Maud; and bottles and bottles of wine to everyone dear to him.[9]

In November 1881, Sam alerted "Dear Dudie":

You will receive a barrel containing
4 doz pts St. Estèphe Claret
2 doz qts Margeaux ditto
freight paid. Have the barrels opened instantly and the wine laid on its side in the cellar. You will find it very good. You ought to drink half a pint a day, at dinner. . . . .
Tomorrow there will be a second consignment of wine, comprising
1 case of champagne, qts;   1 of Nierstein, qts
2 doz Moselle, qts;   1 case glorious sherry, qts
1 case Beychevelle claret, for grand occasions with which I hope you will be able to make Christmas. Put all the wines, save the sherry, on their sides and let the latter stand up. I have added half a doz bottles of Vermouth di Torino, which is a tonic for young women, an appetizer for young men and a sort of universal cocktail ante prandial.

No wonder Julia wrote of the brother she adored in her *Reminiscences*, "I certainly never knew one who took so much delight in giving pleasure to others or whose life was so full of natural, overflowing geniality and beneficence."[10]

In addition to tangible presents like tea pots and paint sets, Sam gave the gift of his newfound time to those of his nieces and nephews open to accepting his attentions. In delightful letters, Sam entertained them with family stories and anecdotes from his life. He took them seriously, listened to their worries and enthusiasms carefully, and almost never preached. Sam was especially concerned about his nephew Marion, who was in his mid-20s and still casting about for his calling. As soon as Marion expressed an interest in writing, Sam went into action, introducing him to his editor friends, getting him assignments as a book reviewer, and cheering him on as he wrote his first novel, *Mr. Isaac's*, which proved a huge success. Marion's letters to "My Dear Uncle" for 1881 and 1882 contained a steady stream of thank yous for theater tickets, books, reporting jobs and book reviews steered his way, for including him at dinners, for money, and for advice.[11]

Marion repaid his uncle's affection by casting him as the wise and utterly delightful Mr. Bellingham in his second novel, another success, *Dr. Claudius*, in 1883. His portrait of Bellingham lovingly captured the image and aura of the aging Sam:

> He was short, decidedly; but a broad deep chest and long powerful arms had given him many an advantage over taller adversaries in strange barbarous lands. He was perfectly bald, but that must have been because Nature had not the heart to cover such a wonderful cranium from the admiring gaze of phrenologists. A sweeping moustache and a long imperial of snowy white sat well on the ruddy tan of his complexion, and gave him an air at once martial and diplomatic. He was dressed in the most perfect of London clothes, and there were superb diamonds in his shirt, while a priceless sapphire sparkled, in a plain gold setting, on his broad, brown hand. . . He moves like a king and has the air of the old school in every gesture. His dark eyes are brighter than his diamonds, and his look, for all his white beard and seventy years, is as young and fresh as the rose he wears in his coat. . . . Mr. Bellingham . . . sparkled with a wit and grace that were to modern table-talk what a rare flagon of old Madeira, crusted with years, but brimming with the imperishable strength and perfume of eternal youth, might be to a gaudily-ticketed bottle of California champagne, effervescent, machine-made, cheap, and nasty.[12]

Sam now had more time for his extensive correspondence. Long, funny letters, full of puns and word plays, left Clinton Place for Rosebery in London, sometimes signed by Sam, sometimes by both Sam and Hurlbert. During Rosebery's visit in 1875, the trio—young, cheeky Rosebery, eccentric and brilliant Hurlbert, and Sam—had formed a very exclusive club, the Mendacious Club, with themselves as the only members, and they referred to each other as the "President" (Sam), the "Member" (Hurlbert), and the "Sycophant" (Rosebery). Barlow was sometimes allowed to attend club sessions, which were always over dinner, but only as the "Perpetual Candidate."[13]

Sam also used his newfound leisure and fortune to travel. He went to England in 1879 and again in 1880 strictly for pleasure. There he watched Liberal William Gladstone stage an exciting comeback from retirement, winning reelection to Parliament with Rosebery as his manager, and once again become prime minister. Rosebery's Dalmeny House was Gladstone's headquarters as well as Sam's. It was presided over by Hannah Rothschild Rosebery, whom Rosebery had married in 1878. Sam liked her enormously and she him. Rosebery had once boasted that he would someday win the Derby, become prime minister, and marry the richest heiress in England, and he eventually did all three.

For Sam, who loved to be loved, these visits to England proved the perfect tonic. On his return in 1880, he wrote Longfellow that he was "quite dazed by the overwhelming kindness I met at every corner." "Strange is it not," he wrote a few days later, "how much they made of me in England? . . . Lady Rosebery writes: 'We have done nothing but miss you.' And he [Rosebery] cabled yesterday, 'Return instantly!' " Sam was not exaggerating. Much *was* made of him by the British. After his visit in 1880, the London *Vanity Fair* ran a glowing article about him, complete with a drawing by the famous caricaturist "Spy," calling Sam, "The Prince of good livers, . . . a man of much experience, observation and wisdom. . . . He has seen much of life in the United States, and has himself often controlled legislation and decided the fate of important measures. His fund of anecdote is inexhaustible; his very presence in a room is enough to put everybody in a good humour."[14]

Sam returned the hospitality. He had always enjoyed squiring foreign visitors around New York and Washington, but now, with time and means, he became an unofficial cicerone to all sorts of visiting Brits. The same *Vanity Fair* article noted: "Every traveler to the United States whose lot has fallen in pleasant places is sure to have met with Samuel Ward, protector of the English and Uncle of the human race." British journalist George Augustus Sala was one of those whom Sam befriended. Sala had enjoyed a dinner at Delmonico's with Sam on a visit to New York in 1863. Back again in 1879, he found Sam as charming and his palate as discriminating as ever: "Whether he rolled logs, or ground axes, or was a lobbyist,

or a mugwump, or bull-dozed anybody, it was no business of mine to inquire."
Sala simply enjoyed Sam's company.[15]

In 1882, Sam received a great deal of press for his hand in introducing Oscar
Wilde to America. Sam had met Wilde in England, and, although he knew of his
outlandish behavior, he also knew that Wilde had studied with John Ruskin at
Oxford and had won the gold medal for Greek at Trinity College and the Newdi-
gate prize with his poem "Ravenna," all of which spoke in the young man's
favor.[16] When Wilde arrived in New York with a letter of introduction from Sam's
good friend Lord Houghton, the poet Monckton Milnes, who was occasionally
allowed to attend a Mendacious Club dinner, Sam welcomed him with open arms.
Sam marked the occasion with a poem, "The Aesthetic," published in Hurlbert's
New York World on January 4, 1882. It began:

> "Father, what is the aesthetic?" Asked a child.
> Puzzled, he said, "Ask the hermetic Oscar Wilde."[17]

Sam took Wilde everywhere in New York and gave several dinners in his
honor. He paired him with Evarts at one dinner and, at another, alluding to
Wilde's self-publicized obsession with the actress Lily Langtry, covered the banquet table with calla lilies, lilies of the valley, and water lilies. Marian Hooper
Adams, wife of Henry Adams, heard rumors about the latter evening all the way
in Washington and wrote her father of Wilde, "We are told that he was carried
home drunk in New York from a dinner given him by 'wicked Sam Ward' at which
a big bowl of punch bore floating lilies!" Both Adamses jokingly differentiated
between Sam Ward of New York and Washington, "wicked Sam Ward," and their
other friend, the more conventional Boston financier Samuel Gray Ward, "good
Sam Ward."[18]

After one five-hour dinner for Wilde hosted by Hurlbert, Sam described the
guest of honor to Maud: "His make-up is very extraordinary, long black hair
hanging to the shoulders, brown eyes, a huge white face like the pale moon . . . a
white waistcoat, black coat and knee breeches, black silk stocking and shoes with
buckles. Until he speaks you think him as uncanny as a vampire." Sam assured a
skeptical Barlow that Wilde had the "capacity to carry all the sail he spreads."[19]

When Wilde traveled to Boston, Sam persuaded Julia to entertain him. As word
got out, Brahmin Boston was scandalized. Author and moralist Thomas Went-
worth Higginson reprimanded Julia in an essay in the *Woman's Journal*, to which
Julia hotly retorted in the *Boston Transcript* that she had every right to entertain whom she pleased and Higginson had no right to say "who should and should

not be received in private houses."[20] As Wilde was about to begin a public lecture in Boston, about sixty Harvard students, mocking him by wearing black wigs, knee breeches, silk stockings, silver buckles, and holding lilies and sunflowers, marched in and caused a ruckus. Sitting in the audience, Julia and Marion Crawford both recognized Sam's grandson Winthrop Chanler among the ringleaders. Sam never mentioned the incident; Wilde was unfazed by it. On the eve of his departure from America, Wilde thanked Sam for all his kindness with a copy of his *Poems* inscribed, "L'art pour l'art, et mes poèms pour mon uncle."[21]

While busy bestowing presents and advice, traveling and being kind to travelers, Sam still found time for politics, politicians, and the lobby. The presidential campaign of 1880 was beginning to heat up just as Sam became a rich man, and, once again, his friend Bayard seemed to have a shot at the Democratic nomination. When Sam was in Washington, he and Bayard discussed strategy over brandy and cigars. When Sam was in New York, a steady stream of letters, some marked "confidential," charted the ups and downs of the run-up to the nomination.[22]

When Bayard lost the nomination to political neophyte General Winfield Scott Hancock at the Democratic convention in Cincinnati that summer, Sam commiserated, lashing out at the "frauds," "arch tricksters," and "flibbertigibbets" who let his friend down.[23] Sam was not sorry, however, when Hancock, whom he barely knew, lost to one of his favorite Republicans, James A. Garfield, that fall. On March 14, 1881, a few days after Garfield's inauguration, Sam happily wrote Julia: "I was detained in Washington by President Garfield's wish to see me. I called at the White House, had an affectionate reception. Everybody seemed glad to see me. Blaine [the new secretary of state] especially kind."[24]

Sam, like the rest of the nation, was horrified when Garfield was shot on July 2, 1881, and he alternated between hope and despair for the president's condition in his letters that summer. The newspapers made note of a one-hundred-year-old bottle of Jamaican rum that Sam sent to the president's sickroom and reported that the White House physicians swore that, added to milk toast, it had done the president good. When Garfield succumbed in September, Sam wrote Daisy that he was "cut up root and branch."[25]

Sam had known the new president, Chester A. Arthur, for years from New York politics, and judged him, more charitably than most, "a man of great practical experience and much ability." In December 1881, he wrote Julia that he was "most warmly welcomed" at the White House; and, while others condemned the expense, Sam noted approvingly that Arthur had "furnished the upper part of the White House most tastily, and for the first time since its erection it looks like a gentleman's habitation."[26] A few months later, he wrote Julia of an evening in

Washington unexpectedly spent with President Arthur at John Sutherland's restaurant, one of Sam's new haunts since the death of John Welcher: "Adolph Mailliard [Annie's husband] and I dined there and were sitting downstairs at the deserted bar counter. . . . he [John Sutherland] shortly returned with the President and two friends who came down to have a private look at the President's old camping ground. The cooks had all gone home, the fires were extinguished, but John contrived to get him a light, cold collation with which they appeared satisfied. This is all *sub rosa*, we did not break up until past 11 p.m."[27]

Sam remained close to Evarts, who served as secretary of state until 1881, when Garfield took office and replaced him with another friend, James G. Blaine. In marked contrast to his one-sided correspondence with Secretary of State Seward fifteen years earlier, letters between Sam and Evarts were warm and made it clear that Evarts valued Sam's skills. He asked Sam to learn what he could about the inner workings of the Prussian government, to check out gold mines in North Carolina as possible investments, to compose menus and choose wines for state dinners, and to find out what Frenchman Ferdinand de Lesseps was up to with his idea to build a canal across Panama. About the latter, he wrote Sam, "I know no one who can make this inquiry more completely and with less ostentation than yourself. . . . Any expense you are put to, send me a memorandum of."[28]

Sam's letters to Evarts, often accompanied by gifts of oysters or cranberries, sometimes asked favors for friends in return. Thanking Sam for one such gift, Evarts paid homage to the "King": "I received a basket of very nice peaches and pears from New York a few days ago without notice from whom. I suppose, as the peasants do, that all good gifts are from the king, that they come from you." When Evarts left office and traveled to England, he took with him a sheaf of letters of introduction from Sam, including one to Rosebery, that opened doors everywhere.[29]

Sam kept his hand in lobbying, sometimes spending as long as a month at a time in Washington, giving dinners several nights a week. He had the luxury to pick and choose only those projects that sounded interesting. He often worked for free, as a favor, but when potential new clients played on his vanity, claiming that only he could help them and begging for his unparalleled skills, his correspondence hinted that he still took on special jobs for pay.

Sam and Barlow saw much of each other now that Sam was ensconced in New York. When apart, their correspondence focused more on personal news (Barlow bragged about his children, Sam about his nephew, Marion) than on lobbying projects. But Sam still lobbied occasionally in Washington for him, and Barlow continued to send special, and especially lucrative, clients Sam's way. Barlow asked often about some large claims Sam was shepherding along for him and referred to one project involving a nickel mine out West and to another involving a gentleman with a project in Mexico, which only Sam could handle.[30]

Sam was missed in Washington by those who had been his frequent dinner guests, but also by those reporters who had enjoyed covering him and had looked forward to his quotable quotes. The "Life in Washington" column in the *Chicago Tribune* explained and lamented Sam's absence to its readers: "Sam Ward, that prince of gastronomy, no longer glides about with his pocket full of real Havana cigars, inviting Congressmen to those wonderful dinners. . . . He cured James Keene of dyspepsia, and the grateful stock-operator settled a competency on him. . . . His great delight used to consist in giving dinners to refractory Congress-men whose votes were needed by those who paid for the repast. . . . He is missed in Washington, for every one, from Sir Edward Thornton [the British minister] down to the correspondent of the Western luminary, used to enjoy his dinners, his reminiscences, and his rare conversational powers."[31]

While she detested lobbyists like Huntington, Emily Briggs missed Sam. She lamented the loss of his dinners, his good cheer, his vast trove of anecdotes. After informing her readers that he had come into a fortune and moved his base of operations to New York, she warned away any aspiring imitators: "The last time Sam Ward was seen he was marching across the Capitol Rotunda. . . . His round, chubby, boyish face and duck legs bore not the slightest resemblance to the lobby. He is the brother of Julia Ward Howe, the author of the Battle Hymn of the Republic. The same kind of spiritual essence that enters this poem made his dinners famous, but let no man attempt the same high art. The solitary vase has been broken, but the odor is left and clings to it still."[32]

In the summer of 1880, Sam's letters to Barlow and other friends had been filled with enthusiastic reports about his grand new moneymaking plan. With his windfall, he was backing two developers, whom he had only recently met but was certain were trustworthy, who were building a grand resort by the ocean at Long Beach on Long Island that would rival popular Long Branch, New Jersey. He had sought advice from no one, and, within a year, to no one's surprise but Sam's, the project was requiring more and more cash, while little seemed to be get-ting built.[33]

By early 1882, even Sam realized that he was in deep trouble. He wrote to Julia: "I am in low spirits in consequence of the dead weight of Long Beach and other enterprises I have to shoulder, and I freely declare to you that I have never been so wretched as since I got some money. . . . This is all *entre nous*." Julia's advice, much the same as she had offered in 1860 when she urged him to live quietly, was wise but, as then, futile: "I am so sorry for the ups and down of the financial world which toss your brilliant bark! Why not retire from Long Beach and all the rest, putting what you have in Boocock's [Samuel Boocock, a family friend] hands? You will be as much a Prince in private life, and without so much expense, as you now are, since nature has distinguished you as money never can."[34]

No doubt embarrassed to have squandered yet another fortune, just as his friends feared he might, Sam kept up a breezy banter about Long Beach to Barlow and others, saving his woes for Julia's ears: "Long Beach is a sore thing, into which I was hurried half dazed by bad men whom I thought good ones. However, I shall pull through, only I will confess I have never in my life endured such wretchedness."[35]

In the midst of this new financial misery, Longfellow died in Cambridge on March 24, 1882. Hurlbert sent word to Sam, who was dining at Sutherland's with Marion. Sam had seen that his old friend was failing when they had spent Thanksgiving together, but still the news was wrenching. He immediately wrote a lovely appreciation of his friend of half a century for Hurlbert's *World* and an even longer one for the *North American Review* and headed to Cambridge for "Longo's" funeral. He was, he wrote Daisy, "unhinged" by the snapping of one more tie to his past.[36]

By the fall of 1882, Sam was making "desperate efforts to extricate myself from all these business entanglements" and losing the battle.[37] He could not "pull through" on his own, and called on Julia for help. She reported to Annie, "Sam sent for me lately, and I passed most of the week at the Brevoort to be near him. Poor dear boy! I think he has income enough to make him comfortable even if he should lose most of his capital. [They] have fooled away most of the $500,000 which he lent them to start with." Julia was wrong about Sam being able to salvage anything. When he finally admitted his situation to Barlow, Hurlbert, and Duncan, who had begged to help him invest prudently, they found that not only was his final fortune, the security for his old age, gone, but Sam had foolishly signed papers making him liable for much more. In her *Reminiscences*, Julia summed up this tumultuous period in a sentence: "Quite late in life, he [Sam] enjoyed a turn of good fortune, and was most generous in his use of the wealth suddenly acquired, and alas! as suddenly lost."[38]

When he had hit bottom in 1849, Sam had bid adieu to New York, family, and friends and sailed west on a Pacific Mail steamer. This time, he slunk out of town by catching a ship bound for England, trying to throw creditors off his scent. In a hasty letter, he told only Julia: "By Hurlbert's advice I am off for Europe tomorrow. This is to avoid servance of process, as they intend to try and make me out a full partner, and, although the firm owes very little money, I don't want to get into the clutches of the law. I gave out that I was going to Boston, just to get away noiselessly. . . . I have sold all my furniture and books . . . and the rooms will be closed for the present. Best love to Maud. Not a word about my whereabouts."[39]

Maud Howe Elliott recalled the consternation Sam's letter caused her mother and Aunt Annie, as it sank in that their brother was on the lam, a fugitive from creditors. The sisters envisioned "Bro. Sam" leading a quiet, chastened life in exile, harboring his few remaining resources. Instead, Sam bobbed up in London unrepentant and was straightaway fêted by the Roseberys, old friends like William Howard Russell and Lord Houghton, and new friends whom he charmed. Soon he was writing jaunty letters back to Julia, who, Maud noted, received them sourly, telling of balls and dinners, staying up to all hours, weekends at country houses, a day at Ascot, chatting with the Prince of Wales, offering advice to Gladstone, and dropping the names of the dukes, duchesses, lords, and ladies whose company he did and did not enjoy.[40]

When Hurlbert, who left the *New York World* rather than work for its new owner Joseph Pulitzer, joined Sam in London, the two old friends were doubly entertaining and doubly entertained, with invitations piling up at their respective doors. Marion, who joined Sam in London and got caught up in the whirlwind, wrote his cousin Maud in astonishment: "You have no conception of what his life is like. I had five days of it, and never met anything less than a baron."[41]

After writing the Roseberys a sheaf of letters of introduction and seeing them off on a trip around the world in the fall of 1883, Sam moved on to join Louisa and her family, first in Sorrento and then in Rome. In Italy, Sam made Marion climb Mount Vesuvius with him; in Sorrento, Sam, just a few months shy of seventy, and Marion took to swimming far out from shore. Spring found Sam in Naples enjoying the pre-Lenten carnival. Suddenly, he became violently ill, possibly from tainted mussels. He staggered back to Rome, and Louisa wrote Julia that she despaired for his life. Sam refused the regimen a doctor prescribed, dictating instead his own recipes.[42]

In May, to escape the summer heat in Rome, Marion, Daisy, and the French nun Louisa had hired to nurse him, moved Sam to Pegli on the Riviera, but the change of scenery failed to revive him. On the morning of May 19, 1884, Sam dictated a light-hearted letter to Rosebery, his faithful "Sycophant," dozed, then whispered to Marion, "I think I am going to give up the ghost." Marion wrote that Sam had not been in pain—his heartbeat just grew more and more faint, then stopped. He died with a dog-eared volume of Horace beneath his pillow.[43]

The task of conveying the sad news was taken up by Marion, who sent tele-grams to the family and to Rosebery and Hurlbert. The latter arrived the next day to help bury his old friend and "President" and then described the scene to Rosebery: "In the little Protestant cemetery there was a vacant nook, shaded by noble ilex trees and oaks, alive with birds and bright with natural flowers. This was at once secured, and everything that must be done was done, not only without delay, but quietly and becomingly and tastefully. . . . There came to us a modest, simple little German pastor, friendly and unpretending, who . . . used the short, simple enough German service of the Lutherans over our dead, in the rich Ger-man tongue he loved."[44]

For Julia, who had so disapproved of Sam's lifestyle in exile, the blow hit hard. In a letter to Louisa, she reproached herself: "Now, I feel how little I appreci-ated his devotion, and how many chimeras, in my foolish wool-gathering head, crowded upon this most precious affection, which was worthy of a much larger place in my thoughts. . . . As I write, the tears come. . . . I believe he is in the heaven accorded to those who have loved their fellow-men, for who ever coined pure kindness into acts as he did?"[45]

Rosebery, back in London, was heartsick over not having seen Sam one last time. Bayard and Barlow consoled each other. Bayard responded to a note from Barlow on May 24, telling him how much it meant to him to write of their mutual friend: "*I wanted some one to feel as I did about him.* . . . Dear, kind old heart, may the recollections of his thoughtful, loving kindness bind together those who are to tarry here a little longer."[46]

Within days of Sam's passing, obituaries appeared in all the leading news-papers in London and America. The *Times* of London, the London *Saturday Review*, the *New York Tribune*, *New York Sun*, *New York Commercial Advertiser*, *New York World*, *New York Herald*, *New York Times*, plus newspapers in Washington, Boston, and Chicago, ran stories with headlines that read, "A Famous Lobbyist Dead," "Sam Ward—Exit," and, from the *National Police Gazette*, "Sam Ward's Career: His Adventures as a Lobbyist, Philosopher, Speculator, and Lover."[47]

Sam would have been highly gratified by so many inches of prose devoted to him. The *New York Times*'s obituary filled two entire columns with more than 4,000 words. He might have wished for more attention to his poetry and early scholarship and less to his failed second marriage and financial embarrassments, but the fact that so few mentioned his father or his genealogy would probably have pleased him. The *National Police Gazette*'s story began, "The announcement of the death of Samuel Ward, the son of Samuel Ward of the once famous banking house of Prime, Ward & King, has no meaning for this generation, but the demise of Sam Ward, King of the Lobby, will stir-up particular memories in many minds." Sam was his own man, and he had carved out his own path. After mentioning his twinkling eyes, his great bald head, his well-cut suits, and his sapphire ring, most of the obituaries focused on several overlapping aspects of Sam's life that made him unique: Sam as gastronomer and genial host, Sam as friend to the world, Sam as "pacificator," and, receiving the most ink, Sam as "King of the Lobby." That his own special brand of lobbying, his social lobbying, was as singular as Sam himself came through in all of the obituaries.

The *Boston Transcript,* in a lovely and fitting phrase, referred to Sam's "true hospitality of soul." He was, noted the *Times* of London, the "most charming of social companions and most genial of hosts." The *New York Tribune* described "the exquisite tact and bonhomie with which he fused heterogeneous elements, and sent every one away pleased alike with his host, his companions, and, chief of all, with himself. . . . The generous but dainty feasts by which he promoted intrigues and pushed claims upon the treasury left in the memory of the participants only the haunting aroma of unparalleled dishes, and the echoes of the best table-talk heard in the United States." Sam had "lived like a prince," the *New York Times* claimed, "entertaining all the brightest and most celebrated men of the country, treating all alike, indifferent to their politics or religion. . . . His gastronomical knowledge was his stock in trade, and upon it he lived like a potentate in Washington for nearly a score of years."

The *New York Herald* began its obituary by announcing "the death of everybody's friend, Sam Ward." "The long, long roll of his friendships," observed the *New York Times,* "would have filled columns if confined to the famous alone, and there were hundreds of the humble and unaspiring whose names were known only to himself." His obituaries claimed that Sam had friends on every continent. The *Saturday Review* of London praised him as being "of that class of Americans who, so to speak, bridge over the Atlantic—who help to make the New World intelligible to the Old, and the Old to the New." Among the many obituaries that referred to Sam's generosity to his friends, the *New York Commercial Advertiser* observed, "If by chance he possessed a thousand dollars in the morning, as he frequently did, by night he had not money enough to pay for a carriage. . . . as long as Sam Ward had a dollar, his friends could have ninety-nine cents of it."

Turning to Sam's career in the lobby, and using language that would have made Sam preen, several obituaries focused on the manner in which Sam had woven these attributes together to create the lobbying style that he had perfected.

The *New York Times* noted, "It was always claimed by his hosts of friends that, although an acknowledged lobbyist, he was not a corrupt man and that he never went beyond his gastronomic feats to influence legislation." The hallmark of Sam's lobbying work, the *Times* continued, was "reconciliation of hostile political factions by means of good dinners and social entertainments. . . . He soon became known as 'the King of the Lobby,' a title of which he was proud, and 'The Great Reconciler,' a name in which he took still greater delight. . . . He . . . gained an amazing influence in national affairs, which he turned to good account for those whom he favored." The "King of the Lobby . . . worked for the best," noted the *Boston Transcript*. "It can truthfully be said of him," claimed the *Washington Post*, "that he made his money without resorting to corrupt methods and spent it like a prodigal, without a prodigal's vices."

"Carp," the reporter Frank Carpenter, relayed word of Sam's death and many particulars of his colorful life to the thousands of readers of his Washington column: "Sam Ward, king of the Washington lobbyists, died this week in Italy, aged seventy-one [he was seventy]. It is five years since he has done any work here in Washington, but his name is still spoken and old politicians will tell stories by the hour of his marvelous dinners and his princely manners. For sixteen years his house was the favorite resort of statesmen, diplomats, and politicians; even the President now and then sat down at his table." Lest his readers mistake Sam for a common sort of lobbyist, "Carp" emphasized, "Sam Ward belonged to the higher class of lobbyists. His operations were on a grand scale and he dealt only with prominent men. He really had influence, and he did not stoop to petty means to gain his ends."[48]

As obituaries usually do, Sam's focused mostly on the pluses, not the minuses. Amid a positive assessment of Sam's life, the *Washington Post* noted that he had "failed to realize upon his intellectual resources, through want of fixedness of purpose," but that remark was mild and quite true. Only one obituary author took the opportunity to criticize Sam. The *New York World* was the lone spoiler. When Manton Marble and then Hurlbert had been at its helm, the *World* and Sam had been on friendly terms. Under Hurlbert's aegis especially, it had run many positive articles about and by Sam. But the new owner, Joseph Pulitizer, styled himself a man of the people, and for him, Sam—cultured, from a rich old family, and dead—was an easy target.

"Now that he is dead, the world may be said to have lost the most elegant spendthrift who ever lived," the *World*'s obituary began. Sam would have been deeply stung by the cheap shot that followed: "[His] first business stroke was characteristic of the history of the man. It was in marrying the daughter of William B. Astor. Practically, Sam Ward was a genteel adventurer all his life. His two marriages show it. . . . Sam Ward's powers decayed very fast, for in rapid succession he became the friend of Oscar Wilde, published a volume of poems, and died." (Sam had brought out a second edition of *Lyrical Recreations* in 1883.)

How to reconcile all of the disparate aspects of this man: loyal friend, doting uncle and brother, adventurer, gastronomer, spendthrift, poet, lover of Horace, *and* the "King of the Lobby"? It was, indeed, an odd assortment of ingredients that anyone but Sam might have found difficult to blend into a single savory dish. Obituary writers had no more success than Sam's relatives in summing up his life. Julia wrote Louisa that she had not the yardstick with which to measure his days. Marion, writing the particulars of Sam's death to his Aunt Julia, reflected on the conundrum that was his Uncle Sam. He did not think Sam was an atheist, but was not sure; he knew that others who lobbied in Washington were viewed with suspicion, but he had never heard Sam tarred with that brush; he finally concluded about the uncle he loved so much: "He died like a good man, and he was one."[49]

"What a puzzle in short was this universal favorite," concluded the *Tribune*'s obituary, "whom the sternest moralist could not find it in his heart to dislike, and the boldest lobby agent could yet call his comrade; who lived by arts which nobody can respect, and adorned a questionable life with so much amiability, so much refinement, so much good breeding!" While the *Tribune* failed in its long obituary to solve the puzzle, it did put its finger on Sam's most significant contribution to the lobby. It correctly concluded that Sam's "greatest achievement was establishing himself in Washington at the head of a profession which, from the lowest depths of disrepute, he raised almost to the dignity of a gentlemanly business." He had never been called corrupt or gross, never fell into obloquy as so many of his colleagues had. "He never resorted to vulgar bribery; he excelled rather in composing the enmities and cementing the rickety friendships which play so large a part in political affairs, and he tempted men not with the purse, but with banquets, graced by vivacious company, and the conversation of wits and people of the world."

Sam would no doubt have found this brief summing up of his life just, even complimentary, but it lacks the spice and flourishes he always favored. He was very fond of and might have enjoyed being eulogized with the lively portrait of his variegated life, closer to his own view of himself, painted in witty words by Rosebery on the eve of sailing back to England after the 1875 visit when the two had first become friends:

Uncle Samuel

Alas! my Samuel, when I think
I stand upon the Ocean's brink;
The time is near, full is my cup,
The buoyant *Russia*'s steam is up,
And I return, an unlicked cub,
Leaving the great "Mendacious Club";
Thy tales no more my mind shall fill,
And Hurlbert's brilliant voice be still! . . .

No more shalt thou approach my bed,
A bandit's hat upon thy head,
Beneath whose brim there beams an eye
That puts to shame the brilliant tie.
Beneath one arm a trout, alack!
The other holds a canvas-back.
The pockets bulge with products rare,—
French novels, prints and caviare,
Two manuscripts of odes and bets,
Old bills of fare and cigarettes,
Two thousand dollar notes,—ye gods!
Welcher's accounts, green pepper-pods,
And pressing calls to various duties,
From railways, senators and beauties.

And then, perhaps, thy bursting brain
Reveals its treasure-room again,
And recollections, lightly wove,
With tales of horror or of love,
Carry the list'ner swiftly through
From Cochin-China to Peru;
And further yet, as in a trance,
From memory sprightly to romance;
He hears thee clothe the arid fact
And scorn the fools who are exact!

He's borne aloft from Piccadilly
To California, willy-nilly;
He sees thee change, without a creak,

To banker, sportsman or cazique.
He sees thee read with deep emotion
The burial service in mid-ocean,
Or play, with one hand on thy knife,
A ruined miner, for thy life.

By Tennyson or Longo sought,
Probing a jockey's inward thought,
Counselling statesmen on finesse,
Counselling ladies on their dress,—
A wit, a scholar and a poet,
A rake we fear, a friend we know it;
It is the lion and the lamb,
And there's your portrait, Uncle Sam!

Some foolish fancy dims my eye,
As, for a time, I say "Goodbye!"[50]

EPILOGUE

Remembered fondly by family, friends, and total strangers; the lobby in Washington after Sam; Sam's chief and enduring legacy: the social lobby lives

S AM LAY beneath the ilex trees on an Italian hillside. All four of his children and both of his wives had predeceased him. His loving-kindness was foremost in the minds of those who mourned him and was reflected in the epitaph on the simple stone cross erected some months after his death, after much consultation, by three of them:

ARCHIBALD, EARL OF ROSEBERY

WILLIAM HENRY HURLBERT

FRANCIS MARION CRAWFORD

IN LOVING REMEMBRANCE OF

SAMUEL WARD

BORN NEW YORK, U.S.A., JAN. 27, 1814

DIED AT PEGLI, MAY 19, 1884

And God gave him largeness of heart even as the sands on the seashore[1]

Sam was remembered by many. Julia, Louisa, and Annie never failed to remember his birthday in their letters. Sam's grandson, Winthrop "Wintie" Chanler, who, despite the Astors' best efforts, was very much like his grandfather in temperament, visited Julia in the weeks after his death to learn more about him. Wintie's marriage to Louisa's daughter Daisy Terry, his first cousin once removed, in 1886 would have pleased Sam.

The wedding in 1887 of his niece Maud Howe and the young Scottish painter John Elliott also would have delighted Sam, who had actively nudged the two together. Fifty years after his death, Maud wrote of her Uncle Sam: "Heady, intoxicating, the very memory of him—half a century dead—stirs me as no living being has the power to do. He drank deep of life, was intoxicated with it!" Still another adoring niece, Maud's sister Laura, remembered her Uncle Sam as "the soul of generosity, the essence of wit, the spirit of kindliness. . . . He came into the house like light."[2]

In 1937, Maud and Sam's granddaughter Alida Chanler Emmet hired a driver to take them to the little Protestant cemetery in Pegli, where they laid an armful of red roses on Sam's grave. He would have been touched by this lovely gesture, but he would have appreciated even more an earlier tribute from two of his grandsons. Wintie and one of his brothers had made the same pilgrimage, but, instead of flowers, they took with them the finest bottle of wine they could find. After each had drunk deeply, they emptied the bottle onto Sam's grave.[3]

Sam had been allowed to do little for his grandchildren while he lived, but his name aided several of his grandsons after his death. Their Astor guardians, fearing they would squander the money coming to them, gave the boys very little spending money; so, as college students, they were always strapped for cash. Their guardians did, however, allow them unlimited credit at certain respectable New York establishments, among them Delmonico's. Sam's name was still golden at the restaurant he had always promoted, and the new generation of Delmonicos was happy to accommodate Sam's grandsons by becoming their informal banking house, charging their guardians for dinners never eaten and turning over the cash to the young Chanlers.[4]

Sam's name was, and still is, memorialized in an unusual and appropriate way. For years, bar patrons enjoyed "Sam Wards," a drink Sam invented (cracked ice in a glass, with a thin peel of lemon laid around the inside, and yellow Chartreuse), even if they did not know its namesake. That the recipe, slightly modified, is still featured, along with a brief biography of Sam, in *Esquire* magazine's cocktail database, and that Columbia University students and alumni, members of Sam's revived Philolexian Society, still raise their "Sam Wards" high on special occasions would please him enormously. That menus at the Union Club, the Down Town Club, and other New York restaurants featured dishes *à la Sam Ward* until at least World War II might please him even more. Boston's Somerset Club and Loche Ober restaurants carried one of Sam's signature chicken dishes on their menus into the 1990s, and patrons of the Algonquin Club there still request *Chicken Sauté Sam Ward.*[5]

Sam's writings fared less well than his recipes. Without him to distribute free copies of *Lyrical Recreations* to all he met, Sam's poetry dropped from sight, and his early scholarly papers on mathematics and history were largely forgotten. His name did, however, live on in the writings of others, and it frequently popped up posthumously in articles about high society and gracious living.

Through the mid-1890s, Sam was often remembered in New York society columns, usually in articles about his pompous younger cousin, Ward McAllister, whom he had tutored in the culinary arts and who, as the whitest of white sheep, was wary of being too closely linked with Sam, the gray sheep of the family. By 1888, McAllister had already been battling for more than two decades to prevent the disintegration of polite society. He was the self-appointed Cerberus guarding the gates against the nouveaux riches trying to buy their way into the old elite. That year, McAllister had informed a reporter that "there are only about four hundred people in fashionable New-York society. If you go outside that number you strike people who are either not at ease in a ball-room or else make other people not at ease." The press pounced on the phrase. Who were "The Four Hundred"? Although begged and badgered to name them, McAllister remained silent.[6]

Although Sam and Ward McAllister had both started out with impeccable pedigrees, the cousins' lives had taken different paths. Ironically, for each, there were Astors at the crossroads. Had Emily Astor lived, Sam might well have enjoyed much happiness, great riches, and a guaranteed rung high up on the social ladder. As it was, after Emily's death, Sam earned the Astors' everlasting enmity by his second marriage, lost his daughter to them, lost his money, and set off on the path that would make him "King of the Lobby." McAllister's unlikely star rose because he had hitched his wagon to the Astors, specifically to Mrs. William Backhouse Astor, Jr. (Caroline Webster Schermerhorn Astor, Sam's former sister-in-law, *the* Mrs. Astor by the mid-1880s), whose ambition to dominate New York's high society McAllister helped her realize.

By the time McAllister's fatuous memoir, *Society As I Have Found It*, appeared in 1890, his standing as the defender of social exclusivity was declining. That he sounded like a conceited prig from first page to last and offended people right and left did not help. (A parody was published, called *Society As It Has Found Me Out*.) His descent accelerated the following year when he agreed to give a dinner party for, of all people, Collis Huntington, the ruthless old "devil fish" of the lobby, and his second wife, who were desperately seeking admittance into New York society. Huntington had, it turned out, agreed to pay McAllister $9,000 for entry into "The Four Hundred"; but, once invited to the ultraexclusive "Patriarchs' Ball" and introduced to Mrs. Astor, he refused to pay up. Indignant, McAllister threatened to sue and spoke rashly to a reporter. Both men were humiliated when the details leaked into the gossip columns.[7]

The next year, possibly hoping to revive interest in himself, on the occasion of Mrs. Astor's annual ball, McAllister finally reeled off his list of the "The Four Hundred." When it was printed, in most of the city's sixteen newspapers, everyone noticed that it contained only 319 names (and some of those individuals were already dead). Nevertheless, every name was scrutinized, which led to the resurrection of the story of Sam, Emily, Maddie, and the "Astor orphans" once again.

The only Ward family members on the list were Ward McAllister and his daughter, Louise Ward McAllister, but four of Sam's grandchildren and one of his nieces were among "The Four Hundred." Mr. and Mrs. Winthrop Chanler, Sam's grandson Wintie and his niece Daisy, were thirty-fourth on the alphabetical list. Thirty-fifth were "The Misses Chanler," three of Sam's heiress granddaughters, Elizabeth Winthrop Chanler, Margaret Livingston Chanler, and Alida Beekman Chanler, who were being presented to society that year by Daisy.[8]

By the time McAllister died in 1895 at 67, he had slipped from his high place in society. Cartoonists had stopped lampooning him, and he was more ignored than ridiculed. Mrs. Astor, his "Mystic Rose," at the peak of her powers in large part due to McAllister's tireless efforts, could not be bothered to attend his funeral. He would not have been pleased to know that nearly all of his obituaries also mentioned Sam.

In the late 1940s, Sam's name cropped up again, this time linked to a tantalizing historical mystery. In 1879, the North American Review ran four installments of "The Diary of a Public Man, Unpublished Passages of the Secret History of the American Civil War," which purported to be entries from a diary kept by someone in Washington and New York from December 28, 1860, through March 15, 1861. The diarist had remarkable access to prominent Republicans and Democrats from both North and South, who talked to him freely, valued his good opinion, and sought his advice during that tense secession winter.[9]

Was the diary genuine? Who was its author? Readers looked for clues in every sentence. Dozens of names were tossed about, including those of Thurlow Weed, Henry Adams, Hamilton Fish, and Allen Thorndike Rice, the Review's editor. Later, some historians would cite the "Diary" as an authentic source, although others were wary and still others continued to scour archives, trying to solve the puzzle. The most dogged researcher was Frank Maloy Anderson. In The Mystery of "A Public Man," published in 1948, Anderson concluded that the entries were not from a genuine diary recorded in 1860–1861 but perhaps had the kernel of a real diary at their heart. Anderson developed criteria by which to isolate the author, applied them to dozens of names, including reporter Ben Perley Poore and Lincoln's private secretary, John Hay, and came up with a match. The author of the "Diary of a Public Man," Anderson was certain, was Sam Ward.

While Anderson's conclusions caused a flurry of renewed interest in Sam, and, while, superficially, Sam did seem to meet many of the criteria, Anderson was wrong. Sam loved intrigue and aliases (Pedro Fernández, Carlos López), but he was not the "Public Man." In December 1860, Sam had been in Washington little more than a year, having spent the better part of the previous decade in California and Central and South America. For a newcomer, he had many important friends in the capital, but he was hardly an insider to whom someone like Stephen A. Douglas would turn for policy advice. Sam made no secret of the fact that he was a Democrat, so he was also not likely to be privy to behind-the-scenes Republican politicking. Furthermore, while Sam had once been a financier, his financial woes were well known: he was not a man on whom to rely for his economic savvy.

Sam was also plenty busy in the winter of 1860–1861, looking after Paraguay's interests, doing jobs for Barlow and other clients by day, and spending his nights organizing the first of his dinners at the little house on F Street. In mid-January, he had also begun acting as intermediary between Seward and Gwin, and, as "Midas, Jr.," churning out several thousand words of action-packed prose each week for *Porter's Spirit of the Times*. And if, as Anderson suspected, the diary was embellished or invented in the mid-1870s, Sam was busy then, too, scratching, as he told Julia, harder than ever for a dollar. Even if Rice was paying handsomely, such a project would have required time and deep concentration, neither of which Sam had ever had. Finally, Sam, who loved to drop names, could never have kept the activities described by the "Public Man" a secret. Even, for instance, if he did not share their enthusiasm for President Lincoln, Sam could not have met with Lincoln three times without bragging of it to Julia and Longfellow, knowing how such encounters would elevate him in their eyes.

Anderson's conclusions continue to be challenged, most recently and most thoroughly by historian Daniel Crofts, who argues that the "diary," while possibly based on some actual events and incorporating some material written in 1860–1861, was actually a clever, after-the-fact construct written shortly before publication. After extensive research and a stylometric analysis of the diarist's word choice, word frequency, and style, Crofts identifies a new author—Sam's brilliant and erratic friend William Henry Hurlbert. Others had glanced at Hurlbert and rejected him. He was just thirty-three in 1860 and already a deeper-dyed

Democrat than Sam, but he was also charming, well-traveled, and well-connected. Crofts offers a great deal of evidence to support his claims and to suggest that both Sam and Rice may have had a hand in helping Hurlbert create the "diary." Whether or not Hurlbert was the "Public Man" and whether or not Sam knew it or helped him, it would undoubtedly have delighted Sam no end to have his name bandied about as part of the speculation that endures more than six score years after his death.[10]

Sam's name has also lived on in articles about the lobby. A 1913 article in the *Nation* noted that "Sam Ward was everywhere recognized as king of the lobby. . . . Not only did he make no secret of his calling, but he established for it a sort of ethical code which he was never loath to expound."[11] Far more important than his name, however, Sam's spirit lives on in the lobby. Whenever lobbyists, clients, and congressmen meet over an excellent meal or share a bottle of good wine—occasions now more circumscribed because of restrictions that would have mystified and annoyed Sam—or enjoy an informal conversation at a select reception, he is there, even though none present may know his name.

The evolution of lobbying after the "King" abdicated can be quickly outlined. Collis Huntington "trolled in Congressional waters" for several years after Sam decamped. Sidney Dillon and Jay Gould continued to pay top dollar for the services of William E. Chandler and Grenville Dodge into the 1880s. For lobbyists tightly tied to the Republicans like Uriah Painter, Democrat Grover Cleveland's election to the White House in 1884 was a blow. One of Painter's compatriots wrote him, "We must clean up all we can before the 4th of March for after that time it will be dry picking in Washington."[12]

The press corps adopted new rules in the House and Senate in 1879 and 1884 to police themselves and cut down on egregious lobbying by journalists.[13] "Lobbyesses" became fixtures in Washington; in 1888, after a careful study of American government, Englishman James Bryce concluded that women were "widely employed and efficient" at lobbying.[14] Both lobbyists and lobbyesses continued to be the brunt of parody and denigration in fiction: Charles T. Murray's *Sub Rosa* (1880), Frances Hodgson Burnett's *Through One Administration* (1883), and Henry James's short story "Pandora" (1884) featured lobbyists of both sexes. The best of the new novels, Henry Adams's *Democracy*, charted the course of several slippery lobbyists; but one, who resembled Sam, escaped Adams's harsh censure. "Mr. Schneidekoupon" of New York brought clients and congressmen together over dinners at "Welckley's."

Through the end of the century, newspapers, journals, and magazines occasionally took shots at the lobby. There was, however, an important change in the tone of many of these articles beginning in the 1880s, as the depression eased, the high tide of scandal receded and Congress, political parties, and the federal government got better organized. There were fewer forecasts of the death of democratic government at the hands of lobbyists and more suggestions that the lobby might be legitimate, even useful.

In 1882, "Carp" assured his readers that "much of the lobbying here is legitimate and honorable." Remember, he chided, that "a man who seeks to influence legislation by convincing Congressmen of the best way to vote, by arguments only, is also called a lobbyist."[15] Englishman Bryce agreed. He concluded that the hysteria over corruption and lobbying in the 1870s had probably been overblown, and in any case, because a better organized Congress was now more effectively meeting constituent demands and thereby unclogging the system, the lamentations of pundits were no longer justified. Bribery, Bryce declared, "exists in Congress, but is confined to a few members, say five per cent of the whole number," and that he seemed to find perfectly acceptable. He urged Americans to remember "that in a new and large country . . . conditions are not the most favourable to virtue."[16] The author of a letter to the editor in *Century Illustrated Magazine* in 1886 took Frances Hodgson Burnett to task for her negative portrayal of lobbyists in her novel *Through One Administration* and defended the practice: "There are some subjects on which senators and members may with propriety be enlightened. They cannot know everything."[17]

Several articles argued for making right what was wrong with the lobby, but after the flurry of activity in the 1870s, little happened in the way of lobby reform on the federal level for the rest of the century (although the states were hotbeds of reform activity). The new century, however, brought several investigations into lobbying, as muckrakers and Progressives like David Graham Phillips and Senator Robert LaFollette of Wisconsin worked from outside and inside Congress to reveal abuses of the public trust. In 1913, President Woodrow Wilson lambasted lobbyists for the National Association of Manufacturers (N.A.M.) and other protectionists for opposing his efforts to lower tariff schedules. Wilson, a historian himself who was fully aware of the excesses of the Gilded Age, fumed, "Washington has seldom seen so numerous, so industrious, or so insidious a lobby. . . . There is every evidence that money without limit is being spent to sustain this lobby."[18]

That same year, a sensational front-page article in the *New York World* shocked Americans who had forgotten or were too young to remember the lobby scandals of the 1870s. Colonel Martin M. Mulhall, a lobbyist for the N.A.M., claimed that he had paid a congressman $2,000 in return for legislative favors. Testimony from the investigation that followed revealed that not only had Mulhall set up his own private office in the Capitol, but he paid the House's chief page $50 a month for inside information from the cloakrooms and had paid House members for information on pending legislation.[19]

More revelations and investigations in the 1920s and 1930s led to several piecemeal efforts at reform, but the first far-reaching lobby-regulatory legislation, the Federal Regulation of Lobbying Act, was passed in 1946 as part of the sweeping Legislative Reorganization Act. This landmark legislation did not restrict lobbyists, but it did require two important things of them: (1) that they register with the clerk of the House or the secretary of the Senate and name their employers, and (2) that they file quarterly financial reports stating the amount and sources of their income and describing their lobby activities.[20]

Although it was almost immediately dubbed "more loophole than law," the Federal Regulation of Lobbying Act not only acknowledged the legitimacy of the lobby but was the beginning of serious efforts to make it more transparent and to end its grossest abuses. A host of congressional investigations into lobbying practices have taken place in the decades since—into lobbying by retired military officers and foreign lobbyists in the 1950s and '60s, "Koreagate" in the late '70s, "Abscam" and investigations into activities of aides to President Ronald Reagan in the '80s, foreign money and campaign finance abuses in the '90s, and into the activities of lobbyist Jack Abramoff as the twentieth-first century opened. Hearings have resulted in continuing efforts, most notably the Lobbying Disclosure Act of 1995 and a sweeping package of changes to lobbying laws and to internal House and Senate ethics rules known as the Honest Leadership and Open Government Act of 2007, to plug up loopholes and keep up with changes in Congress, the culture, and the lobby itself.[21]

As the hearings into Samuel Colt's and the Pacific Mail Steamship Company's lobbying did in the nineteenth century, the twentieth- and twenty-first-century investigations have revealed much about changes in the lobby, such as in its size. Just as the number of lobbyists mushroomed after the Civil War, it jumped again after another calamity, the Great Depression, and for some of the same reasons, mainly increases in federal spending and expansion of the government's authority into areas in which a change in federal policy could spell success or failure, fortunes won or lost, for a host of special interests. Lobbyists' numbers spiked again in the 1970s, when a series of congressional reforms weakened the seniority system, increased the power of subcommittees, and decentralized power on Capitol Hill, changes that multiplied the people to be contacted and access points to be covered and spawned a proliferation of large, multifaceted lobbying firms, trade associations, and corporate lobbying offices.

By 1979, just as doctors and dentists had done more than a century earlier, lobbyists banned together to establish their own professional association, the American League of Lobbyists (ALL), with a code of ethics and a certification program. Gilded Age reporters had been alarmed when they estimated lobbyists to number in the hundreds in Washington in the 1870s; by 2007, there were 2,744 lobbying firms and 31,193 lobbyists registered to represent 12,762 clients in the capital, with thousands more lobbyists falling outside the guidelines for registration but lobbying just the same.[22]

Hearings have also made clear that, while some aspects of the lobby have remained constant, others have changed. The importance of access, for example, for a lobbyist's success has never diminished, while that of accurate information has increased. To be on a first-name basis with members of Congress, many of whom may also be old friends or colleagues, is still an asset, but so are well-researched reports, speeches ready for presentation on the Senate floor, and lists of possible cosponsors at the ready. A lobbyist's all-important foot in a congressperson's door is more often used to make a client's case with facts and figures than with the modern equivalents of Colt's revolvers or Huntington's railroad passes, although, as the Abramoff investigations made clear, a few lobbyists still find members of Congress who rise to the bait of golfing trips to Scotland and sky boxes at sporting events.

So where is Sam's hand still seen in the lobby that has evolved over the century and a quarter that he has been gone? Sam enjoyed access: important doors opened to him all around town. He had expertise: with his prodigious memory, he had vast amounts of timely information at his finger-tips. But so did others. These were not the assets that set him apart from other Gilded Age lobbyists or helped him expand the definition of what it meant to lobby. It was what Sam did for his clients after hours and away from Capitol Hill, and how he did it, that made him unique and constitutes his chief and enduring contribution to the lobby. Sam was in the vanguard of the social lobby, and it is his lobbying by means of entertaining that is his legacy.

Sam's select lobby dinners at Welcher's in the 1870s, with each course and each seating assignment carefully planned, were much like lobbyist Jack Abramoff's lobby dinners in the 1990s at the lavishly appointed Signatures restaurant on Pennsylvania Avenue, just a few blocks from Sam's old haunt. The main difference, which Sam might have envied, was that Abramoff *owned* Signatures. Sam certainly would have appreciated Signatures' Villeroy & Boch china and the flat-ware from Christofle, both old European firms already known for elegance in Sam's day.

Sam did not invent the social lobby—in 1790 William Maclay had groused about the merchants who were wining and dining his congressional colleagues— but Sam perfected it. No one had ever used canvas-back ducks and Maryland terrapin to lobby as systematically, with as much forethought, or to better effect than Sam. Aside from the time he delayed a congressman's arrival for a vote by causing the man's boots to be mislaid, Sam never used dirty tricks or bribery to win his ends. He used fine dinners and good conversation. Carefully crafted evenings where, as he said, his guests went home pleased with themselves and each other, were Sam's supremely effective lobbying tactic.

Sharp-eyed reporter Emily Briggs had recognized and admired Sam's unique style of lobbying, and she was certain that only he had elan enough to pull it off. She had warned away all who would attempt to follow in his footsteps: "let no man attempt the same high art." But Briggs's admonition fell on deaf ears, as anyone familiar with the pragmatic lobby could have told her it would. When outright bribes of cash were found to work, lobbyists offered more of them; when stock certificates bought votes, lobbyists passed out stacks of them. And when genteel entertainments got results for Sam, it did not go unnoticed. Here was a fresh arrow for lobbyists to add to their quivers. So, of course, many a man and many a woman did attempt the same high art.[23]

Some of them found that the methods of the social lobby were not for them; the results were and are subtle, often intangible, usually deferred, and rarely closely linked to specific legislation. Collis Huntington, Colonel Mulhall, and their successors were too impatient to wait for the warm glow of friendship, nurtured over many dinners and glasses of wine, to shine eventually in their favor. The careful cultivation of contacts and potential allies who might prove useful in the future was not their style, but it was definitely Sam's. It was this addition to the lobbyist's bag of tricks—social lobbying—that made Sam, not Grenville Dodge, not Collis Huntington, the "King of the Lobby" and that has long out-lived his other works, like *Lyrical Recreations*. While there have been many potential aspirants for Sam's crown over the years, no man or woman has won it. There have been and there are princes and princesses of the lobby, but no king or queen. As a man who deep down was vain and insecure, Sam would be grateful for that.

By the 1890s, the social lobby was in full bloom, and reporters covered it avidly. A 1906 guidebook to Washington informed readers, "Men who wish to push a

measure through Congress will sometimes take a house here and entertain roy-
ally for a month or two."[24] The 1913 investigation into the frenzied lobbying over
tariff schedules that had so angered President Wilson revealed that much of the
money spent by both high-tariff and low-tariff lobbyists had gone for entertaining.

Magazine articles and serious scholarly works examined how the social lobby
worked. A 1927 article entitled "Lawmaking by Means of Dinners" explained that,
"after a Senator new to the ways of Washington has sat about an evening or two in
the company of delightful folk having social and financial distinction, he is half
ashamed to find that his views and theirs are not in accord. He thinks to himself:
'These are wonderfully fine people and they don't agree with my views. Maybe
I'm wrong.'"[25] Writing about the ways of the social lobby, political scientist Pendleton Herring noted in 1929 that business and measures before Congress were
not discussed at its entertainments at all. Rather, the attempt was made to introduce persons of like thoughts, to "break down animosities by bringing political
enemies together in a friendly social atmosphere." Sam could not have said it
better himself.[26]

Nearly three-quarters of a century later, new hearings into lobbying activities
confirmed that the social lobby is still alive and well in Washington. So well, so
important, and so effective, in fact, that dinners and entertaining were specifically
singled out for special rules in the 1995 Lobbying Disclosure Act, rules that were
tightened further in 2007. One can almost hear Sam sputter with indignation
upon learning that neither members nor their aides can accept free meals from
registered lobbyists.

Despite tighter rules and closer scrutiny, the social lobby endures. It endures in
part because loopholes (such as the "toothpick rule"—food served on toothpicks,
rather than on plates, does not constitute a meal—and the "reception exception"—
members may still attend events where at least twenty-five people who are not
congressmen or congresswomen are present) endure. But the social lobby lives on
primarily because, as Sam, "the gastronomic facilitator," shrewdly recognized
when he arrived in the capital in 1859, bringing people together over good food,
wine, and conversation remains a fruitful way to "break down animosities," make
a point, and conduct business. What was a sure-fire *plan de campagne* for Sam is
often a successful strategy still.

The skills that were Sam's currency during the Gilded Age and those of many
of today's successful lobbyists are of the same metal. Sam almost certainly could
slip into a well-appointed office at one of today's top public relations firms on K
Street and, in his well-cut suit, armed with statistics and a BlackBerry, make the
rounds on Capitol Hill by day and, dressed in a dinner jacket with his diamond

studs and sapphire ring, host and lobby at receptions, dinners, and benefits by night.

Sam would be happy to see that the social lobby, while just one of many avenues leading to influence in Washington, is still going strong and that entertaining remains an important opportunity for communication in the capital. As Arthur Schlesinger, Jr., another keen observer of Washington, noted a hundred years after Sam's death, exaggerating just a bit as Sam was wont to do, "Every close student of Washington knows half the essential business of government is still transacted in the evening . . . where the sternest purpose lurks under the highest frivolity."[27] Sam's art was to guarantee that the men and women who enjoyed his *noctes ambrosianae* never focused on the purpose that lurked beneath his perfectly poached *poisson*.

ACKNOWLEDGMENTS

Sam, who lived and breathed graciousness, loved giving gifts—ripe peaches, lustrous pearls, fine Madeira. His generosity of spirit has been inherited by those of his descendants, direct and collateral, and even by the spouses of descendants, whose paths have crossed with mine. J. Winthrop Aldrich, Sam's great-great-grandson, kindly shared not only family lore but many of the images from the Astor family archives at Rokeby in Barrytown-on-Hudson in New York that appear in this book with his permission. When I first met the late Deborah Clifford, who was both Sam's great-great-granddaughter and great-niece (her grandfather was Sam's grandson Wintie Chanler and her grandmother was Louisa's daughter Daisy), she said that she had something to show me. As she carefully unwrapped a miniature of little Sam, Louisa, and Annie passed down through generations to her, she told me the family stories that had been passed down with it. Her biography of her great-aunt, *Mine Eyes Have Seen the Glory: A Biography of Julia Ward Howe*, has been most helpful, and her enthusiasm for me to write Sam's most encouraging.

Julia Terry, another of Louisa's great-granddaughters, not only shared family stories but brought along to our first lunch a little sack. When she shook it, out fell Sam's beautiful sapphire and diamond ring, which still glitters with the same fire it gave off when he testified before the House Ways and Means Committee in 1875. She urged me to slip it on, and there I sat with Sam's ring—the ring that had graced his right hand through thick and thin for so many years—on my hand. For that electric moment and for her enthusiasm for this project, I can't thank her enough. Monk Terry, Julia's brother, also gave me information about the Ward family. This included the news that the handsome portrait of a pensive Sam wearing his sapphire ring, painted by John Elliott in 1884, of which I have only a poor reproduction, was stolen from his parents' home years ago, and the happier news that a new little Julia was born into the family in 2007.

Many of Annie Ward Mailliard's descendants still live in the San Francisco area, and several kindly responded to my query as to the whereabouts of a lovely portrait of a young, carefree Sam in Dresden in 1836. They steered me to Mrs. William Mailliard, the widow of Annie's great-grandson, the late congressman William S. Mailliard, who not only confirmed that the painting hangs in her dining room but graciously allowed me to reproduce it here.

Perhaps it was Sam's beneficent ghost hovering over all of the librarians and archivists who care for the tangible remains of his life—his letters to Barlow marked "On the □," his correspondence with "Longo" and "Dearest Dudie," his poems—that made them all so accommodating. My thanks go to the staff of the following institutions who generously shared their collections and their expertise: the Huntington Library, the Manuscript Division and the Prints and Photographs Division of the Library of Congress, the New York Public Library, the New-York Historical Society, Columbia University Archives, the Frick Art Reference Library, New Hampshire Historical Society, Carey Library in Lexington, Massachusetts, and to all of the staff but especially to Anita Israel at the Longfellow National Historical Site in Cambridge, Massachusetts.

Many at Harvard University have given me invaluable gifts for which I am deeply appreciative. The staff at Houghton, Widener, and Lamont Libraries helped me mine their riches. My colleagues at the Schlesinger Library at Harvard's Radcliffe Institute have listened to stories about Sam for years and offered good cheer, encouragement, and help with translations, scanning, and elusive sources. Nancy Cott, Pforzheimer Foundation Director of the Schlesinger Library and Jonathan Trumbull Professor of American History at Harvard, and Marilyn Dunn, the library's executive director, have been unfailingly supportive. A Bryant Fellowship in 2003 and an Extended Professional Development Opportunity grant in 2007–8, both generous programs available to Harvard library staff, gave me the gifts of travel and time for research and writing.

Daniel W. Crofts, whose forthcoming book is titled *A Secession Crisis Enigma: William Henry Hurlburt and "The Diary of a Public Man,"* kindly shared with me his innovative efforts to unmask the diary's author. Tom Vinciguerra provided information about Sam and Columbia University's Philolexian Society and the delightful news that current members and alumni of the "Philo" still lift their "Sam Wards" high in toasts each year. Jeff Kleinman of Folio Literary Management and Robert J. Brugger and Anne Whitmore of the Johns Hopkins University Press win prizes for patience and understanding. My thanks go to them all.

Sam was often in debt. At times, he owed money—a lot of it—to many people, and he sometimes skipped town to dodge his obligations. I've accumulated debts, too—debts of gratitude—in the course of writing about Sam's life and the lobby, and I am quite happy to acknowledge them here. I am indebted to Jean Baker, whose courses at Goucher College turned me into a history major, and to the late John Higham, my Ph.D. advisor at Johns Hopkins University, who, from the beginning, saw in Sam Ward's life a tale worth telling. I am grateful to many, many good friends and colleagues for their kindness, support, and advice over many years. Special thanks go to Susan Ware, whose books are models of how to write about a life and its times, Marshall A. Cohen, Polly Jo Kemler, and Katherine Kraft, who read the manuscript and whose collective critique improved every page.

My greatest debt of gratitude is to my family. Sam loved his family dearly, and it was to them that he gave, in addition to rugs, a ranch, and Rieslings, intangible gifts of his time and attention. My own family—my mother, Doris Allamong; my husband, Robert Jacob; my daughters, Charlotte and Annie; and my son-in-law, Daniel Fixler, who joined our family midway through this project—all of whom I love dearly, have given me time to write, their attention as they have patiently listened to yet one more story about Sam, and, as Sam would surely appreciate, plenty of good dinners. I am very, very grateful to them and for them.

NOTES

Ward Papers, Houghton   Samuel Ward (1814–1884) Papers, Houghton Library, Harvard
                         University, Cambridge, MA
WEC   William E. Chandler
WHS   William Henry Seward
WME   William M. Evarts

INTRODUCTION

1. SW to HWL, January 25, 1875, HWLL.

2. John Forney, *Anecdotes of Public Men* (New York: Harper & Brothers, 1873), 394.

3. Emily Edson Briggs, *The Olivia Letters* (New York: Neal Publishing, 1906), 91.

4. George Alfred Townsend, *Washington, Outside and Inside* (Hartford, CT: Betts & Co., 1873), 75.

5. Everit Brown and Albert Strauss, eds., *The Dictionary of American Politics* (New York: A. L. Burt, 1892), 315.

6. *Vanity Fair*, January 10, 1880.

7. *Vanity Fair*, January 10, 1880; Henry Adams, *The Education of Henry Adams* (1918; reprint, New York: Modern Library, 1931), 253.

8. SW to JWH, March 6, 1860, HFP, Houghton.

CHAPTER ONE

1. The following works chronicle the life of Daniel Sickles and the Sickles-Key affair and its aftermath: Nat Brandt, *The Congressman Who Got Away With Murder* (Syracuse, NY: Syracuse University Press, 1991); Thomas Keneally, *American Scoundrel: The Life of the Notorious Civil War General Dan Sickles* (New York: Doubleday, 2002); W. A. Swanberg, *Sickles the Incredible* (New York: Charles Scribner's Sons, 1956); *Trial of the Hon. Daniel E. Sickles for Shooting Philip Barton Key* (New York: R. M. DeWitt, 1859).

2. *Washington Evening Star*, February 27–March 4, 1859; Virginia Clay-Clopton, *A Belle of the Fifties: Memoirs of Mrs. Clay of Alabama* (New York: Doubleday, Page, 1904), 96–97.

3. *Trial of the Hon. Daniel E. Sickles*, 42.

4. *Washington Evening Star*, April 4–27, 1859; *National Intelligencer*, February–April 1859.

5. The Gwins' $75,000 would be the equivalent of about $1,500,000 in 2000. Arthur Quinn, *The Rivals: William Gwin, David Broderick, and the Birth of California* (New York: Crown Publishers, 1994), 229–30; Clay-Clopton, *A Belle*, 86.

6. Clay-Clopton, *A Belle*, 126–37; *Harper's Weekly*, April 24, 1858; *Washington Evening Star*, April–May 1858, and April 1859.

7. Lately Thomas [Robert Steele], *Sam Ward, "King of the Lobby"* (Boston: Houghton Mifflin, 1965), 239; Mary Elizabeth Wilson Sherwood, "Washington Before the War," *Lippincott's Monthly Magazine*, August 1894.

8. Constance Green, *Washington: A History of the Capital, 1800–1950* (Princeton: Princeton University Press, 1962), vol. 1, 21, 179–80; Elliott Coues and D. Webster Prentiss,

Avifauna Columbiana (Washington, DC: Smithsonian Institution, 1883), quoted in Frank Graham, Jr., *Potomac: The Nation's River* (Philadelphia: J. B. Lippincott, 1976), 42.

9. Sherwood, "Washington Before the War."

10. Mark Twain and Charles Dudley Warner, *The Gilded Age: A Tale of To-Day* (1873; reprint, New York: Oxford University Press, 1996), 221–22.

11. *National Intelligencer*, January–December 1859; *New York Tribune*, November 5, 15, 16, 1858; *Washington Evening Star*, January–December 1859; Benjamin Perley Poore, *Perley's Reminiscences of Sixty Years in the National Metropolis* (Philadelphia: Hubbard Brothers, 1886), vol. 2, 43–44; *Harper's Weekly*, December 4, 1858.

12. Margaret Bayard Smith, *The First Forty Years of Washington Society*, ed. Gaillard Hunt (New York: C. Scribner's Sons, 1906), 165; Kathryn Allamong Jacob, *Capital Elites: High Society in Washington, D.C., after the Civil War* (Washington, DC: Smithsonian Institution Press, 1995), 14–45; James Sterling Young, *The Washington Community: 1800–1828* (New York: Columbia University Press, 1966), 89.

13. Two articles focusing on lobbying during the first years of the new government appear in *The House and Senate in the 1790s: Petitioning, Lobbying, and Institutional Development*, ed. Kenneth R. Bowling and Donald R. Kennon (Athens, OH: Ohio University Press, 2002): William C. diGiacomantonio, "Petitioners and Their Grievances: A View from the First Federal Congress," 29–56; and Jeffrey L. Pasley, "Private Access and Public Power: Gentility and Lobbying in the Early Congress," 57–99. Vol. 7, *Petition Histories: Revolutionary War-Related Claims*, and vol. 8, *Petition Histories and Non-Legislative Official Documents*, of *The Documentary History of the First Federal Congress of the United States of America, March 4, 1789–March 3, 1791*, ed. Charlene Bangs Bickford, William C. diGiacomantonio, and Kenneth R. Bowling (Baltimore: Johns Hopkins University Press, 1997, 1998), discuss the flurry of petitioning that began as soon as the First Congress got under way.

14. William Maclay, *The Diary of William Maclay and Other Notes on Senate Debates*, ed. Kenneth R. Bowling and Helen E. Veit (Baltimore: Johns Hopkins University Press, 1988), vol. 9 of *The Documentary History of the First Federal Congress*, 215.

15. *Gazette of the United States*, April 21, 1792; Roy Swanstrom, *The United States Senate, 1787–1801* (Washington, DC: U.S. Government Printing Office, 1962), 213–16.

16. Karl Schriftgiesser, *The Lobbyists* (Boston: Little, Brown, 1951), 6–7.

17. Daniel Webster, *The Papers of Daniel Webster, 1830–1834*, ed. Charles M. Wiltse (Hanover, NH: University Press of New England, 1977), vol. 3, 288.

18. Thompson Westcott, *The Life of John Fitch, Inventor of the Steamboat* (Philadelphia: Lippincott, 1857), 356–70; John Fitch, *The Autobiography of John Fitch, Memoirs of the American Philosophical Society*, ed. Frank D. Prager (Philadelphia: American Philosophical Society, 1976), 184.

19. Poore, *Perley's Reminiscences*, vol. 2, 43–44; *Harper's Weekly*, December 4, 1858; *New York Tribune*, November 5, 15, 16, 1858.

20. Bern Keating, *The Flamboyant Mr. Colt and His Deadly Six-Shooter* (New York: Doubleday, 1978), 110–11; William Hosley, *Colt, The Making of an American Legend* (Amherst: University of Massachusetts Press, 1996), 81–85; Herbert Houze, *Samuel Colt, Arms, Art, and Invention* (New Haven: Yale University Press, 2006), 9–10.

21. U.S. Congress, House Report 353, "Colt Patent, &c., &c.," 33rd Cong., 1st sess., 1854.

22. House Report 353, "Colt Patent," 1–15, 19–32, 39–50, 71–84.

23. House Report 353, "Colt Patent," 1–20, 44–49.

24. Samuel Colt to Major William H. B. Hartley, December 12, 1859, Samuel Colt Papers, Connecticut Historical Society, quoted in Houze, *Samuel Colt*, 81.

25. Glyndon Van Deusen, *Thurlow Weed, Wizard of the Lobby* (Boston: Little, Brown, 1947), 1–26.

26. Michael F. Holt, "The Anti-Masonic and Know Nothing Parties," in *The History of Political Parties*, ed. Arthur Schlesinger, Jr. (New York: Chelsea House, 1973), vol. 1, 575–620.

27. Van Deusen, *Thurlow Weed*, 70–92, 166–92, 212–19, 282.

28. Mark Wahlgren Summers, *The Plundering Generation: Corruption and the Crisis of the Union, 1849–1861* (New York: Oxford University Press, 1987), 112; Van Deusen, *Thurlow Weed*, 220–24.

29. U.S. Congress, House Report 414, "Alleged Corruption in the Tariff of 1857," 35th Cong., 1st sess., 1858, 6.

30. House Report 414, "Alleged Corruption," 3–86.

31. House Report 414, "Alleged Corruption,"107.

32. *New York Herald*, May 9, 12, 1858; *New York Tribune*, May 10, 1858.

33. Michael Spangler, "Benjamin Brown French in the Lincoln Period," *White House History* 8 (Fall 2000): 4–17; BBF, *Benjamin Brown French, Witness to the Young Republic, A Yankee's Journal, 1828–1870*, ed. Donald B. Cole and John J. McDonough (Hanover, NH: University Press of New England, 1989), 1–11, 54–56, 165–66.

34. BBF diary, March 9, 1851, Benjamin Brown French Papers, Library of Congress, Washington, DC; BBF, *Witness to the Young Republic*, 165–66.

35. BBF diary, March 9, 17, 1851; BBF to Henry French, January 22, March 17, 1851; April 17, 1853; April 1 and December 23, 1855; January 21, July 24, 1856; September 11, 1858, BBF Papers.

36. BBF, *Witness to the Young Republic*, 230–31, 278–79, 326–30. Shortly after his inauguration, President Lincoln renamed French commissioner of public buildings. His responsibilities included care of the White House. Mrs. Lincoln and French "cottoned to each other," and she came to depend on him. When Willie Lincoln died in February 1862, French took charge of the funeral arrangements; he was on the speaker's stand at Gettysburg when Lincoln dedicated the national cemetery with his stirring address in November 1863; and he stood by the dying president's bedside in April 1865. BBF, *Witness to the Young Republic*, 346–47, 410–11; Spangler, "Benjamin Brown French," 76–85.

37. James Buchanan to Franklin Pierce and others, summer 1852, James Buchanan Papers, Library of Congress, Washington, DC; and June 21, 1852, letter cited in Summers, *Plundering Generation*, 306, and Schriftgiesser, *Lobbyists*, 7.

38. Thurlow Weed to Hamilton Fish, August 16, 1852, cited in Summers, *Plundering Generation*, 306.

39. Walt Whitman, "The Eighteenth President," in *Complete Poetry and Collected Prose*, ed. Justin Kaplan (New York: Viking Press, 1982), 1307–25.

40. *Washington Evening Star*, October 3, 1859.

41. Clay-Clopton, *A Belle*, 126–37.

42. Green, *Washington*, vol. 1, 53–54, 95–96, 178.

43. Jacob, *Capital Elites*, 38–41.

44. Elizabeth Blair Lee, *Wartime Washington: The Civil War Letters of Elizabeth Blair Lee*, ed. Virginia Laas (Urbana: University of Illinois Press, 1991), 23.

45. *Washington Evening Star*, May 16, October 2–30, 1860; Margaret Leech, *Reveille in Washington* (New York: Harper & Brothers, 1941), 20–26.

46. SW to SLMB, correspondence 1859–1860, Barlow Papers.

47. Milton S. Latham, "The Day Journal of Milton S. Latham, January 1 to May 6, 1860," ed. Edgar Eugene Robinson *Journal of the California Historical Society* 11 (March 1932): 3–28.

48. Latham, "Day Journal," 16–19.

49. Latham, "Day Journal," 16–19.

50. SW to JWH, May 10, 1860, HFP, Houghton.

51. JWH to SW, December 18, 1856, in Maud Howe Elliott, *Uncle Sam Ward and His Circle* (1938; reprint, New York: Arno Press, 1975), 446.

52. SW to JWH, March 6, 1860, HFP, Houghton.

53. Pablo Max Ynsfran, "Sam Ward's Bargain with President López of Paraguay," *Hispanic American Historical Review* 34 (August 1954): 313–31; Perez Acosta, *Carlos Antonio López Obrero Maximo* (Asunción, Paraguay: Editorial Guarania, 1948), 459–61; Jan M. G. Kleinpenning, *Paraguay: 1515–1870* (Frankfurt, Germany: Vervuert, 2003), vol. 1, 66–67.

54. Latham, "Day Journal," 17–18.

55. SW to JWH, May 10, 1860, HFP, Houghton.

56. SW to SLMB, June 11 and 27, 1860, Barlow Papers.

57. SW to SLMB, February 23, March 16, July 7, 1860, Barlow Papers. In 1859, a would-be lodge member who had been rejected appealed to Sam to lobby on his behalf, and Sam took up his case with Barlow. SW to SLMB, June 27, 1859, Barlow Papers.

58. SW to JWH, October 20, 1860, HFP, Houghton.

59. *Washington Evening Star*, November 7–8, December 1–24, 1860.

60. Sara A. R. Pryor, *Reminiscences of Peace and War* (New York: Macmillan, 1905), 111–12.

CHAPTER TWO

1. Ward Papers, NYPL; JWH, *Reminiscences, 1819–1899* (Cambridge, MA: Riverside Press, 1899), 3–4; Ward McAllister, *Society As I Have Found It* (New York: Cassell Publishing, 1890), 3–7; Deborah Clifford, *Mine Eyes Have Seen the Glory: A Biography of Julia Ward Howe* (Boston: Little, Brown, 1979), 8–12.

2. "Memoirs"; miscellaneous family papers, Ward Papers, NYPL.

3. Philip Hone, *The Diary of Philip Hone, 1828–1851*, ed. Allan Nevins (New York: Dodd, Mead, 1927), 433; JWH, *Reminiscences*, 6, 10–13, 18. Stephen Frank, in *Life with Father: Parenthood and Masculinity in the Nineteenth-Century American North* (Baltimore: Johns Hopkins University Press, 1998), and E. Anthony Rotundo, in *American Manhood: Transformations in Masculinity from the Revolution to the Modern Era* (New York: Basic Books, 1993),

note that many, many fathers in the early nineteenth century shared a deep anxiety about the moral and material welfare of both their sons and their daughters and a horror of the profligate life. Banker Ward's dread of dissipation tended toward the obsessive end of the scale.

4. SW to Samuel Ward, January 23, 1826, and Samuel Ward to SW, January 27, 1826, Ward Papers, NYPL; Letters between Samuel Ward and Sam Ward, Samuel Ward (1789–1839): Letters to Various Correspondents, Houghton Library, Harvard University, Cambridge, MA.

5. Louise Hall Tharp, *Three Saints and a Sinner* (Boston: Little, Brown, 1956), 35–44; George Bancroft to Samuel Ward, March 22 or 25, 1827, Ward Papers, NYPL.

6. "Memoirs." Although Sam did not possess the size, strength, and endurance that Rotundo describes in *American Manhood*, 38–42, as the traits boys admired in one another, he excelled in loyalty and daring, which were also prized.

7. Nathaniel Prime, the Prime in Prime, Ward, and King, was the first president of the New York Stock Exchange and one of the wealthiest men in New York. The "prime rate," the baseline interest rate charged by banks to their most credit-worthy borrowers, is named for him. Howard Wachtel, *Street of Dreams—Boulevard of Broken Hearts: Wall Street's First Century* (London: Pluto Press, 2003), 41; Henry Lanier, *A Century of Banking in New York, 1822–1922* (New York: Gilliss Press, 1922), 42, 57, 92, 139; "Memoirs."

8. Draft history of Delmonico's, Ward Papers, NYPL; Lately Thomas [Robert Steele], *Delmonico's: A Century of Splendor* (Boston: Houghton, Mifflin, 1967), 4–23.

9. Samuel Ward file, Columbia University Archives, New York, NY; information about Columbia's Philolexian Society shared with the author by alumnus Thomas Vinciguerra, who spearheaded the society's revival in 1985.

10. "Memoirs"; Sam's introduction to Young's *Algebra* is full of an eighteen-year-old's braggadocio. J. R. Young, *An Elementary Treatise on Algebra Theoretical and Practical: Intended for the Use of Students, With Improvements by Samuel Ward, Junior* (Philadelphia: Carey & Lea, 1832).

11. "Memoirs"; SW to Samuel Ward, November 28/29, 1832, and letters from 1832 to 1836, Ward Papers, Houghton.

12. SW pocket diaries and miscellaneous papers, 1832–1835, Ward Papers, NYPL.

13. Jules Gabriel Janin, *The American in Paris, during the Summer* (New York: Burgess, Stringer & Co., 1844); Amy Trubek, *Haute Cuisine: How the French Invented the Culinary Profession* (Philadelphia: University of Pennsylvania Press, 2000), 35–41.

14. "Memoirs"; pocket diaries, 1832–1836, Ward Papers, NYPL.

15. "Memoirs"; Longfellow, seven years older than Sam, and his wife, Mary, had gone to Europe so he could prepare for the new post. Mary had a miscarriage and died in November 1835, and Henry was still in mourning the following spring when he met Sam.

16. Sam's diploma from Tübingen is among the Ward family papers that are at the New-York Historical Society, New York, NY. Samuel Ward file, Columbia University Archives; SW to CFM, spring 1836, Ward Papers, NYPL. Mersch, a native of Luxembourg and from a family of modest means, had gone to Paris to study mathematics at the same time as Sam.

17. SW to Samuel Ward, March 7, 1833, Ward Papers, Houghton.

18. SW to Samuel Ward, late June 1836, Ward Papers, Houghton; SW to CFM, July 1, and October 19, 1836, Ward Papers, NYPL.

19. Hone, *Diary*, 433, 838; JWH, *Reminiscences*, 44–45; Jerry E. Patterson, *The First Four Hundred: Mrs. Astor's New York in the Gilded Age* (New York: Rizzoli, 2000), 46.

20. George Templeton Strong, *The Diary of George Templeton Strong*, ed. Allan Nevins and Milton Halsey Thomas (New York: Macmillan, 1952), vol. 1, 55.

21. JWH, *Reminiscences*, 15, 48–49, 68; Eric Homberger, *Mrs. Astor's New York: Money and Social Power in the Gilded Age* (New Haven: Yale University Press, 2002), 93–97.

22. JWH, *Reminiscences*, 46–49, 68.

23. SW to CFM, January 24, 1837, HFP, Houghton.

24. SW to CFM, January 24, 1837, HFP, Houghton.

25. JWH, *Reminiscences*, 69.

26. SW to CFM, July 23, 1837, HFP, Houghton.

27. HWL to SW, April 2, 1837, HWLL, Houghton. E. Anthony Rotundo, in *American Manhood*, 75–89, and Donald Yacovone, in "Surpassing the Love of Women: Victorian Manhood and the Language of Fraternal Love," *A Shared Experience: Men, Women, and the History of Gender*, ed. Laura McCall and Donald Yacovone (New York: New York University Press, 1998), 195–221, offer helpful perspective on the intimate male friendships of the nineteenth century, when there was no stigma associated with fraternal love and no context for a term like "homosexuality."

28. HWL to George Greene, March 25, 1836, in Henry Wadsworth Longfellow, *The Letters of Henry Wadsworth Longfellow*, ed. Andrew Hilen (Cambridge: Belknap Press of Harvard University Press, 1966), vol. 1, 542.

29. "Memoirs." Frank, in *Life with Father*, 139–58, and Rotundo, in *American Manhood*, 20–27, explore the tension between nineteenth-century fathers, who, usually with the best of intentions, tried to force sons into a career like their own, and the young men who resisted. As Sam realized, his problem was compounded by the facts that he loved the life of luxury his father's money made possible and that he was still living under his father's roof.

30. SW to CFM, December 31, 1836, Ward Papers, NYPL.

31. *New York American*, November 5, 1837.

32. SW to CFM, March 7, April 3, November 24, 1837, HFP, Houghton.

33. Daniel Wilson, *The Astors* (New York: St. Martin's Press, 1993), 34–57, 83–92; Axel Madsen, *John Jacob Astor, America's First Millionaire* (New York: John Wiley and Sons, 2001), 75, 168–71, 219; JWH, *Reminiscences*, 73–76; Virginia Cowles, *The Astors* (New York: Alfred A. Knopf, 1979). In addition to her trunks filled with her trousseau, Emily came with a trust worth $200,000, carefully designed by her father to preserve the principal for her and her "issue." Homberger, *Mrs. Astor's New York*, 100.

34. JWH to Henry Ward, January 8, 1838, HFP, Houghton; JWH, *Reminiscences*, 64–67.

35. SW to HWL, January 27, 1838, HWLL, Houghton.

36. In a scrapbook with pink and green marbled pages, Sam, or perhaps Emily, carefully clipped, glued, and annotated the favorable notices he had begun to receive. Scrapbook, Ward Papers, NYPL; Samuel Ward file, Columbia University Archives.

37. Household account books, 1838–1839, Ward Papers, NYPL.

38. Samuel Ward file, Columbia University Archives; Hone, *Diary*, November 27, 1839, vol. 1, 433; SW to HWL, December 11 and 31, 1839, June 21, 1840, and autumn (no date), 1840, HWLL, Houghton.

39. SW to HWL, November 27, 1840, HWLL, Houghton. Prime had become delusional and imagined he had lost all of his money. Wachtel, *Street of Dreams*, 42.

40. SW to HWL, February 16, 18, 21, 23, 1841, HWLL, Houghton.

41. SW to HWL, April 3, 1841, HWLL, Houghton.

42. In addition to letters to Julia, Marion, and Longfellow, during this period Sam wrote many letters to his friend Dr. Francis Lieber, a historian and political writer. SW to Francis Lieber, 1841−1842, Francis Lieber Papers, Huntington Library, San Marino, CA.

43. Charles Sumner to SW, November 9, 1842, HFP, Schlesinger; Tharp, *Three Saints*, 87−89; HWL to SW, June 2, 1841, "Longfellow's Letters to Samuel Ward," *Putnam's Monthly*, November 1907. Felton became president of Harvard in 1860. His death, in 1862, was the first among "the boys." The letters exchanged by the five "boys" mirror the language of male friendship discussed by Rotundo in *American Manhood*, 75−89, and Yacovone in "Surpassing the Love of Women," 195−221, in which they unabashedly declare their fondness for one another and the pleasure they derive from their associations.

44. SW to SGH, April 4, 1843, HFP, Houghton.

45. Marion Ward to SW, February 3, 1843, Ward Papers, NYPL.

46. SW to HWL, February 6 or 8, 1843, HWLL, Houghton; HWL to SW, March 2, 1843, HWL, *Letters of Henry Wadsworth Longfellow*, vol. 2, 512−13.

47. Charles Sumner to SW, January 19, 1842, and July 25, 1843, HFP, Schlesinger.

48. *Chicago Daily Tribune*, September 26, 1885.

49. Marion Ward to Louisa Ward, July 1843, Samuel Ward (1786−1839): Letters, Houghton Library.

50. HWL to SW, April 13, 1843, HWLL, Houghton.

51. Clippings, HFP, Schlesinger; *Chicago Daily Tribune*, September 26, 1885.

52. Cowles, *The Astors*, 82−83; Madsen, *John Jacob Astor*, 220; Clifford, *Mine Eyes*, 78−79.

53. Henry Brevoort, *Letters of Henry Brevoort to Washington Irving*, ed. George Hellman (New York: G. P. Putnam's Sons, 1916), vol. 2, 133−35; Tharp, *Three Saints*, 105; SW to Samuel Gridley Howe, October 14, 1843, HFP, Houghton.

54. There are many clippings about the smash-up of Prime, Ward and Company in the Samuel Ward file, Columbia University Archives, and in the Ward Family Papers at the New-York Historical Society.

55. JWH, *Reminiscences*, 69.

56. SW to HWL, December 26, 1847, HWLL, Houghton.

57. SW to HWL, October 26, 1848, HWLL, Houghton.

58. Pamela Herr, *A Biography of Jessie Benton Frémont* (New York: Franklin Watts, 1987), 195; shipboard notebook, Ward Papers, NYPL; Sam Ward, *Sam Ward in the Gold Rush*, ed. Carvel Collins (Stanford: Stanford University Press, 1949), 11−15.

59. McAllister, *Society*, 19−25; James P. Delgado, "A Gold Rush Enterprise: Samuel Ward, Charles Mersch, and the Storeship 'Niantic'," *Huntington Library Quarterly* 46 (Autumn 1983): 321−24; Ward, *Gold Rush*, 3−13.

60. Delgado, "A Gold Rush Enterprise," 321–24; Lately Thomas [Robert Steele], *Sam Ward, "King of the Lobby"* (Boston: Houghton Mifflin, 1965), 158–65; Susan Johnson, "Bulls, Bears, and Dancing Boys: Race, Gender, and Leisure in the California Gold Rush," in *Across the Great Divide: Cultures of Manhood in the American West*, ed. Matthew Basso, Laura McCall, and Dee Garceau (New York: Routledge, 2001), 45–50; Susan Johnson, *Roaring Camp: The Social World of the California Gold Rush* (New York: W. W. Norton, 2000), 11–13, 105.

61. SW to JWH, February 7, 1852, HFP, Houghton; Ward, *Gold Rush*, 11–16, 19–22, 89, 145–148; Delgado, "A Gold Rush Enterprise," 326–27.

62. Sam described his time in Mexico in a long letter dated 1859, possibly to a family friend, the poet Fitz-Greene Halleck. Ward Papers, NYPL.

63. Strong, *Diary*, vol. 2, June 10, 1852, 96. Lately Thomas identifies the man with whom Medora's name was linked in innuendo as Russian Paul Damidoff, not a prince but a very rich man. Thomas, *Sam Ward*, 193.

64. SW to JWH, March 30, 1856, in Maud Howe Elliott, *Uncle Sam Ward and His Circle* (1938; reprint, New York: Arno Press, 1975), 447–48.

65. Longfellow was touched by Sam's plight: "It makes my heart ache to think of your calamities and perplexities." HWL to SW, September 10 and 15, 1857, in Longfellow, *Letters*, vol. 4, 47–48.

66. Pablo Max Ynsfran, "Sam Ward's Bargain with President López of Paraguay," *Hispanic American Historical Review* 34 (August 1954): 313–15.

67. Ynsfran, "Sam Ward's Bargain," 313–31. Sam's journal from his trip to Paraguay is among the Ward Papers, NYPL; *Paraguay: A Concise History* (London: Effingham Wilson, 1867), 17–19.

68. Ynsfran, "Sam Ward's Bargain," 322–24; Perez Acosta, *Carlos Antonio López Obrero Maximo* (Asunción, Paraguay: Editorial Guarania, 1948), 459–61. Sam's obituary in the *Chicago Daily Tribune*, May 20, 1884, included a detailed account of his adventures in Paraguay.

CHAPTER THREE

1. *Richmond Examiner*, December 25, 1860; *Washington Evening Star*, January 2, 5, 10, 15, 1861.

2. Virginia Clay-Clopton, *A Belle of the Fifties: Memoirs of Mrs. Clay of Alabama* (New York: Doubleday, Page, and Co., 1904), 151.

3. *Washington Evening Star*, February 22–March 6, 1861.

4. *Washington Evening Star*, March 3–7, 1861; SW to WHS, no date but probably March 4, 1861, Seward Papers.

5. SW to SLMB, February 15, 1861, Barlow Papers.

6. SW to WHS, February 16, 1861, Seward Papers; Margaret Butterfield, "Samuel Ward, Alias Carlos Lopez," *University of Rochester Library Bulletin* 12 (Winter 1957): 23–33.

7. SW to WHS, April 5, 1860, Seward Papers.

8. Gwin's personal account of these weeks in 1861, with many references to the "mutual friend," is included in Evan Coleman, "Gwin and Seward—A Secret Chapter in Ante-

bellum History," *Overland Monthly and Out West Magazine* 18 (November 1891): 469; Lately Thomas [Robert Steele], *Between Two Empires: The Life Story of California's First Senator* (Boston: Houghton Mifflin, 1969), 236–43; Glyndon Van Deusen, *William Henry Seward* (New York: Oxford University Press, 1967), 243; Arthur Quinn, *The Rivals: William Gwin, David Broderick, and the Birth of California* (New York: Crown, 1994), 277; John M. Taylor, *William Henry Seward, Lincoln's Right Hand* (New York: Harper Collins, 1991), 146–49.

9. SW to WHS, February 26, 1861, Seward Papers.

10. The letter, intact, is among Seward's papers. SW to WHS, February 21, 1861, Seward Papers.

11. SW to WHS, no date but likely March 4, 1861, Seward Papers; Frederic Bancroft, *The Life of William H. Seward* (New York: Harper & Brothers, 1900), vol. 2, 542–45.

12. SW to WHS, no date but likely March 4, 1861, Seward Papers; Coleman, "Gwin and Seward," 465–69; Bancroft, *Life of William H. Seward*, vol. 2, 25–26, 108; Van Deusen, *William Henry Seward*, 277; Thomas, *Between Two Empires*, 239–43.

13. Sam Ward, *Sam Ward in the Gold Rush*, ed. Carvel Collins (Stanford: Stanford University Press, 1949), 19–21.

14. Ward, *Gold Rush*, 25, 65, 89, 128, 141, 158.

15. Ward, *Gold Rush*, 172.

16. SW to WHS, April 9, 1861, Seward Papers.

17. William Howard Russell, "Recollections of the American Civil War," *North American Review* 166 (February 1898), 237.

18. William Howard Russell, *My Diary North and South* (Boston: T.O.H.P. Burnham, 1863), 10–110; Alan Hankinson, *Man of Wars: William Howard Russell of the Times* (London: Heinemann, 1982), 156.

19. SW to SLMB, April 9 or 10, 1861, Barlow Papers.

20. SW to SLMB, April 8, 9, 10, and an undated letter most likely April 11, 1861, Barlow Papers; Taylor, *William Henry Seward*, 172–73.

21. Russell, *Diary North and South*, 111–94.

22. There is no question that the letters signed Charles Lopez were written by Sam—his handwriting is unmistakable and, when he was in a hurry, almost impossible to read—or that they were intended for and read by Seward. The letters, although addressed to "Dear George," bear marginal comments in Seward's hand and were preserved and indexed among Seward's own correspondence, now at the University of Rochester.

23. SW to WHS, April 19, 1861, Seward Papers.

24. SW to WHS, April 25, 1861, Seward Papers.

25. SW to WHS, May 2, 1861, Seward Papers.

26. SW to WHS, May 9, 1861, Seward Papers.

27. SW to WHS, June 18 and 21, 1861, Seward Papers; Russell, *Diary North and South*, 154–204, 265–86, 325–37, 366–77.

28. SW to WHS, June 18, 1861, Seward Papers; Russell, *Diary North and South*, 265–70, 410–23.

29. SW to WHS, June 21, 1861, Seward Papers.

30. SW to WHS, June 21, 1861, Seward Papers. Daniel Sickles became one of the most

prominent of the political generals. His insubordination at the Battle of Gettysburg cost many Union soldiers their lives. Sickles himself lost his leg to cannon fire during the battle.

31. Ward, *Gold Rush*, 172.

32. SW to WHS, July 15 and October 16, 1861, Seward Papers.

33. Russell, *My Diary North and South*, 442–66; *Washington Evening Star*, July 20–25, 1861.

34. *Washington Evening Star*, July 22–25, 1861; Walt Whitman, *The Complete Poetry and Prose of Walt Whitman*, ed. Malcolm Cowley (New York: Pellegrini & Cudahy, 1948), vol. 2, 17–18.

35. Russell, *Diary North and South*, 468, 491–591.

36. This was the period of greatest activity in Sam's letters to Seward. SW to WHS, October 6, 7, 10, 11, 15, 16, 19, 20, 22, 24, 28, 29, 1861, Seward Papers.

37. SW to WHS, October 11, 28, 1861, Seward Papers.

38. SW to SLMB, May–December 1861, Barlow Papers.

39. SW to HWL, July 9, 1862, HWLL, Houghton.

40. SW to WHS, June 21, October 16, 1861, Seward Papers.

41. Lately Thomas [Robert Steele], *Sam Ward, "King of the Lobby"* (Boston: Houghton Mifflin, 1965), 290–91.

42. SW to WHS, June 7, 18, July 22, 1862, Seward Papers; SW to HWL, January 20, 1863, HWLL, Houghton.

43. SW to WHS and Frederick Seward, October–November, 1861, Seward Papers.

44. SW to WHS and Frederick Seward, October 16, 19, 22, 1861, Seward Papers.

45. SW to WHS and Frederick Seward, December 3, 16, 24, 25, 30, 1861, January 8, February 4, 1862, Seward Papers.

46. SW to WHS and Frederick Seward, January 8, 30, March 8, 1862, Seward Papers.

47. SW to WHS, April 23, 1862, Seward Papers.

48. SW to WHS, July 23, 1862, Seward Papers.

49. SW to HWL, July 9, 1862, HWLL, Houghton.

50. The Halleck-Ward letters are among the Ward Papers, NYPL.

51. SW to HWL, August 9, 1862, HWLL, Houghton.

52. SW to SLMB, autumn of 1863, Barlow Papers; SLMB to SW, autumn of 1863, Ward Papers, NYPL.

53. SLMB to SW, December 2, 1863, Ward Papers, NYPL.

54. SW to HWL, December 15, 1863, HWLL, Houghton.

55. SW to SLMB, December 28, 1863, Barlow Papers.

56. SW to SLMB, January 27, 1864, Barlow Papers.

57. SW to SLMB, February 13, 1864, Barlow Papers.

58. Maud Howe Elliott, *Uncle Sam Ward and His Circle* (1938; reprint, New York: Arno Press, 1975), 477.

59. Sam to HWL, August 26, 1864, HWLL, Houghton.

60. SW to JWH, June 15, 1864, HFP, Houghton.

61. *New York Times*, March 18, 1875; undated newspaper article, HFP, Schlesinger.

62. Thomas, *Sam Ward*, 234; SW to HWL, March 9, 1863, HWLL, Houghton. Upon Medora's death, the Ward mansion at 32 Bond Street, which Sam had given her upon their

marriage and then, after their estrangement, helplessly watched her rent out, finally reverted to him. SW to JWH, September 15, 1872, HFP, Houghton.

63. SW to SLMB, July 2, 1864, Barlow Papers.

64. SW to HWL, July 9, 1860, HWLL, Houghton.

65. Samuel Ward, *Lyrical Recreations* (New York: D. Appleton, 1865).

66. Halleck to SW, January to May 1865, Ward Papers, NYPL; SW to HWL, February 15, March (no date), April 21, August (no date), 1865, HWLL, Houghton.

67. SW to HWL, April 21, 1865, HWLL, Houghton.

68. SW to JWH, spring–summer 1865, in Elliott, *Uncle Sam*, 492, and Thomas, *Sam Ward*, 331.

CHAPTER FOUR

1. Constance Green, *Washington: A History of the Capital, 1800–1950* (Princeton: Princeton University Press, 1962), vol. 1, 261–77, 290–303; James Whyte, *The Uncivil War: Washington during the Reconstruction, 1865–1878* (New York: Twayne Publishers, 1958), 13–27.

2. Whyte, *Uncivil War*, 15.

3. Ernest Duverzier de Hauranne, *A Frenchman in Lincoln's America*, ed. Ralph Bowen (Chicago: Lakeside Press, 1974–75), vol. 1, 51–52.

4. L. U. Reavis, *A Change of National Empire, or, Arguments in Favor of the Removal of the National Capital from Washington City to the Mississippi Valley* (St. Louis: J. F. Torrey, 1869); Alan Lessoff, *The Nation and Its City* (Baltimore: Johns Hopkins University Press, 1994), chapters 1, 2, and 3.

5. BBF, *Witness to the Young Republic*, ed. Donald B. Cole and John J. McDonough (Hanover, NH: University Press of New England, 1989), 490; Donn Piatt quoted in John B. Ellis, *Sights and Secrets of the National Capital* (New York: United States Publishing, 1869), 416–18.

6. In the 35th Congress (1857–59), there had been 39 Democrats, 20 Republicans, and 5 "others" in the Senate; 131 Democrats, 92 Republicans, and 14 "others" in the House. In the 41st Congress (1869–71), there were 11 Democrats and 61 Republicans in the Senate; 73 Democrats and 170 Republicans in the House. U.S. Senate, *Senate Campaign Information* (Washington, DC: Government Printing Office, 1978), 396–97.

7. Henry Adams, *The Education of Henry Adams* (1918; reprint, New York: Modern Library, 1931), 237.

8. Margaret Thompson, *The Spider Web: Congress and Lobbying in the Age of Grant* (Ithaca: Cornell University Press, 1985), 45–46.

9. *Historical Statistics of the United States, Colonial Times to 1957* (Washington, DC: U.S. Department of Commerce, 1960), 7–13, 427–28; Thompson, *Spider Web*, 41–45.

10. Thompson, *Spider Web*, 41–45.

11. Thompson, *Spider Web*, 44–54; Morton Keller, *Affairs of State* (Cambridge: Harvard University Press, 1977), 101; Kathryn Allamong Jacob, *Capital Elites, High Society in Washington, D.C., after the Civil War* (Washington, DC: Smithsonian Institution Press, 1995), 58–

59; Edward Winslow Martin [James Dabney], *Behind the Scenes in Washington* (New York: Continental Publishing, 1873), 5.

12. James Sterling Young, *The Washington Community: 1800–1828* (New York: Columbia University Press, 1966), 28; *Historical Statistics*, 710; Thompson, *Spider Web*, 45–46.

13. *Historical Statistics*, 959–60; Keller, *Affairs of State*, 20–22; Thompson, *Spider Web*, 44–46; Lauros G. McConachie, *Congressional Committees* (New York: Crowell, 1898).

14. Keller, *Affairs of State*, 101–2.

15. John Walter, *First Impressions of America* (London: privately printed, 1867), 118.

16. The story of the development of the "New Washington" and the short life of the Territory of the District of Columbia is told best in Constance Green's *Washington*, in chapters 13 and 14 of volume 1. The best analysis of the meaning of the story is told briefly in Morton Keller's *Affairs of State*, 98–101, and at length in Alan Lessoff's *The Nation and Its City*.

17. Keller, *Affairs of State*, 6–7, 45–46, 106–7; Joel Parker, *The Three Powers of Government* (New York: Hurd & Houghton, 1869), 76.

18. E. L. Godkin to Frederick Law Olmsted, no date, quoted in Keller, *Affairs of State*, 45–46; Ernest Samuels, *The Young Henry Adams* (Cambridge: Harvard University Press, 1965), (1948), 145–46.

19. Arinori Mori, *Life and Resources in America* (Washington, DC: no publisher, 1871), 39; Keller, *Affairs of State*, 122–61, 177; Thompson, *Spider Web*, 46–48; Gaines Foster, *Moral Reconstruction: Christian Lobbyists and the Federal Legislation of Morality, 1865–1920* (Chapel Hill: University of North Carolina Press, 2002), 3, 27.

20. George Alfred Townsend, *Washington, Outside and Inside* (Hartford, CT: Betts & Co., 1873), 22.

21. Mark Wahlgren Summers, *The Plundering Generation: Corruption and the Crisis of the Union, 1849–1861* (New York: Oxford University Press, 1987); Mark Wahlgren Summers, *The Era of Good Stealings* (New York: Oxford University Press, 1993), chapter 1.

22. Keller, *Affairs of State*, 165; Whyte, *Uncivil War*, 194.

23. Robert Sharkey, *Money, Class, and Party: An Economic Study of Civil War and Reconstruction* (Baltimore: Johns Hopkins Press, 1959), 57–59; Hugh McCulloch, *Men and Measures of Half a Century* (New York: Charles Scribner's Sons, 1888).

24. Sharkey, *Money, Class, and Party*, 61–89, chapter 3; Irwin Unger, *The Greenback Era: A Social and Political History of American Finance, 1865–1879* (Princeton: Princeton University Press, 1974), 41–124.

25. McCulloch, *Men and Measures*, 210–57; Frank Carpenter, *"Carp's" Washington*, ed. Frances Carpenter (New York: McGraw Hill, 1960), 280; SW to SLMB, October 1865–December 1866, Barlow Papers; Herbert Schnell, "Hugh McCulloch and the Treasury Department, 1865–1869," *Mississippi Valley Historical Review* 17 (December 1930): 404–21; SW to unnamed correspondent, no date but almost certainly late 1870s, Ward Papers, NYPL.

26. Lately Thomas [Robert Steele], *Sam Ward, "King of the Lobby"* (Boston: Houghton Mifflin, 1965), 342. Several of his obituaries recount Sam's involvement with both McCulloch and Morrissey.

27. Thomas, *Sam Ward*, 249.

28. *Oxford Encyclopedia of Food and Drink in America* (New York: Oxford University Press, 2004), vol. 1, 625–35; Waverly Root and Richard De Rochemont, *Eating in America: A History* (New York: William Morrow and Co., 1976), 146–47, 213–34.

29. Amy Trubek, *Haute Cuisine: How the French Invented the Culinary Profession* (Philadelphia: University of Pennsylvania Press, 2000), 8–10, 98–100; Jerry E. Patterson, *The First Four Hundred: Mrs. Astor's New York in the Gilded Age* (New York: Rizzoli, 2000), 16–18.

30. Mrs. E. F. Ellet, *The New Cyclopedia of Domestic Economy, and Practical Housekeeper* (Norwich, CT: Henry Bill Publishing, 1872), 98; Lately Thomas [Robert Steele], *Delmonico's: A Century of Splendor* (Boston: Houghton Mifflin, 1967), 89–91, 118–21, 148, 174–75; Ward McAllister, *Society As I Have Found It* (New York: Cassell Publishing, 1890), 233.

31. Benjamin Perley Poore, *Perley's Reminiscences of Sixty Years in the National Metropolis* (Philadelphia: Hubbard Brothers, 1886), vol. 1, 221; Emily Edson Briggs, *The Olivia Letters* (New York: Neal Publishing, 1906), 199–204, 416–17.

32. Lillie de Hegermann-Lindencrone, *The Sunny Side of Diplomatic Life, 1875–1912* (New York: Harper & Brothers, 1914), 8–9.

33. *Oxford Encyclopedia of Food and Drink*, vol. 1, 380–81; Thomas, *Delmonico's*, 146, 198.

34. Whyte, *Uncivil War*, 180; George Alfred Townsend, *Washington, Outside and Inside* (Hartford, CT: Betts & Co., 1873), 176–78.

35. Carpenter, *"Carp's" Washington*, 280.

36. Thomas, *Sam Ward*, 418–19; *Chicago Daily Tribune*, May 15, 1875; Robert Steele compiled "Sam Ward's gastronomic sayings" and included them in a letter to amuse food writer M. F. K. Fisher. Robert Steele to M. F. K. Fisher, February 12, 1972, Fisher Papers.

37. SW to HWL, July 30, 1873, HWLL, Houghton.

38. McAllister, *Society*, 158–59.

39. Thomas, *Sam Ward*, 412; Briggs, *The Olivia Letters*, 417.

40. Thomas, *Sam Ward*, 414–15.

41. Thomas, *Sam Ward*, 416–18, 429.

42. Briggs, *The Olivia Letters*, 417; Hegermann-Lindencrone, *Sunny Side of Diplomatic Life*, 78–79.

43. John Forney, *Anecdotes of Public Men* (New York: Harper & Brothers, 1873), 394; Whyte, *Uncivil War*, 193.

44. "Uncle Joe," *Literary Digest*, 76 (March 17, 1923): 48; Carpenter, *"Carp's" Washington*, 280.

45. Poore, *Perley's Reminiscences*, vol. 2, 246–47.

46. Lloyd Lewis and H. J. Smith, "King of the Lobby," *American Mercury* 37 (February 1936): 211–16.

47. Carpenter, *"Carp's" Washington*, 280.

48. SW to HWL, February 27, 1874, HWLL, Houghton.

49. SW to HWL, no date, mid-December 1870, HWLL, Houghton.

50. Albert House, "The Samuel Latham Mitchill Barlow Papers in the Huntington Library," *Huntington Library Quarterly* 28 (August, 1965): 342–51.

51. House, "Barlow Papers in the Huntington," 347–51; *New York Times*, October 11, 1868.

52. SLMB to SW, March 23, 1868, Barlow Papers.

53. SLMB to SW, March 27, 28, April 1, 2, 1868, Barlow Papers.

54. SW to SLMB, March 4, 1869, Barlow Papers.

55. SLMB to SW and SW to SLMB, March, April, and May, 1869, Barlow Papers.

56. SLMB to SW, June 19, 1875, Barlow Papers.

57. SLMB to SW, no date, January and February 15, 1869, Barlow Papers.

58. SW to unnamed correspondent, no date but almost certainly late 1870s, Ward Papers, NYPL.

59. SW to unnamed correspondent, no date but almost certainly late 1870s, Ward Papers, NYPL.

60. Hans Trefousse, *Ben Butler: The South Called Him Beast* (New York: Twayne Publishers, 1957), 80–174; Chester Barrows, *William M. Evarts* (Chapel Hill: University of North Carolina Press, 1941), 138–63.

61. SW to SLMB, February 25, 27, 1868, Barlow Papers.

62. George Wilkes to Benjamin Butler, May 20, 21, 23, 27, 1868, Benjamin Butler Papers, Library of Congress, Washington, DC.

63. U.S. Congress, House Report 75, "Raising of Money To Be Used in Impeachment," 40th Cong., 2nd sess., 1868. Wilkes's letters to Butler were full of serious charges against Sam and a great number of other prominent men. Some of them were almost certainly true: Sam *was*, it seems clear, betting on the outcome of the impeachment trial. Others, such as Wilkes's claim that Sam had tried to pass off a mistress, dressed as a man, as his cousin—a story that seemed designed to feed on Butler's dislike of Sam and to make Wilkes look more "in the know"—were almost certainly not true. No other hint, not even a veiled one, of such a relationship appears anywhere. George Wilkes to Benjamin Butler, May 20, 21, 23, 27, 1868, Benjamin Butler Papers.

64. House Report 75, "Raising of Money To Be Used in Impeachment."

65. Poore, *Perley's Reminiscences*, vol. 2, 246–47; SW to SLMB, June 19, 1868, Barlow Papers.

66. SW to SLMB, May–August, 1868, Barlow Papers; SLMB to SW, May–August, 1868, Ward Papers, NYPL; SW to Manton Marble, May–August, 1868, Marble Papers; Manton Marble to SW, May–August, 1868, Ward Papers, NYPL; George T. McJimsey, *Genteel Partisan: Manton Marble* (Ames: Iowa State University Press, 1971), ix–xi, 1–76, 105.

67. SW to Manton Marble, July 31, 1868, Marble Papers.

68. SW to Manton Marble, August 4, 16, 19, 1868, Marble Papers.

69. After sculptor Thomas Crawford's death, Louisa married painter and American expatriate Luther Terry. They lived in Rome with their two children and Louisa's children from her first marriage. In 1846, Annie Ward, Sam's shy, youngest sister, married dashing Frenchman Adolph Mailliard, an illegitimate grandson of Joseph Bonaparte, brother of Napoleon. Annie and Mailliard, called "Uncle Do" within the family, moved to California, where Annie came to love their ranch north of San Francisco.

70. Several books chronicle the stormy Ward-Howe marriage: Valerie Ziegler, *Diva*

Julia: The Public Romance and Private Agony of Julia Ward Howe (New York: Trinity Press, 2003); Deborah Clifford, *Mine Eyes Have Seen the Glory* (Boston: Little, Brown, 1979); Gary Williams, *Hungry Heart: The Literary Emergence of Julia Ward Howe* (Amherst: University of Massachusetts Press, 1999); Mary Grant, *Private Woman, Public Person* (New York: Carlson Publishers, 1994).

71. SW to JWH, May 30, 1869, HFP, Houghton. After the war, Sam and Sumner were again on somewhat friendly terms.

72. *Every Saturday: A Journal of Choice Reading* (October 29, 1870).

CHAPTER FIVE

1. Benjamin Perley Poore, *Perley's Reminiscences of Sixty Years in the National Metropolis* (Philadelphia: Hubbard Brothers, 1886), vol. 2, 525.

2. Frank Carpenter, *"Carp's" Washington*, ed. Frances Carpenter (New York: McGraw Hill, 1960), 280; Lately Thomas [Robert Steele], *Sam Ward, "King of the Lobby"* (Boston: Houghton Mifflin, 1965), 358; Maud Howe Elliott, *Three Generations* (Boston: Little, Brown, 1923), 69.

3. SW to SLMB, no date, 1873, Barlow Papers.

4. SW to SLMB, December 9, 1873, Barlow Papers.

5. SW to SLMB, no date, 1873, Barlow Papers.

6. SW to SLMB, July 15, 1874, July 7, 1875, and November–December 1875, Barlow Papers.

7. Mary Crawford, unpublished memoir, quoted in Maud Howe Elliott, *Uncle Sam Ward and His Circle* (1938; reprint, New York: Arno Press, 1975), 507.

8. Laura Howe Richards, unpublished account, quoted in Elliott, *Uncle Sam*, 508.

9. James A. Garfield, *The Diary of James A. Garfield*, ed. Harry James Brown and Frederick D. Williams (East Lansing: Michigan State University Press, 1967), vol. 2, February 27, 28, March 6, 12, April 2, May 2, 1872.

10. Garfield, *Diary*, vol. 2, January 21, 1873.

11. Garfield, *Diary*, vol. 2, December 3, 4, 1873.

12. Garfield, *Diary*, vol. 2, December 8, 1873.

13. Garfield, *Diary*, vol. 2, February 2, 1874.

14. Garfield, *Diary*, vol. 2, July 7–8, 1874; Alvin F. Harlow, "William Henry Hurlbert," *Dictionary of American Biography* (New York: Charles Scribner's Sons, 1932), vol. 9, 424.

15. Charles Tansill, *The Congressional Career of Thomas Francis Bayard, 1869–1885* (Washington, DC: George Washington University Press, 1946), 1–49; Carpenter, *Carp's Washington*, 262.

16. TFB to SW, December 24, 1873, August 30, 1874, Ward Papers, NYPL; SW to TFB, March 24, 1872, Bayard Papers.

17. SW to TFB, February 23, 27, March 24, 1872, and TB to SW, August 30, 1874, Bayard Papers. Sickles's first wife died in 1867. In 1871, he married a young Spanish woman he had met while U.S. minister to Spain.

18. Carpenter, *Carp's Washington*, 26.

19. Ellis Oberholtzer, *A History of the United States Since the Civil War* (New York:

Macmillan, 1922), vol. 2, 391; Chester Barrows, *William M. Evarts* (Chapel Hill: University of North Carolina Press, 1941), 197–213; Adrian Cook, *The Alabama Claims: American Politics and Anglo-American Relations, 1865–1872* (Ithaca: Cornell University Press, 1975), 207–16.

20. SW to HWL, January 31, 1871, in Samuel Longfellow, *Life of Henry Wadsworth Longfellow, with Extracts from His Journals and Correspondence* (Boston: Houghton, Mifflin, 1896), vol. 3, 165–66.

21. SW to WME, summer 1872 through December 1874, Evarts Papers; Barrows, *William M. Evarts*, 214–27; SW to SLMB, December 1970 through January 1871, Barlow Papers.

22. WME to SW, December 19, 1873, February 8, 17, April, May 6, 7, 1874, Ward Papers, NYPL; Barrows, *William M. Evarts*, 216.

23. WME to SW, May 11, June 17, July 23, 29, 1874, Ward Papers, NYPL.

24. SW to HWL, no date, January 1874, HWLL, Houghton.

25. SW to HWL, January 27, 1873, April 17, 1873, HWLL, Houghton.

26. SW to HWL, December 27, 30, 1873, and no date but probably January or February 1874, HWLL, Houghton; HWL journal, February 22, 1874, Samuel Longfellow, *Life of Henry Wadsworth Longfellow*, vol. 3, 219–22.

27. Gail Hamilton [Mary Abigail Dodge], *Gail Hamilton's Life in Letters*, ed. H. Augusta Dodge (Boston: Lee & Shepard, 1901), 683; Elliott, *Uncle Sam*, 501.

28. SW to JWH, May 19, 1870, HFP, Houghton.

29. SW to SLMB, April 13, 1874, Barlow Papers.

30. Emily Edson Briggs, *The Olivia Letters* (New York: Neale Publishing, 1906), 91.

31. Briggs, *The Olivia Letters*, 92–93.

32. Collis Huntington to Mark Hopkins, June 6, 1868, and Collis Huntington to E. B. Crocker, December 7, 1867, and July 2, 28, 1868, in David Lavender, *The Great Persuader* (New York: Doubleday, 1970), 151, 222–23.

33. Briggs, *The Olivia Letters*, 94.

34. Lavender, *The Great Persuader*, 305–11.

35. Oberholtzer, *History of the United States*, vol. 1, 284, 341; Pitt Cooke to Jay Cooke, February 18, 1869, in Henrietta Larson, *Jay Cooke, Private Banker* (Cambridge: Harvard University Press, 1936), 201, and also 101–8, 186, 227.

36. Constance Green, *Washington: A History of the Capital, 1800–1950* (Princeton: Princeton University Press, 1962), vol. 1, 357–58; Larson, *Jay Cooke*, 123.

37. Ronald Jensen, *The Alaska Purchase and Russian-American Relations* (Seattle: University of Washington Press, 1975), 105–6; James Shenton, *Robert John Walker: A Politician from Jackson to Lincoln* (New York: Columbia University Press, 1961), 109–202.

38. Jensen, *Alaska Purchase*, 100–130; Jordan H. Donaldson, "A Politician of Expansion: Robert J. Walker," *Mississippi Valley Historical Review* 19 (December 1932), 362–81; Paul Holbo, *Tarnished Expansion: The Alaska Scandal, the Press, and Congress, 1867–1871* (Knoxville: University of Tennessee Press, 1983), 30–73.

39. Stanley Hirshson, *Grenville M. Dodge: Soldier, Politician, Railroad Pioneer* (Bloomington: Indiana University Press, 1967), 3–36.

40. Hirshson, *Grenville M. Dodge*, 185–96.

41. Hirshson, *Grenville M. Dodge*, 185–96; Maury Klein, *The Life and Legend of Jay Gould* (Baltimore: Johns Hopkins University Press, 1986), 162–74.

42. Leon Burr Richardson, *William E. Chandler: Republican* (New York: Dodd, Mead, 1940), 1–5, 38–57.

43. Richardson, *William E. Chandler*, 63–67; SW to WEC, August 31, 1866, Chandler Papers.

44. Richardson, *William E. Chandler*, 73–82; WEC to William J. Palmer, April 1, 1867, Chandler Papers.

45. Grenville Dodge to WEC, December 26, 1875, in Richardson, *William E. Chandler*, 162–63.

46. Lavender, *The Great Persuader*, 197.

47. Collis Huntington to David Colton, November 27, 1875, in Lavender, *The Great Persuader*, 310–11, also 106, 150, 197.

48. James Olson, *J. Sterling Morton* (Lincoln: University of Nebraska Press, 1942), 134–42, 214–30, 291.

49. Olson, *J. Sterling Morton*, 216–19.

50. Mark Wahlgren Summers, *The Era of Good Stealings* (New York: Oxford University Press, 1993), 50–51; Charles F. Adams, Jr., "Railway Problems in 1869," *North American Review* 110 (January 1870): 116–51; Robert W. Fogel, *The Union Pacific Railroad—A Case of Premature Enterprise* (Baltimore: Johns Hopkins Press, 1960).

51. Charles Ames, *Pioneering the Union Pacific: A Reappraisal of the Building of the Railroad* (New York: Appleton-Century-Crofts, 1969), 204–7, 431–68; Summers, *Era of Good Stealings*, 51–52; U.S. Congress, House Report 77, "Credit Mobilier," 42nd Cong., 3rd sess., 1871, 4–7, 30–32.

52. *The Nation*, January 30, 1873.

53. House Report 77, "Credit Mobilier."

54. John B. Ellis, *Sights and Secrets of the National Capital* (New York: United States Publishing, 1869), 183.

55. Mrs. John A. Logan, *Thirty Years in Washington* (Hartford, CT: A. D. Worthington & Co., 1901), 122.

56. Catherine Allgor, *Parlor Politics: In Which the Ladies of Washington Help Build a City and a Government* (Charlottesville: University Press of Virginia, 2000), chapters 2 and 3.

57. Grenville Dodge to Anne Dodge, March 30, 1867, in Hirshson, *Grenville M. Dodge*, 149.

58. Briggs, *The Olivia Letters*, 91–92.

59. Mary Clemmer Ames, *Ten Years in Washington: Life and Scenes in the National Capital as a Woman Sees Them* (Hartford, CT: A. D. Worthington & Co., 1873), 120–24.

60. *New York Daily Graphic*, March 18, 1876.

61. George Alfred Townsend, *Washington, Outside and Inside* (Hartford, CT: Betts & Co., 1873), 455–57.

62. Briggs, *The Olivia Letters*, 92; Summers, *Era of Good Stealings*, 113.

63. Ellis, *Sights and Secrets*, 183–84; Mark Twain and Charles Dudley Warner, *The Gilded Age: A Tale of To-Day* (1873; reprint, New York: Oxford University Press, 1996), 145;

Cincinnati Enquirer, February 6, 1875; *New York World,* January 2, 1870; *Chicago Tribune,* February 20, 1869.

64. Poore, *Perley's Reminiscences,* vol. 2, 513–15.

65. James Parton, "The Small Sins of Congress," *Atlantic Monthly* 24 (November 1869): 524.

66. Sidney Teiser, "Life of George Williams: Almost Chief Justice," *Oregon Historical Quarterly* 47 (September 1946): part 1, 271–74; *Oregon State Journal,* May 9, 1868.

67. *Oregon State Journal,* April 10, 1869; Teiser, "Life of George Williams," part 1, 278–80.

68. Sidney Teiser, "Life of George Williams: Almost Chief Justice," *Oregon Historical Quarterly* 47 (December 1946): part 2, 418–25; Mrs. John A. Logan, *Reminiscences of a Soldier's Wife* (New York: C. Scribner's Sons, 1916), 271.

69. Teiser, "Life of George Williams," part 2, 424–27; Hamilton, *Gail Hamilton's Letters,* 682–83.

70. C. H. Hill to Benjamin Bristow, December 19, 1873, Benjamin Bristow Papers, Library of Congress, Washington, DC; *Congressional Record,* 43rd Cong., 1st sess., 3375–78; Logan, *Reminiscences of a Soldier's Wife,* 271–73.

71. Hamilton Fish diary, January 5, 1874, in Alan Nevins, *Hamilton Fish: The Inner History of the Grant Administration* (New York: Dodd, Mead, 1937), 663; Jerome Stillson to Charles A. Dana, December 3, 1873, enclosed in Dana's letter to Manton Marble, December 4, 1873, Marble Papers.

72. Teiser, "Life of George Williams," part 2, 427–34.

73. U.S. Congress, House Report 353, "Colt Patent, &c., &c.," 33rd Cong., 1st sess., 1854, 4–15.

74. Donald Ritchie, *Press Gallery: Congress and the Washington Correspondents* (Cambridge: Harvard University Press, 1991), 1–6, 73–78; Mark Wahlgren Summers, *The Press Gang: Newspapers and Politics, 1865–1878* (Chapel Hill: University of North Carolina Press, 1994), 2–24.

75. James Parton, "The Pressure Upon Congress," *Atlantic Monthly* 25 (February 1870): 157; Ritchie, *Press Gallery,* 92–130; Summers, *Press Gang,* 2–24, 112.

76. *Cincinnati Gazette,* January 23, 1875.

77. Ritchie, *Press Gallery,* 4; Summers, *Press Gang,* 5; Poore, *Perley's Reminiscences,* vol. 2, 513–15.

78. Summers, *Press Gang,* 116–19.

79. U.S. Congress, House Report 799, "Management of the War Department: Testimony Regarding Contracts with Cowles and Brega," 44th Cong., 1st sess., 423–55; Summers, *Press Gang,* 123–42.

80. Ritchie, *Press Gallery,* 92–98; Jensen, *Alaska Purchase,* 124–25; Holbo, *Tarnished Expansion,* 4–5, 23–58; U.S. Congress, House Report 35, "Alaska Investigation," 40th Cong., 3rd sess., 1869, 11–12, 23–41; Summers, *Press Gang,* 108–16.

81. House Report 35, "Alaska Investigation," 11–30; Holbo, *Tarnished Expansion,* 23–68.

82. House Report 35, "Alaska Investigation," 1–41; Holbo, *Tarnished Expansion,* 68–75.

83. Ritchie, *Press Gallery*, 99–101; Summers, *Press Gang*, 109–12; Hirshson, *Grenville M. Dodge*, 201; Oberholtzer, *History of the United States*, vol. 2, 91, vol. 3, 335–47.

84. Townsend, *Washington, Outside and Inside*, 520.

85. Ritchie, *Press Gallery*, 102–7; House Report 77, "Credit Mobilier," 31–32; Wilbur W. Allan, "The Credit Mobilier Scandal, 1873," in *Congress Investigates: A Documented History, 1792–1974*, ed. Arthur M. Schlesinger, Jr., and Roger Bruns (New York: Chelsea House, 1975), vol. 3, pp. 1849–63.

CHAPTER SIX

1. John Haskell Kemble, "The Genesis of the Pacific Mail Steamship Company," *California Historical Society Quarterly* 13 (September 1934): 240–54 and (December 1934): 386–406; John Haskell Kemble, "A Hundred Years of the Pacific Mail," *American Neptune* 10 (April 1950): 123–43; John Haskell Kemble, "The Transpacific Railroads, 1869–1915," *Pacific Historical Review* 18 (August 1949): 331–43; *The Nation*, December 17, 24, 1874, January 7, 14, 28, February, 4, 1875; Leonard Alexander Swann, Jr., *John Roach, Maritime Engineer: The Years as a Naval Contractor, 1862–1886* (Annapolis: U.S. Naval Institute, 1965).

2. Mark Wahlgren Summers, *The Press Gang: Newspapers and Politics, 1865–1878* (Chapel Hill: University of North Carolina Press, 1994), 106; Donald Ritchie, *Press Gallery: Congress and the Washington Correspondents* (Cambridge: Harvard University Press, 1991), 107–8; Kemble, "Transpacific Railroads," 333–35; U.S. Congress, House Report 268, "China Mail Service," 43rd Cong., 2nd sess., 1874, 12.

3. House Report 268, "China Mail Service," 344, 362, 618.

4. House Report 268, "China Mail Service," v–xix, 344, 362–75, 618; *Chicago Times*, January 16, 1875.

5. *Chicago Daily Tribune*, January 20, 1875. All quotations of Sam's testimony come from House Report 268, "China Mail Service," 408–10.

6. *Chicago Daily Tribune*, January 20, 1875; *New York Sun*, January 15, 1875.

7. *New York Daily Graphic*, December 20, 1876.

8. *New York Times*, February 8, 1875.

9. SW to HWLL, January 25, 1875, HWLL, Houghton.

10. SW to Edmund Stedman, January 17, 1875, transcript in Ward Papers, NYPL.

11. James A. Garfield, *The Diary of James A. Garfield*, ed. Harry James Brown and Frederick D. Williams (East Lansing: Michigan State University Press, 1967), vol. 3, 1875–1877; Evarts, Bayard, and Cox letters, Ward Papers, NYPL.

12. SW to HWL, March 15, 23, June 11, 1875, HWLL, Houghton.

13. SW to HWL, March 23, 1875, HWLL, Houghton.

14. *New York Times*, March 18, 1875.

15. SW to HWL, December 19, 1875, HWLL, Houghton.

16. Lately Thomas [Robert Steele], *Sam Ward, "King of the Lobby"* (Boston: Houghton Mifflin, 1965), 384–93; Lately Thomas [Robert Steele], *A Pride of Lions: The Astor Orphans* (New York: William Morrow and Co., 1971), 18–31.

17. SW to JWH, January 10, 1876, HFP, Houghton.

18. SW to HWL, undated, spring of 1876, in Maud Howe Elliott, *Uncle Sam Ward and His Circle* (1938; reprint, New York: Arno Press, 1975), 537.

19. SW to Maud Howe, February 6, 1876, in Elliott, *Uncle Sam*, 534–35.

20. SLMB to SW, no date, late 1875, Barlow Papers.

21. SW to HWL, May 23, 1875, HWLL, Houghton.

22. SW to TFB, April 30, 1876, Bayard Papers.

23. SW to TFB, November 2, 3, 1875, April 30, May 2, December 8, 1876, January 17, 1877, Bayard Papers; SW to SLMB, July and August, 1876, Barlow Papers; SW to Julia Romana Anagnos, December 31, 1876, HFP, Schlesinger.

24. *Cleveland Plain Dealer*, August 30, 1870, in Mark Wahlgren Summers, *The Era of Good Stealings* (New York: Oxford University Press, 1993), 9.

25. Among the studies of corruption in the 1850s, Mark Wahlgren Summers's *The Plundering Generation* offers the most detailed analysis and creates a vivid context in which to view antebellum lobbying. Mark Wahlgren Summers, *The Plundering Generation: Corruption and the Crisis of the Union, 1849–1861* (New York: Oxford University Press, 1987).

26. Horace Elisha Scudder, *James Russell Lowell: A Biography* (Boston: Houghton Mifflin, 1901), vol. 2, 192.

27. James Russell Lowell, "An Ode for the Fourth of July, 1876," in *The Poems of James Russell Lowell* (Boston: Houghton, Mifflin, 1890), vol. 4, 96.

28. Summers, *Era of Good Stealings*, 62–85.

29. Summers, *Press Gang*, 1–6, 25–42.

30. Morton Keller, *Affairs of State* (Cambridge: Harvard University Press, 1977), 1–121; Charles Calhoun, "The Political Culture: Public Life and the Conduct of Politics," in *The Gilded Age: Essays on the Origins of Modern America*, ed. Charles Calhoun (Wilmington, DE: Scholarly Resources, 1996), 185–214; Margaret Thompson, *The Spider Web: Congress and Lobbying in the Age of Grant* (Ithaca: Cornell University Press, 1985), 52–53, 66–67: Summers, *Era of Good Stealings*, chapter 1.

31. Henry Adams, "The Session," *North American Review* 111 (July 1870): 29.

32. Gamaliel Bradford, "Congressional Reform," *North American Review* 111 (October 1870): 334.

33. Margaret Thompson's exploration of how lobbyists became the scapegoat of those looking for a simple explanation for the corruption they saw engulfing the federal government offers keen insight into their demonization and informs the discussion that follows. Thompson, *Spider Web*, 32–56; Summers, *Era of Good Stealings*, 6–8.

34. Thompson, *Spider Web*, 54–56.

35. Gail Hamilton [Mary Abigail Dodge], *Biography of James G. Blaine* (Norwich, CT: H. Bill Publishing, 1895), 439.

36. "The Existence of the Lobby," *The Nation*, July 22, 1869, 65; *New York Herald*, April 10, 1875.

37. Benjamin Perley Poore, *Perley's Reminiscences of Sixty Years in the National Metropolis* (Philadelphia: Hubbard Brothers, 1886), vol. 2, 513; "Is There Anything In It," *Continental Monthly*, June 1863, 690; John B. Ellis, *The Sights and Secrets of the National Capital* (New York: United States Publishing, 1869), 188–90; "The Congressional Lobby," *The*

Republic 1 (April 1873): 71; Edward Winslow Martin [James Dabney], *Behind the Scenes in Washington* (New York: Continental Publishing, 1873), 217–20; *Harper's Weekly*, January 30, 1869, 9; James Parton, "Logrolling at Washington," *Atlantic Monthly* 24 (September 1869): 368.

38. James Parton, "The Small Sins of Congress," *Atlantic Monthly* 24 (November 1869): 522.

39. Gordon Milne's *The American Political Novel* (Norman: University of Oklahoma Press, 1966) offers insightful analysis of the Gilded Age novels of Twain and Warner, John De Forest, and Henry Adams.

40. Mark Twain and Charles Dudley Warner, *The Gilded Age: A Tale of To-Day* (1873; reprint, New York: Harper & Brothers, 1901), vol. 1, 306–7.

41. John William De Forest, *Playing the Mischief*, introduction by Joseph Jay Rubin (1875; reprint, State College, PA: Bald Eagle Press, 1961), 7; John William De Forest, *Honest John Vane* (New Haven: Richmond & Patten, 1875), 100; Robert Falk, *The Victorian Mode in American Fiction* (East Lansing: Michigan State University Press, 1965), 37–39; Leo Levy, "Naturalism in the Making: De Forest's Honest John Vane," *New England Quarterly* 37 (March 1964): 92.

42. De Forest, *Honest John Vane*, 102–3.

43. De Forest, *Honest John Vane*, 104.

44. De Forest, *Playing the Mischief*, introduction by Rubin, 7, 29–30.

45. De Forest, *Honest John Vane*, 102.

46. De Forest, *Playing the Mischief*, 374.

47. Twain and Warner, *The Gilded Age* (Harper & Brothers, 1901), vol. 2, 268.

48. "The Lobby," *The Republic* 1 (1873): 74.

49. Thompson, *Spider Web*, 58–60.

50. *Congressional Record*, 43rd Cong., 2nd sess. (1875), 648.

51. *Congressional Record*, 43rd Cong., 2nd sess. (1875), 2235.

52. *Congressional Record*, 44th Cong., 1st sess. (1876), 3230–31.

53. *Congressional Record*, 44th Cong., 1st sess. (1876), 3230–31.

54. Thompson, *Spider Web*, 65–66.

CHAPTER SEVEN

1. JWH to SW, March 25, 1878, in Maud Howe Elliott, *Uncle Sam Ward and His Circle* (1938; reprint, New York: Arno Press, 1975), 542.

2. William Bristol Shaw, "James R. Keene," *Dictionary of American Biography* (New York: Charles Scribner's Sons, 1933), vol. 10, 283; Edward Bowen, *Legacies of the Turf: A Century of Great Thoroughbred Breeders* (Lexington, KY: Eclipse Press, 2003), vol. 1, 5–26; *Chicago Daily Tribune*, February 13, 1879; Mary Simon, "James R. Keene: The Man Who Loved Racing," *Thoroughbred Times*, August 18, 2000.

3. SW to HWL, February 29, March 11, 1880, HWLL, Houghton.

4. William Butler Duncan to SW, August 22, 1879, HFP, Schlesinger.

5. TFB to SW, September 28, 1879, Ward Papers, NYPL.

6. SW to HWL, March 17, 1880, HWLL, Houghton; Lately Thomas [Robert Steele], *Sam Ward, "King of the Lobby"* (Boston: Houghton Mifflin, 1965), 402–3.

7. Sam's gift was Julia's home for the last thirty years of her life. Laura Richards and Maud Howe Elliott, *Julia Ward Howe, 1819–1910* (Boston: Houghton Mifflin, 1916), vol. 2, 71, 81; Deborah Clifford, *Mine Eyes Have Seen the Glory: A Biography of Julia Ward Howe* (Boston: Little, Brown, 1979), 220–27; Elliott, *Uncle Sam*, 612; JWH to SW, April 13, 1881, HFP, Houghton.

8. Clifford, *Mine Eyes*, 220–21; Margaret Chanler, *Roman Spring: Memoirs* (Boston: Little, Brown, 1934), 98, 120; Richards and Elliott, *Julia Ward Howe*, vol. 2, 67; SW to SLMB, no date, autumn, 1881, Barlow Papers.

9. Mary Sherwood, *New York Times*, February 25, 1899.

10. SW to JWH, November 17, 1881, HFP, Houghton; Julia Ward Howe, *Reminiscences, 1819–1899* (Cambridge, MA: Riverside Press, 1899), 73.

11. Francis Marion Crawford to SW, May 1881–July 1882, F. Marion Crawford Letters, Library of Congress, Washington, DC.

12. Marion Crawford, *Dr. Claudius: A True Story* (New York: Macmillan, 1883), 181–85.

13. Letters to Sam from "Member" and "Sycophant" are in the Ward Papers, NYPL. Three biographies provide useful background about Lord Rosebery: Robert Crewe, *Lord Rosebery* (New York: Harper & Brothers, 1931); Robert James, *Rosebery, A Biography of Archibald Philip Fifth Earl of Rosebery* (New York: Macmillan, 1964); Leo McKinstry, *Rosebery: Statesman in Turmoil* (London: John Murray, 2005); Elliott, *Uncle Sam*, 580–600.

14. SW to HWL, February 29, March 11, 1880, HWLL, Houghton; *Vanity Fair*, January 10, 1880.

15. Lately Thomas [Robert Steele], *Delmonico's: A Century of Splendor* (Boston: Houghton Mifflin, 1967), 197–98.

16. Lloyd Lewis and Henry Justin Smith, *Oscar Wilde Discovers America* (New York: Harcourt, Brace, 1936), 49; Richard Ellmann, *Oscar Wilde* (New York: Alfred A. Knopf, 1988), 82–161.

17. *New York World*, January 4, 1882.

18. Marian Hooper Adams, *The Letters of Mrs. Henry Adams, 1865–1883*, ed. Ward Thoron (Boston: Little, Brown, 1936), 339; Lewis and Smith, *Oscar Wilde Discovers America*, 50.

19. SW to Maud Howe, January 12, 1884, in Elliott, *Uncle Sam*, 604; Lewis and Smith, *Oscar Wilde Discovers America*, 60; SW to SLMB, January 13, 1882, Barlow Papers.

20. *Woman's Journal*, February 4, 1882; *Boston Transcript*, February 16, 1882; *New York Daily Tribune*, February 18, 1882; Richards and Elliott, *Julia Ward Howe*, vol. 2, 71–72.

21. Elliott, *Uncle Sam*, 609; *Boston Transcript*, February 1, 2, 1882; Ellmann, *Oscar Wilde*, 161–62, 182–84.

22. SW to TFB, May 20, 1879, and May–June 1879, Bayard Papers; TFB to SW, June 10, 1879, and May–June, 1879, Ward Papers, NYPL.

23. TFB to SW, July–August 1879, Ward Papers, NYPL; SW to TFB, June 28, 1880, and July–August 1879, Bayard Papers.

24. SW to JWH, March 4, 1881, in Elliott, *Uncle Sam*, 570.

25. SW to Margaret Terry, September 29, 1881, Samuel Ward: Letters to Margaret Terry Chanler, Houghton Library, Harvard University, Cambridge, MA; Chanler, *Roman Spring*, 102.

26. SW to JWH, December 12, 1881, HFP, Houghton.

27. SW to JWH, June 7, 1882, HFP, Houghton.

28. WME to SW, June 5, 1879, in Elliott, *Uncle Sam*, 558.

29. WME to SW, in Thomas, *Sam Ward*, 392–93; WME to SW, 1879–1882, Ward Papers, NYPL; SW to WME, 1879–1882, Evarts Papers; Chester Barrows, *William M. Evarts* (Chapel Hill: University of North Carolina Press, 1941), 363–68.

30. SW to SLMB, June 6, 1879; February 6, 1880; April–July 1880, Barlow Papers.

31. *Chicago Tribune*, January 6, 1881.

32. Emily Edson Briggs, *The Olivia Letters* (New York: Neale Publishing, 1906), 417–18.

33. SW to SLMB, July–August 1880, Barlow Papers.

34. SW to JWH, March 9, 1882, and JWH to SW, undated but soon thereafter, HFP, Houghton; JWH to SW, spring 1882, Julia Ward Howe Papers, Houghton Library, Harvard University, Cambridge, MA.

35. SW to JWH, undated, March 1882, HFP, Houghton.

36. SW to Margaret Terry, no date, spring 1882, Samuel Ward: Letters to Margaret Terry Chanler, Houghton; Sam Ward, "Days With Longfellow," *North American Review* 134 (May 1882). Just three months earlier, Siro Delmonico, the last of his generation and a man from whom Sam had learned so much, had died, and Sam was still mourning the passing of this old friend. Thomas, *Delmonico's*, 197.

37. SW to Margaret Terry, no date, October 1882, Samuel Ward: Letters to Margaret Terry Chanler, Houghton.

38. JWH to Annie Ward Mailliard, November 4, 1882, HFP, Houghton; JWH, *Reminiscences*, 72–73.

39. SW to JWH, November 14, 1882, HFP, Houghton.

40. Louise Hall Tharp, *Three Saints and a Sinner* (Boston: Little, Brown, 1956), 331–34; Elliott, *Uncle Sam*, 638.

41. Sam's letters to Maud Howe (Ward Papers, Houghton) and to Daisy Terry (Samuel Ward: Letters to Margaret Terry Chanler, Houghton Library), who were less judgmental than Julia, were filled with details of food and fashion from London and the English countryside. Sam's letters to Barlow also give a lively account of his and Hurlbert's activities. Among the most detailed are SW to SLMB, July 10, July 31, August 7, 16, 18, 1883, Barlow Papers.

42. Elliott, *Uncle Sam*, 671–80; Chanler, *Roman Spring*, 155–58; SW to SLMB, October 5, 1883, January 30, March 2, 1884, letters from fall and winter 1883–84, Barlow Papers.

43. Elliott, *Uncle Sam*, 682–84; Chanler, *Roman Spring*, 156–58.

44. Hurlbert to Rosebery, in Thomas, *Sam Ward*, 482–84; Chanler, *Roman Spring*, 158.

45. JW to Louisa Ward Crawford Terry, in Thomas, *Sam Ward*, 484; Richards and Elliott, *Julia Ward Howe*, vol. 2, 93–96.

46. TFB to SLMB, May 24, 1884, Barlow Papers.

47. While most of Sam's obituaries appeared on May 20 and May 21, 1884, the *National Police Gazette* ran its tribute on June 7, 1884.

48. Frank Carpenter, *"Carp's" Washington*, ed. Frances Carpenter (New York: McGraw Hill, 1960), 279–80.

49. Marion Crawford to JWH, in Thomas, *Sam Ward*, 487.

50. Lord Rosebery, "Uncle Sam," Ward Papers, NYPL; *Daily Graphic*, February 1, 1875.

EPILOGUE

1. Maud Howe Elliott, *Uncle Sam Ward and His Circle* (1938; reprint, New York: Arno Press, 1975), 686.

2. Elliott, *Uncle Sam*, 677, 686; Laura Richards and Maud Howe Elliott, *Julia Ward Howe, 1819–1910* (Boston: Houghton Mifflin, 1916), vol. 1, 56.

3. Elliott, *Uncle Sam*, 685–86; "Anecdote told by Chanler Chapman, of Barrytown, Sam Ward's great-grandson," included in a letter from Robert Steele to M. F. K. Fisher, April 18, 1965, Fisher Papers.

4. Robert Steele to M. F. K. Fisher, July 27, 1965, Fisher Papers.

5. Margaret Chanler, *Roman Spring: Memoirs* (Boston: Little, Brown, 1934), 101. For directions for making a "Sam Ward" and to see the attractive drink, see www.esquire.com/drinks/sam-ward-drink-recipe. Information about Columbia's Philolexian Society was shared with the author by Thomas Vinciguerra of New York. Sam's recipe for Chicken Sauté still sounds delicious: "Using three 2-lb. broilers separate breasts and legs. Remove excess bones and sauté in butter until done. Remove chicken from pan and in the same pan sauté one pint of sliced mushrooms. Add one pint of cream sauce, salt and pepper, and let simmer for about five minutes." Ward Papers, NYPL; conversations with staff at the Somerset Club, Loche Ober restaurant, and the Algonquin Club, Boston, 2008.

6. The story of Ward McAllister, Sam, the Astors, and what and who "The Four Hundred" was and were is well told in the following: Eric Homberger, *Mrs. Astor's New York: Money and Social Power in a Gilded Age* (New Haven: Yale University Press, 2002), 149–219; Ward McAllister, *Society As I Have Found It* (New York: Cassell Publishing, 1890); Jerry E. Patterson, *The First Four Hundred: Mrs. Astor's New York in the Gilded Age* (New York: Rizzoli, 2000), 71–84, 147–48, 207–33; *New York Daily Tribune*, March 25, 1888.

7. (New York) *Town Topics*, March 12 and February 26, 1891; Homberger, *Mrs. Astor's New York*, 216–17. A year after his wife of nearly forty years died in 1883, Collis Huntington married thirty-four-year-old widow Arabella D. Worsham, who was eager to enter society. After Collis Huntington's death in 1900, she married his nephew, Henry Huntington, another railroad tycoon, and, upon his death in 1924, she was said to be the richest woman in America.

8. Wintie and Daisy and their large family lived in luxury all over the world, "wherever thrills were to be had," according to Maud Howe Elliott. A friend of Theodore Roosevelt's, Wintie served with the "Rough Riders" and was wounded in the right arm. Patterson, *First Four Hundred*, 147–48.

9. Discussion of the "Diary of a Public Man" draws on the following: F. Lauriston Bullard, *The Diary of a Public Man* (New Brunswick: Rutgers University Press, 1946); Frank Maloy Anderson, *The Mystery of "A Public Man"* (Minneapolis: University of Minnesota Press, 1948); Roy N. Lokken, "Has the Mystery of 'A Public Man' Been Solved?" *Mississippi*

Valley Historical Review 40 (December 1953): 420–40; Benjamin Price, "That Baffling Diary," *South Atlantic Quarterly* 54 (January 1955): 56–64.

10. Daniel W. Crofts, *A Secession Crisis Enigma: William Henry Hurlbert and "The Diary of a Public Man"* (Baton Rouge: Louisiana State University Press, forthcoming). In 1895, Hurlbert, like Sam, died an expatriate in Italy, escaping troubles. Sam's troubles were financial, Hurlbert's legal. After leaving the *World* in 1883, Hurlbert had spent most of his time in England; but he had bolted from London for Italy in 1891, fleeing a breech of promise suit by a British actress and a warrant for his arrest. Alvin F. Harlow, "William Henry Hurlbert," *Dictionary of American Biography* (New York: Charles Scribner's Sons, 1932), vol. 9, 424.

11. *The Nation*, June 12, 1913.

12. George Spencer to Uriah Painter, November 20, 1884, in Stanley Hirshson, *Grenville M. Dodge: Soldier, Politician, Railroad Pioneer* (Bloomington: Indiana University Press, 1967), 211–12; Donald Ritchie, *Press Gallery: Congress and the Washington Correspondents* (Cambridge: Harvard University Press, 1991), 110–11.

13. Ritchie, *Press Gallery*, 109–21.

14. James Bryce, *The American Commonwealth* (New York: Macmillan, 1888), vol. 2, 732, and vol. 1, 681.

15. Frank Carpenter, *"Carp's" Washington*, ed. Frances Carpenter (New York: McGraw Hill, 1960), 278–79.

16. Bryce, *American Commonwealth*, vol. 1, chapters 13–19, and vol. 2, 121–33.

17. "Lobbying and its Remedy," *Century Illustrated Magazine* 31 (April 1886): 96.

18. *Guide to Congress* (Washington, DC: CQ Press, 2000), vol. 1, 719.

19. U.S. Congress, House Report 113, "A Report of the Select Committee of the House of Representatives, under H. Res. 198, on Charges Against Members of the House and Lobbying Activities of the National Association of Manufacturers of the United States, and Others," 63rd Cong., 2nd sess., 1913.

20. U.S. Congress, Senate, S. Print 99–161, Committee on Governmental Affairs, "Congress and Pressure Groups: Lobbying in a Modern Democracy," 99th Cong., 2nd sess., 1986, 41–45; Karl Schriftgiesser, *The Lobbyists* (Boston: Little, Brown, 1951), 26–30; James Deakin, *The Lobbyists* (Washington, DC: Public Affairs Press, 1966), 70–74.

21. Helpful summaries of the 2007 changes to lobbying laws and regulations are found in "Lobbying Disclosure: Themes and Issues, 110th Congress," RL 33798, May 2007, and "Lobbying Law and Ethics Rules Changes in the 110th Congress," RL 34166, September 18, 2007, Reports of the Congressional Research Service, Library of Congress, Washington, DC.

22. The American League of Lobbyists' web site (www.allcd.org) includes the ALL's code of ethics and history. *Guide to Congress* (Washington, DC: CQ Press, 2008), vol. 1, 805–8.

23. Emily Edson Briggs, *The Olivia Letters* (New York: Neal Publishing, 1906), 417–18.

24. Florence H. Hall, *Social Usages at Washington* (New York: Harper & Brothers, 1906), 132.

25. "Lawmaking by Means of Dinners," *Literary Digest*, July 16, 1927.

26. Pendleton Herring, *Group Representation Before Congress* (Baltimore: Johns Hopkins Press, 1929), 38–40.

27. *Washington Post*, October 14, 1980.

ESSAY ON SOURCES

Philadelphia newspaperman John Forney was right when he made this observation about Sam in 1873: "What a delicious volume . . . what a jewel of a book he could make of the good things he has heard at his thousand *noctes ambrosianae!*" Two years later, after Sam testified before Congress, he told Longfellow that publishers were beating a path to his door, but the closest Sam came to writing about his life in any sustained way were the stories of his sojourn in the California wilderness in 1851 and the memoir he began to compose after being "cudgeled" into it by Lady Rosebery during his last exile in 1883.

The fourteen picaresque installments of "Incidents on the River of Grace" appeared from January through April 1861, in *Porter's Spirit of the Times* and were edited into a lively volume, *Sam Ward in the Gold Rush*, by Carvel Collins in 1949 (Stanford: Stanford University Press). Sam's memoir, which he began dictating first to Lady Rosebery herself and later to a secretary whom she hired for him, carried him only up to his return from his extended stay in Europe as a young man in 1837. The only known copy, with Sam's unmistakable handwriting in the margins, resides at Harvard's Houghton Library. While Frank Maloy Anderson claimed in *The Mystery of "A Public Man"* (Minneapolis: University of Minnesota Press, 1948) that the "The Diary of a Public Man," which ran in the *North American Review* in 1879, was a third example of Sam's autobiographical writing, he was mistaken. Daniel W. Crofts's forthcoming *A Secession Crisis Enigma: William Henry Hurlbert and "The Diary of a Public Man,"* sections of which he kindly shared, does an excellent job of proving Anderson wrong.

Not only did Sam never write a book himself, but he went out of his way to make it difficult for anyone else to do so, or at least he meant to. Among the Howe family papers at the Schlesinger Library at Harvard's Radcliffe Institute, there is a tantalizing, unsigned, handwritten note—it is not Julia's handwriting nor does it appear to be that of her daughters—from 1903 that reads:

> Mr. Samuel Ward, fourth of that name, and well-known in New York and Washington a generation ago, as "Uncle Sam" or "Sam Ward" was very decidedly a man of sentiment who could not bear to destroy aught that might remind him of his friends. Hence the mass of his correspondence found after his death some nineteen years ago, was very voluminous. In the several large chests needed to contain it, were found interesting letters from many distinguished men, notes of invitation, recipes

and menus of the dinners for which he was famous, and mementos of many sorts. Among these were the two locks of hair which suggested the subject for his friend the poet Longfellow's well-known poem. They belonged to Mr. Ward's first wife, Emily Astor, and to the infant son whose birth cost his mother her life.

Sadly, no large chests full of Sam's letters and mementos survive. In another note in the same collection, his niece Laura wrote that her Uncle Sam had instructed her mother to burn all of his professional correspondence, and, probably with a sense of relief, sometime between 1903, when the note was written, and 1910, when she died, Julia did just that.

Despite Sam's and Julia's best efforts, two authors did persevere and write books about him. *Uncle Sam Ward and His Circle* by Maud Howe Elliott (1938; reprint, New York: Arno Press, 1975) is a sweet, uncritical volume of heavily edited letters to, from, and about Sam—many of which have not found their way into any repository—compiled by his adoring niece. There is little commentary, even less analysis, and the "circle" of the title is Sam's family circle only, so there is little mention of Sam as lobbyist. *Sam Ward, "King of the Lobby,"* by Lately Thomas, the pseudonym of Robert Steele (Boston: Houghton Mifflin, 1965), is a straightforward biography based on sources available in the early 1960s. One-third of the book deals with the years before Sam bobbed up in Washington; another third with the years after Sam left Washington; and another third with the years between 1860 to 1878 when Sam earned his crown. Although there is little about the lobby over which Sam reigned, Steele did travel to England to use the Rosebery archives, and he provides delightful detail about the members of the Mendacious Club.

While much of Sam's writing went up in flames, some papers escaped Julia's bonfire. A great deal of Sam's correspondence, literally hundreds and hundreds of his letters, still exists among the papers of his many family members, who, happily, seem to have saved just about everything and made certain that it found homes in appropriate repositories. The largest group of Sam's personal papers at the New York Public Library fill eight thin boxes. These include letters from his father to Sam when he was at Round Hill School and about money matters while Sam was in Europe, a meticulous household account book kept as he and Emily started their life together, the only note in Medora's handwriting, and Sam's diary from aboard the "Panama" bound for California.

In addition to the only copy of Sam's unpublished memoir and several copies of *Lyrical Recreations* (New York: D. Appleton, 1865), one of which is inscribed to Longfellow, several collections of Sam's papers and those of his family members are at Harvard's Houghton Library. One collection, "Samuel Ward (1814–1884): Letters to Margaret Terry Chanler," consists of his letters to his niece Daisy; another, "Samuel Ward (1814–1884): Papers," includes, among letters he wrote to others, more than 150 letters from Sam to his niece Maud Howe Elliott. The Margaret Terry Chanler family papers, the F. Marion Crawford papers, and two collections of the papers of Sam's father, Samuel Ward (1789–1839), all at Houghton Library, also contain significant material on Sam. Two other large collections there—the Julia Ward Howe papers and the largest of several collections of Howe family papers (MS Am 2119)—are gold mines not only for letters to and from Sam but for intrafamilial correspondence in which Sam is discussed.

The Julia Ward Howe papers and the Howe family papers at the Schlesinger Library at the Radcliffe Institute at Harvard contain much material by and about Sam, including many letters to Julia, who is sometimes "Dearest Dudie" and sometimes "My Dear Old Bird." Several collections at the New-York Historical Society, notably the Ward family papers, include material about Sam and his ancestors. The F. Marion Crawford papers at the Library of Congress consist of a beautifully bound book of Marion's letters to Sam thanking him for his many kindnesses. The Samuel Ward file at the Columbia University Archives includes information on Sam's academic career, on the years right after his return from Europe, and on the Prime, Ward and Company debacle.

Many correspondents besides Sam's family members saved his letters, and some who had secretaries even saved copies of their letters to him. These primary sources are invaluable for the flavor of Sam's personality which they impart and the details of his lobbying work which they reveal. The two most important of these caches are the collection of Sam's letters to Henry Wadsworth Longfellow at Houghton Library, with copies at the Longfellow National Historical Site in Cambridge, and the Samuel Latham Mitchill Barlow papers at the Huntington Library, in San Marino, California.

In a correspondence that documented their friendship and spanned nearly half a century, from their meeting in Heidelberg as young men until Longfellow's death in 1882, Sam and Longfellow delighted in one another's successes, traded jokes and gossip, and consoled one another over loves and losses. With no one else but Julia did Sam share so much of himself. Longfellow's 358 letters from Sam are in the largest of several Longfellow collections at Houghton Library: "Henry Wadsworth Longfellow: Letters to Henry Wadsworth Longfellow."

Letters between Sam and Barlow (copies of many from Barlow to Sam are also in the collection) spanned nearly thirty years and, while some are just brief notes, are even more numerous than the letters to Longfellow. Barlow was Sam's friend before he was Sam's chief employer and their correspondence reflects this dual relationship. Birthday greetings and discussions of wines are mixed in with candid discussions of Barlow's specific legislative goals and Sam's *plan de campagne* to realize them.

Many other manuscript collections help to illuminate Sam's life and work and the Gilded Age lobby. Especially helpful are the papers of William Henry Seward at the University of Rochester; of Sam's friends James A. Garfield, Thomas A. Bayard, and William M. Evarts, all at the Library of Congress; those of Francis Lieber at the Huntington Library; and of Charles Sumner at Houghton Library. The James G. Blaine, Benjamin Bristow, Benjamin Butler, Salmon Chase, Hamilton Fish, Benjamin Brown French, and Manton Marble papers at the Library of Congress, the William Chandler papers at the New Hampshire Historical Society, and the M. F. K. Fisher papers at the Schlesinger Library, which include her correspondence with Robert Steele, all open windows onto various aspects of Sam's career and onto the lobby.

A number of published first-hand accounts, memoirs, and autobiographies by

Sam's contemporaries offer rich detail about Washington, the lobby, and Sam, and create a context in which his life and work can be placed. These include: Virginia Clay-Clopton, *A Belle of the Fifties: Memoirs of Mrs. Clay of Alabama* (New York: Doubleday, Page, 1904); Lillie de Hegermann-Lindencrone, *The Sunny Side of Diplomatic Life, 1875–1912* (New York: Harper & Brothers, 1914); Mary Clemmer Ames, *Ten Years in Washington: Life and Scenes in the National Capital as a Woman Sees Them* (Hartford, CT: A. D. Worthington & Co., 1873); *Reminiscences of a Soldier's Wife*, by Mrs. John A. Logan (New York: C. Scribner's Sons, 1916); Mary Elizabeth Wilson Sherwood's articles in various magazines; the published diaries of Benjamin Brown French and James A. Garfield; John B. Ellis, *The Sights and Secrets of the National Capital* (New York: United States Publishing, 1869); *Washington, Outside and Inside* by reporter George Alfred Townsend (Hartford, CT: Betts & Co., 1873); *The Education of Henry Adams* by Henry Adams (1918; reprint, New York: Modern Library, 1931); Hugh Mc-Culloch, *Men and Measures of Half a Century* (New York: Charles Scribner's Sons, 1888); Edward Winslow Martin, *Behind the Scenes in Washington* (New York: Continental Publishing, 1873); William Howard Russell, *My Diary North and South* (Boston: T.O.H.P. Burnham, 1863); Benjamin Perley Poore, *Perley's Reminiscences of Sixty Years in the National Metropolis* (Philadelphia: Hubbard Brothers, 1886); *The Olivia Letters* by Emily Edson Briggs (New York: Neal Publishing, 1906); Gail Hamilton, *Gail Hamilton's Life in Letters* (Boston: Lee & Shephard, 1901); Frank Carpenter's columns collected in *"Carp's" Washington* (New York: McGraw Hill, 1960); John Forney's *Anecdotes of Public Men* (New York: Harper & Brothers, 1873); and Ward McAllister's *Society As I Have Found It* (New York: Cassell Publishing, 1890).

Julia's *Reminiscences: 1819–1899* (Cambridge, MA: Riverside Press, 1899), published when she was eighty, convey her tender memories of the brother she loved. In her memoir, *Roman Spring* (Boston: Little, Brown, 1934), Daisy (Margaret Chanler) writes vividly of her Uncle Sam, while her step-brother, Marion Crawford, immortalized Sam as the delightful Mr. Bellingham in his novel *Doctor Claudius* (New York: Macmillan, 1883).

Congressional hearings into possible abuses by the lobby offer insights into the details of its workings. Samuel Colt's gifts of French gloves to the wives and daughters of members came out in the 1854 hearings about his fights for patent extensions; how congressional employees and the press could be enlisted to pass or kill tariffs and how a skilled lobbyist like Thurlow Weed could seem to advocate both sides of an issue at once were revealed in the investigation that began at the Lawrence, Stone and Company woolen mill in 1858. Benjamin Butler's investigation in 1868 into how money might have influenced the outcome of President Johnson's impeachment trial brought Sam to a hearing room and made clear how intense the behind-the-scenes maneuvering had been; the hearings into the Alaska Purchase in the 40th Congress brought to light the value of a former member's floor privileges and the importance of having the press behind an issue. The Credit Mobilier hearings in the 42nd Congress showed the importance of a congressional insider to a railroad and the panic among the beneficiaries when its largesse was exposed. The Pacific Mail hearings in 1875 not only featured Sam and his defense of his profession and his dinners but gave a glimpse of how money was doled out in a lobbying campaign.

Because so many of Sam's friends, family members, predecessors, and contemporaries were prominent men and women, a great many biographies shed light on the times, the capital, and the lobby. Sam himself pops up in many of them. The long list of subjects of biographies, whose variety underscores Sam's many facets, includes the Astor family, Thomas Bayard, Benjamin Butler, Samuel Colt, William Evarts, Samuel Gridley Howe, Henry Wadsworth Longfellow, James Sterling Morton, Lord Rosebery, William Russell, William Henry Seward, Daniel Sickles, Charles Sumner, and the most flamboyant, Oscar Wilde.

Many biographers and literary scholars have written about Julia. Because Sam held a special place in Julia's heart, he figures in the following works: the two-volume biography by two of Julia's daughters, Laura Howe Richards and Maud Howe Elliott, *Julia Ward Howe* (Boston: Houghton Mifflin, 1916); Louise Hall Tharp, *Three Saints and a Sinner* (Boston: Little, Brown, 1956), in which Julia, Louisa, and Annie are the saints and, no surprise, Sam is the sinner; Deborah Clifford, *Mine Eyes Have Seen the Glory: A Biography of Julia Ward Howe* (Boston: Little, Brown, 1979); Mary Grant, *Private Woman, Public Person* (New York: Carlson Publishers, 1994); Gary Williams, *Hungry Heart: The Literary Emergence of Julia Ward Howe* (Amherst: University of Massachusetts Press, 1999); and Valerie Ziegler, *Diva Julia: The Public Romance and Private Agony of Julia Ward Howe* (New York: Trinity Press, 2003).

Three other books by Robert Steele (writing as Lately Thomas), two of them collective family biographies, focus on important places and people in Sam's life: *Delmonico's: A Century of Splendor* (Boston: Houghton Mifflin, 1967); *Between Two Empires: The Life Story of California's First Senator*, a biography of William Gwin (Boston: Houghton Mifflin, 1969); and *A Pride of Lions: The Astor Orphans*, about Sam's grandchildren (New York: W. Morrow, 1971). Two recent books offer rich detail about and wonderful images of the Astors, the "Astor orphans," Ward McAllister, and "The Four Hundred": Eric Homberger, *Mrs. Astor's New York: Money and Social Power in a Gilded Age* (New Haven: Yale Universiety Press, 2002); and Jerry E. Patterson, *The First Four Hundred: Mrs. Astor's New York in the Gilded Age* (New York: Rizzoli, 2000). Finding out more about other aspects of Sam's life and other members of the cast of Gilded Age characters led to some interesting sources: for example, to books on the history of Samuel Colt's guns, to books on horse breeding and to *Thoroughbred Times* for information on Sam's benefactor, James Keene, and to *Esquire* magazine's cocktail database (www.esquire.com/drinks/sam-ward-drink-recipe) for the recipe for a "Sam Ward."

Well-prepared food and fine wines were extremely important to Sam. Among the books that help to explain nineteenth-century American culinary history and why Sam's dinners stood out are Steele's book on Delmonico's, Waverly Root and Richard De Rochemont's *Eating in America: A History* (New York: William Morrow, 1976), Amy Trubek's *Haute Cuisine: How the French Invented the Culinary Profession* (Philadelphia: University of Pennsylvania, 2000), portions of Jerry Patterson's *The First Four Hundred*, and *The Oxford Encyclopedia of Food and Drink in America* (New York: Oxford

University Press, 2004). Mrs. E. F. Ellet's, *The New Cyclopedia of Domestic Economy, and Practical Housekeeper* (Norwich, CT: Henry Bill Publishing, 1872), is just one of the many cookbooks, domestic manuals, and marketing guides filled with recipes and instructions for tasks like ironing linens that were published after the war and not only make the reader hungry and tired but convey a very real sense of the work and forethought involved in carrying off an elegant dinner.

Sam's relationships with his father, his siblings, and his friends were also central to his life, and it is important to see these in the context of his times, when the language of male friendship sounded very different than it does in ours. Among the many recent books that explore issues of masculinity, male friendship, and manhood, the following were especially helpful: E. Anthony Rotundo, *American Manhood: Transformations in Masculinity from the Revolution to the Modern Era* (New York: Basic Books, 1993); Stephen Frank, *Life with Father: Parenthood and Masculinity in the Nineteenth-Century American North* (Baltimore: Johns Hopkins University Press, 1998); Donald Yacovone, "Surpassing the Love of Women: Victorian Manhood and the Language of Fraternal Love," in *A Shared Experience: Men, Women, and the History of Gender* (New York: New York University Press, 1998), edited by Laura McCall and Donald Yacovone; and Susan Johnson, "Bulls, Bears, and Dancing Boys: Race, Gender, and Leisure in the California Gold Rush," in *Across the Great Divide: Cultures of Manhood in the American West* (New York: Routledge, 2001), edited by Matthew Basso, Laura McCall, and Dee Garceau.

Although many of the oversized personalities of the Gilded Age have received a great deal of attention, the nineteenth-century lobby has received much less. While shelves of books—some with catchy titles like *Showdown at Gucci Gulch: Lawmakers, Lobbyists, and the Unlikely Triumph of Tax Reform* (Jeffrey Birnbaum and Allan S. Murray [New York: Random House, 1987]), *Still the Best Congress Money Can Buy* (Philip Stern [Washington, DC: Regnery Gateway, 1992]), and *Club Fed: Power, Money, Sex, and Violence on Capitol Hill* (Bill Thomas [New York: Charles Scribner's, 1994])— by journalists and lobbyists themselves and many with more sober titles by political scientists and public policy experts examine special interests and the lobby in post–World War II, post–Federal Regulation of Lobbying Act, post–Legislative Reorganization Act of 1946 Washington, few look back to see what came before. Even books that claim to offer a history of lobbying, such as Carl Schriftgiesser's *The Lobbyists; the Art and Business of Influencing Lawmakers* (Boston: Little, Brown, 1951) and James Deakin's *The Lobbyists* (Washington, DC: Public Affairs Press, 1966), race over the eighteenth and nineteenth centuries on their way to the twentieth. Journalist Kenneth Crawford's *The Pressure Boys: The Inside Story of Lobbying in America* (New York: J. Messner, 1939) picks up the story in the 1920s.

Several books about the "Great Barbecue" written in the late 1920s and 1930s, another period of great upheaval and fear for the nation's future—among them Claude Bowers's *The Tragic Era: The Revolution After Lincoln* (Cambridge, MA: Houghton Mifflin, 1929), Matthew Josephson's *The Robber Barons* (New York: Harcourt, Brace, 1934) and *The Politicos* (New York: Harcourt, Brace, 1938), and David Loth's *Public Plunder: A History of Graft in America* (New York: Carrick & Evans, 1938)—heaped scorn on these years but missed the bigger picture of which the corruption they decried was a part.

The universe of recent scholarly books that examine the lobby in the Gilded Age within the context of the times is small. Two, both excellent, are Margaret Thompson's *The Spider Web: Congress and Lobbying in the Age of Grant* (Ithaca, NY: Cornell University Press, 1985) and Mark Summers's *The Era of Good Stealings* (New York: Oxford University Press, 1993). Thompson explores how and why the lobby became the scapegoat for those looking for a simple explanation for the corruption they feared was engulfing the nation and offers keen insights into how this demonization reflected frightening, disorganized times. Summers argues that the Gilded Age, while certainly not the best of times, was not the worst of times either. While very real corruption, of which lobbying abuses formed only one genre, seemed about to swamp local, state, and the national government, Summers places it in the context of important changes that were developing before the Civil War and continued to evolve after it.

Other studies also offer important insights into lobbying and Congress in these years and those that came before. For the first years of the government, *The House and Senate in the 1790s: Petitioning, Lobbying, and Institutional Development*, edited by Kenneth R. Bowling and Donald R. Kennon (Athens: Ohio University Press, 2002), and volumes 7 (*Petition Histories: Revolutionary War-Related Claims, 1997*) and 8 (*Petition Histories and Non-Legislative Official Documents, 1998*) of *The Documentary History of the First Federal Congress of the United States of America* (Baltimore: Johns Hopkins University Press) discuss the flurry of petitioning that began as soon as the First Congress got underway. Mark Summers's reevaluation of the 1850s in *The Plundering Generation: Corruption and the Crisis of the Union, 1849–1861* (New York: Oxford University Press, 1987) roots many of the issues, especially corruption, with which Americans would grapple after the Civil War squarely in this antebellum decade. The essays in *The Gilded Age: Perspectives on the Origins of Modern America*, edited by Charles Calhoun (Lanham, MD: Rowman & Littlefield, 2007), especially Calhoun's own, "The Political Culture: Public Life and the Conduct of Politics," all help to explain the world in which Sam and the lobby flourished. Morton Keller's *Affairs of State* (Cambridge, MA: Belknap Press of Harvard University Press, 1977) grapples with the coalescing of factors that made the Gilded Age what it was, which was much more than most frightened, bitter, or disappointed Americans realized. The first of the fervent Christian lobbyists that Gaines Foster examines in *Moral Reconstruction: Christian Lobbyists and the Federal Legislation of Morality 1865–1920* (Chapel Hill: University of North Carolina Press, 2002) offer an interesting contrast to the Huntingtons, Weeds, and Wards in Washington.

David Rothman's *Politics and Power: The United States Senate, 1869–1901* (Cambridge, MA: Harvard University Press, 1966) and books and articles on the nineteenth-century House of Representatives by Nelson Polsby, Garrison Nelson, and others (see especially essays in *Congress in Change: Evolution and Reform*, edited by Norman Ornstein [New York: Praeger, 1975], and *Congressional Behavior*, edited by Polsby [New York: Random House, 1971]) examine the changes Congress was undergoing during these years. Alan Lessoff's *The Nation and Its City: Politics, Corruption, and Progress in Washington, D.C., 1861–1902* (Baltimore: Johns Hopkins University Press, 1994) explains how the capital was affected by the turmoil. Mark Summers's *The Press Gang: News-*

papers and Politics, 1865–1878 (Chapel Hill: University of North Carolina Press, 1994) and chapters dealing with Gilded Age journalists in Donald Ritchie's *Press Gallery: Congress and the Washington Correspondents* (Cambridge: Harvard University Press, 1991), both as entertaining as they are enlightening, examine the ties binding the press and the lobby during the years after the war.

Ritchie and Summers help fit wily Uriah Painter into the postwar drama. Biographies of Samuel Colt, Jay Gould, Collis Huntington, and Jay Cooke do the same. All examine their "Washington work" during the years of the "Great Barbecue." There is only a handful of biographies about the key lobbyists who pulled up chairs for the feast. Biographies of two of Sam's colleagues, Grenville M. Dodge (Stanley Hirshson, *Grenville M. Dodge: Soldier, Politician, Railroad Pioneer* [Bloomington: Indiana University Press, 1967]; Gerald Painter, *The Tie that Binds: Grenville M. Dodge and the Building of the First Transcontinental Railroad* [Northfield, VT: Norwich University Press, 1985]; and J. T. Granger's 1893 biography, reprinted in 1981, *A Brief Biographical Sketch of the Life of Major-General Grenville Dodge* [New York: Press of Styles & Cash, 1893]) and William E. Chandler (Leon Burr Richardson, *William E. Chandler: Republican* [New York: Dodd, Mead, 1940]), describe the power these two master craftsmen wielded. Glyndon Van Deusen's *Thurlow Weed, Wizard of the Lobby* (Boston: Little, Brown, 1947), detailing how Weed kept the New York legislature and the U.S. Congress in his back pocket, and James Shenton's *Robert John Walker: A Politician from Jackson to Lincoln* (New York: Columbia University Press, 1961), Ronald Jensen's *The Alaska Purchase and Russian-American Relations* (Seattle: University of Washington Press, 1975), and Paul Holbo's *Tarnished Expansion: The Alaska Scandal, the Press, and Congress, 1867–1871* (Knoxville: University Press of Kentucky, 1983), describing how ex-senator Robert S. Walker worked for the Russians to get his former colleagues to vote for "Seward's Icebox," convey the trials and excitement of prowling for enough votes to insure success for a client's bill.

The political fiction of the 1870s and 1880s, filled with outrageously corrupt lobbyists, still offers a banquet of wonderful reading. Gordon Milne's *The American Political Novel* (Norman: University of Oklahoma Press, 1966) and Robert Falk's *The Victorian Mode in American Fiction* (East Lansing: Michigan State University Press, 1965) help place these novels within American fiction specifically and American history in general. The best of the nineteenth-century Washington novels are Mark Twain and Charles Dudley Warner's *The Gilded Age: A Tale of To-Day* (1873; reprint, New York: Oxford University Press, 1996) and Henry Adams's *Democracy* (1918; reprint, New York: Modern Library, 1931). The worst, but still great fun to read, is Charles T. Murray's hard-to-find *Sub Rosa* (New York: G. W. Carleton, 1880); and in between are the bitter works of John William De Forest, *Playing the Mischief* (1875; reprint, State College, PA: Bald Eagle Press, 1961), *Honest John Vane* (New Haven: Richmond & Patten, 1875), and *Justine's Lovers* (New York: Harper, 1878); Frances Hodgson Burnett's, *Through One Administration* (Boston: J. R. Osgood, 1883); and Henry James's short story "Pandora." Characters like Mr. Schneidekoupon, Darius Dorman, and Laura Hawkins are as delicious as the real-life Sam.

INDEX

The notation "*gallery*" refers to the illustration gallery that follows page 90.